THE DEACONS OF DEADWOOD MOTORCYCLE CLUB

Sam Allen

A Route66 MC Publication

Copyright: 2014 Samuel N. Allen

All rights reserved

This book may not be reproduced in whole or in part or in any form or format without the written permission of the publisher.

Published by Route 66 MC Publications
1200 Smith St, Suite 1600
Houston, TX 77002

Manufactured in the United States of America
ISBN: 978-0-9904932-9-7

First Edition

Library of Congress Cataloging-in-Publication Data

Allen, Samuel N., 1955-

The Deacons of Deadwood Motorcycle Club/Sam Allen

Cover design by Brian Love

Photos on pages 43 and 55 provided by Bert Silverstein
All other photos provided by Jay McKendree
Outlaw Biker article reprinted courtesy of Outlaw Biker Magazine.

Print layout and interior design by Booknook.biz

This book is dedicated to all my Deacons brothers, past, present and future, except for Dan Bezborn, David Lee, Bruce McDonald and Dick Tate, who other than being referenced herein are *damnatio memoriae*.

DFFD

CONTENTS

	Foreword	*vii*
Chapter 1:	Before the Beginning	1
Chapter 2:	Founding the Deacons of Deadwood	21
Chapter 3:	The Early Years	31
Chapter 4:	Ricky's Turn	49
Chapter 5:	The Rocket Launches	63
Chapter 6:	The Reign of King Jay I	81
Chapter 7:	Steve Lamb and the *Pax Deacona*	101
Chapter 8:	The Deaconess Chapter	125
Chapter 9:	Rodeo	131
Chapter 10:	Rides	135
Chapter 11:	The Deacons Have Big Balls	161
Chapter 12:	Patches	187
Chapter 13:	In Memoriam	199
Chapter 14:	Where No Man Has Gone Before	223
	Epilogue	233
	Acknowledgments	239
Appendix A:	Membership	241
Appendix B:	Directors and Officers	255
Appendix C:	Deaconess Chapter Members, Directors and Officers	259
Appendix D:	Website Articles by Members	265
Appendix E:	*Outlaw Biker* Article	293

FOREWORD

One week from today will be the 12th anniversary of the founding of the Deacons of Deadwood Motorcycle Club, and I am just now beginning to chronicle our history. I have a box of old materials containing minute books, records of public filings, old Charity Ball records and who knows what else. I have not looked at any of it yet. I suspect it will be an incomplete record, and it surely will not include many of the anecdotes that have made our Club so rich. But, it is a starting place.

Although I have been named Club Historian, making this chronicle a success will require a collaborative effort involving input from our past presidents and long-term members, as well as from our most recently inducted members. This history will cover over 12 years of lore. For the first eight years or so, I knew all our members well; however, our membership never exceeded about 60, and active membership generally hovered at around 40. Today we have nearly 100 members, over half of whom have been in our Club for three or fewer years, but virtually 100% of whom are active. So, although I rarely miss a meeting, I simply do not have the same kind of first-hand knowledge of our newer members as I had of our original members. So the newer history will present some challenges.

We have waited too long to begin this project. Some of our early members have long since resigned or passed away. Still, I have a pretty solid memory of the founding of the Deacons of Deadwood and its evolution from a small band of businessmen whose main objective was to form a loose knit gathering of motorcycle riders to one of the largest motorcycle clubs in the Houston area.

This project is going to be fun. I suspect many of our members will remember things differently than I have remembered them. But, by the

Sam Allen

time this book is completed, we will have a realistic and accurate history of our Club. Our longer-standing members will have a source of fond remembrances and our newer members will learn how our traditions emerged and developed. Most importantly, we will have started a process to assure that our heritage is preserved.

So, enough of this. I now am going to turn my computer off and pick up the first volume of the Minutes of the Meetings of the Deacons of Deadwood Motorcycle Club. I can't wait to see what I will find.

Sam Allen
January 19, 2014

CHAPTER 1

BEFORE THE BEGINNING

"If you're going to be a bear you might as well be a grizzly."
— David Cook

"In the beginning, the earth was without form and void, with darkness over the face of the Abyss..."
— Genesis

The founding of the Deacons of Deadwood Motorcycle was a product of the motorcycle riding environment in Houston, coupled with the gathering of a group of people who were not likely to have met outside the motorcycle world. Any understanding of how the Deacons of Deadwood was formed and how the Club became what it is today requires an understanding of these people and of the events that predated the Deacons.

I bought my first motorcycle in December 1996. It was a 1995 Road King. I was driving my Corvette around Houston's 610 Loop and saw a billboard for Mancuso Harley-Davidson. I thought to myself that I could afford one of those. I called Sue Dailey, the only person I knew who owned a motorcycle, and Sue introduced me to David Cook. I bought the Road King from David the next day and we were friends from then on. I had to go to motorcycle driving school to learn how to ride it.

David Cook and Janis: Girlfriend No.3.

Being around David Cook was like being in an Elmore Leonard novel. There always were nefarious people around. Guys like "Gigolo Gene," who specialized in marrying wealthy elderly ladies and screwing around on them. There was "DC," who ran a biker bar and at age 66 went to prison for selling dope. Charlie G ran a flooring company that fronted for his book making business. The list goes on.

David had a scam for everything. For $150 he would sell you a package that had a fake auto insurance card, an authentic handicapped parking tag, a press pass, an ordained minister's license and a variety of other credentials and forms of identification. Once when the Astro's were in the National League playoffs, we went to the Astrodome. He got us into the parking lot by flashing his press pass. We parked in the front using his handicapped parking tag then watched the game from the press box. The seats up there were great and there was a lot of free food and beer.

David was the kind of guy who would swindle you in the morning and pick up your bar tab that night. He ran a used car lot at the corner of the 610 Loop and Shepherd for years. He closed the car lot and opened

The Deacons of Deadwood Motorcycle Club

a motorcycle custom and repair shop called Luxury Cycles Unlimited. David was one of the most likable characters in Houston and had a large following. Many of the founding and future members of the Deacons of Deadwood had known David Cook before they knew each other.

David was a creative motorcycle shop owner, especially when it came to billing. It was not unusual for someone to drop a bike off for an oil change, and upon pick up, to find several hundred dollars of unordered parts and work. David would tell the customer that he put on the new parts and did the extra work because he knew the customer really wanted them anyway, and the customer rarely would complain.

Customers had to pay close attention to their invoices. Without care, they might miss the fact that they had been charged for the same part two or three times or charged for parts that were not put on the bike at all.

One of the easier things was getting a state inspection done. He wouldn't bother with actually getting the bike inspected. Instead he would just buy a valid sticker from the inspection station across the street and add an extra convenience charge.

David would charge for work that never was done. One customer dropped his bike off at Luxury Cycles to get its heads "tubbed." That is a process in which the factory heads of a motorcycle are removed and a portion of them are filled in, leaving a small area roughly the shape of a bathtub, thus "tubbed" heads. The purpose is to get more compression and power.

David had the heads on the bike removed and told the customer that they had been sent out for the necessary machine work. A couple of weeks later, the heads were back on the bike. David gave the customer a discounted deal on the price for the work. The customer was delighted with the discount and with his newly tubbed heads. He told everybody how great the bike was running and that he could especially feel a burst of power between second and third gears.

Sam Allen

A year later, the customer was having problems with his engine so he took the bike to Mancuso Harley-Davidson and asked them to take a look. He told Mancuso that the problem might be due to the increased compression he had because of having had the heads tubbed. Mancuso pulled the bike apart and told the customer that the heads had not been tubbed, and that his engine heads were the same as on any stock Harley.

But David's real talent was selling. David had a beautiful Fat Boy in his shop that he had been trying to sell for $25,000. The bike was worth the money. There were only 400 miles on it and it was totally tricked out. It had a wonderful "Ghost Wolf" paint job that made the bike appear to be a solid deep black cherry color unless the sun shined on the tank in just the right way. When that would happen, a life-like Wolf with piercing yellow eyes would emerge from the undercoat.

One night, David and a bunch of guys, including me, hired a limo to hit some bars. We were so rowdy that the limousine was stopped by a police officer who threatened to arrest the driver and everybody in the limo. David talked the police out of arresting us. Later that night he told me he would sell me the Fat Boy for $20,500, but I had buy the bike next day.

I understood. David did not own the bike. Instead, he was selling it for somebody else and got to keep everything over a $20,000 sales price, and David needed $500. I knew this was the cheapest David would be able to go, so I agreed to buy the bike.

The next morning, I got a call from David who was asking what time I was going to pick up my new Fat Boy. By this time, I had forgotten about the deal, but this motorcycle was a steal at $20,500, so I told David I would be by at lunchtime with a cashier's check. I delivered the check at the appointed time. David handed me the keys and told me I would get the title the next day.

The Deacons of Deadwood Motorcycle Club

Six months went by and I still didn't have the title. I wasn't too worried about it because, after all, I had the bike. However, the time was coming to renew the registration and I was worried I would need a title for the renewal.

A few more months went by, so I called the Texas DOT to find out who had title to the bike. It turned out that the bike was owned by David Osuch. I called Mr. Osuch, and told him I expected we had a common friend named David Cook. Osuch confirmed he had been at friend of David's for years.

Then I told Osuch that I had bought his Fat Boy and I still didn't have the title. Osuch said that was because Cook still owed him money on the bike.

Cook had told Osuch that when I bought the bike, I had only $10,000 in cash, that the rest of my assets were tied up in limited partnerships in England, and that it was going to take me 30 days to get liquid and pay the other ten grand. Osuch kept trying to get his money. Cook finally told Osuch that I had been arrested for selling drugs and that the DEA had confiscated the bike.

I had expected that the delay in getting the title was because David spent the money on something else, and of course, that turned out to be true. I headed to Floyd's Cajun Shack because I figured I would find Cook at the bar. Sure enough, he was there with a VO and Coke in hand. I told David that I had spoken with Osuch and of the news that Osuch had not been paid.

David didn't stumble. He told me I was right and started into a soliloquy justifying the lack of payment. After about a minute, David stopped talking and looked at me and said, "You want your title, don't you," and promised me I would get it the next day. Sure enough, I met David at Floyd's the next day and got the title. Who knows what money had to be shuffled around for David to come up with 10 Large overnight.

As an aside, I sold the Fat Boy two years later to a drug dealer who showed up in a purple Caddy and with a green garbage bag with $23,000 in cash.

David liked to drink and his drink of choice was VO and Coke. Late one night (or early one morning) David was pulled over by the police and David obviously had been drinking. The policeman asked David what a guy David's age was doing out drunk at that time of night?"

David replied "I'm on my paper route."

The next morning in the Harris County Jail when they were passing out the bologna sandwiches, David asked "Do you have any Grey Poupon?"

When David got out of jail the court ordered a Breathalyzer to be put on David's truck so he could not start it if he had been drinking. Some mornings, David would have so much alcohol in his bloodstream from the night before that he still couldn't start his truck. He would call me up and I would have to drive over from work and blow into the Breathalyzer to crank up David's truck.

But the police are smart and knew people would try that kind of dodge. So I would have to ride around the Loop for 45 minutes or so until a beeper would go off signaling that the Breathalyzer had to be reactivated to keep the car moving. So, there I would be riding around in David's truck with my head down blowing into the Breathalyzer looking like I was blowing David. I probably was happier than Cook the day the Breathalyzer was removed.

David Cook was more than just a charming charlatan. He was a whirling dervish who always had something in the planning stages. Each year David would organize a trip to the Sturgis Motorcycle Rally, and his crowd would stay at the Bullock Hotel in Deadwood, South Dakota. Everyone in David's group would receive a personalized welcome gift from the Bullock. One afternoon David and a bunch of his Houston contingent were walking the streets of Deadwood and David said "There are so many of us here they should call us the Deacons of Deadwood."

The Deacons of Deadwood Motorcycle Club

David also organized charitable events like his annual "Ride to Fuad's." Fuad's is a restaurant just west of the Galleria in Houston that has no menu and will prepare whatever a customer orders. Unfortunately, Fuad's also does not have a price list, so there's no telling what a customer will be charged for any particular meal on any particular day. The only thing of which anyone can be assured is that it will be expensive. This is a dark place to take your girlfriend instead of your wife.

The Ride to Fuad's was limited to 35 couples and tickets had to be purchased in advance. David would tell everybody that he would do his best to get them in, but that tickets were in such demand he couldn't guarantee anything. Of course, all of David's friends would get in and it was always a good party.

It was a "Biker Formal" event and guests put a lot of care in selecting their attire. At my first Ride to Fuad's, I took a hot blond and she won the "Best Dressed" award. All she wore was a white tuxedo jacket. Just the jacket: no bra, no panties, no nothing!

There always was a silent auction and door prizes were donated by all of the big motorcycle shops and biker attire places. After deduction of expenses (of which there were many), the event typically would raise something shy of $10,000 to be donated to charity. Fuad's had framed pictures of these parties on its walls for years.

Despite being willing to swindle his friends, David could be generous. At one time David kept two boats in Clear Lake. He would throw parties on the weekends and his guests would shuttle back and forth between the boats in a golf cart. One of David's friends at these gatherings was his long-time girlfriend Marva. Marva is edgy. She is a sexy broad who looks a lot like Angelica Houston in *The Grifters*.

One year at the Sturgis Rally, Marva was riding her own bike, which had a side car. She and the rest of the crowd were at a stop light on their way to the Buffalo Chip campground. A kid in a truck hauling a trailer lost control of his vehicle and the trailer hit Marva hard. Her arm was nearly torn off, and if it had not been for the side car, she likely would have been killed.

Marva was taken to a hospital in Rapid City. The doctors considered amputating her arm, but David would have none of it. She later was taken to a hospital in Houston where she had many surgeries.

Neither David nor Marva had medical insurance. David paid Marva's medical bills in cash out of his own assets. He never quite recovered from the financial loss and the days of two boats in Clear Lake were over. But Marva's arm was saved.

In the mid-1990s through the beginning of the 21st-century, motorcycle riders from all over Houston would gather on Thursday nights at Stelter's Restaurant, which at one time was called Sonora Del Norte. Stelter's was owned and operated by Bubba Stelter. It was in the building that once housed Houston's original Harley-Davidson dealership, which had been owned by Bubba's mother and father. Thursday nights at Stelter's was a bawdy time. Hundreds of bikers would attend. There was loud live music, cold beer, free-flowing tequila, whiskey and lots of shooters. Stelter's had food, but nobody was there for that.

Bikes usually started rolling into Stelter's at around 6:00 and the crowd would increase until around 9:30. After that, different groups would peel off and head to other biker spots around Houston, like Dick Heads and the Big Easy.

Before heading to Stelter's, David Cook usually would host a gathering at his motorcycle shop for a few drinks. At one time or another, all of the founders of the Deacons of Deadwood were at these gatherings. That's where I met David's son, Ricky.

Ricky tried to give the impression that he was the same kind of street smart hustler as the "Old Man." Ricky surely is street smart, but he just as surely is not like his father.

The Deacons of Deadwood Motorcycle Club

Ricky Cook and me at the Ride to Fuad's.

Ricky had been a local high school football star in the North Shepherd area of Houston. He went to the University of Tennessee and tried out for the football team as a walk-on during the Bill Battle and Johnny Majors eras. Ricky made the team but never got into a game. Nonetheless, he gutted it out and remained a University of Tennessee Volunteer until he graduated. Despite being on the football team, Ricky graduated in 3 ½ years.

After graduating from Tennessee, Ricky became a captain in the Marine Corps and traveled the world flying heavy hauler helicopters. During this time, Ricky was called into his Colonel's office and was told that he was about to be dishonorably discharged for running up credit card bills without making any payments. Ricky told the Colonel that he didn't have any credit cards. It turned out the Old Man had taken the credit cards out in Ricky's name. It took Ricky years to do it, but he paid that debt.

After his honorable discharge from the Marines, Ricky put himself through law school, again graduating early. He has been in private practice as a criminal defense lawyer ever since.

Sam Allen

One time a bunch of us were drinking at David's shop getting ready to go to Stelter's. Ricky mentioned that he would be late getting there because he had to pick up some money from a client. The local TV news was on and it showed a drug dealer who had been murdered being wheeled out of a Houston motel. It turned out to be the client that was supposed to pay Ricky that night. Ricky said "Man, how am I ever going to get rich if my clients keep getting whacked."

Another time, Ricky was in a bar in Galveston and the bartender directed Ricky to a customer that had an amputated leg. The guy told Ricky that he had been in the Harris County Jail, and they failed to give him the medication needed to control his diabetes. As a result, this guy's leg had been amputated and he wanted to sue Harris County. He asked Ricky what kind of case he had and Ricky told him "You don't have a leg to stand on."

I also met Elza Smith through David Cook.

Elza is a short fire hydrant built guy with tall Napoleonic complex. He was a police officer and later a firefighter.

Elza is one of those kinds of guys who enjoys kicking up shit. But as exasperating as Elza can be, he also can be a thoughtful and good friend. In 1998, Elza and I took off from Houston on our motorcycles and headed for Vancouver, British Columbia. The plan was to ride through Texas and New Mexico, then cut north to Jackson Hole, Wyoming, head north and west through Canada, come back through the Canadian Rockies and then on to the Sturgis Motorcycle Rally then back to Houston

We were in Kamloops, BC, and were going to ride from there to Jasper and Banff in the Canadian Rockies over the next two days. To get there, we would have a day's ride northeast from Kamloops to Jasper, then a day's ride southeast to Banff, then on to Calgary and into Montana. This was before cell phones were reliable, especially in remote places. I wound up on a five hour call from a phone booth outside of Kamloops. It became evident that I would be held up with work for a couple of days. I told

The Deacons of Deadwood Motorcycle Club

Elza to take off to Jasper and I would meet him in Banff two days later by cutting straight across from Kamloops without going to Jasper. That way, at least one of us would be able to make the Canadian Rockies ride.

Elza told me that we started the ride together and we would finish it together. He stayed with me in Kamloops. Two days later we took the ride from Kamloops to Jasper then down to Banff so we both got to make the trip. I thought then, as I had many times previously and would many times in the future, that Elza could be a real pain in the ass, but he always has been a loyal friend.

Ted Ricketson was another one of David Cook's friends who was in that early riding group. Ted was a general contractor and an entrepreneur who once owned the 11th St. Bar in Bandera, Texas, where he keeps a country home. During the early Deacons days, he lived in Pearland, so he wasn't around as often as some others at David Cook's Thursday night gatherings. Ted liked to spend weekends in his RV at barbeque cook offs and similar events. That's where Ted was seen the most.

Ted's wife was named Rene'. Apparently, Ted's previous wife was corpulent, and when David Cook met Rene' and compared her to Ted's ex, he said "You're no bigger than a fly." The name stuck, and Rene' is now known as the "Fly."

Ted wound up getting the first Deacons of Deadwood tattoo, which was a garish character with a top hat and a Dead Man's Hand.

I had not kept up with my brother Tolly for many years, but motorcycles brought us back together. Tolly had gone to college at the University of Washington and after that entered the military where he was stationed in Germany. After leaving the military, Tolly moved back to Seattle and later to Philadelphia.

Tolly and I were talking on the phone one night and I mentioned that a group was going to ride to the Texas Hill Country in a few weeks. Tolly said he would love to go, so I told him to come on and that I had an extra motorcycle that he could ride.

Sam Allen

It was a thrill a minute watching Tolly trying to ride out of Houston. He came inches from running up on the sidewalk while leaving a restaurant parking lot and had a half a dozen other close calls until getting on to I-10; however, once on the Interstate, he did fine.

After riding through the Hill Country for a weekend, Tolly went back to Philly and bought his own motorcycle. A year later, he shipped it to Seattle and rode to Sturgis to meet everyone at the Rally, and then rode on home to Philadelphia. On the way home he saw a statue of the Jolly Green Giant, the one and only Beer Nuts factory and the place where Eskimo Pies were invented.

I was having dinner at the original Ninfa's Restaurant in Houston with the same hot long legged Houston honey who had worn only a Tux jacket to the Ride to Fuad's when a gangly guy came and sat at my table uninvited and introduced himself as Carroll Kelly. Carroll said "Is that your bike outside?" I said that it was.

Carroll said "I've got a bike."

I replied "Good for you," and thought to myself "Who is this guy and why won't he go away?"

Carroll asked "Have you ever been to that Sturgis Motorcycle Rally?" I said that I had not been, but I planned to go in just a few weeks. I really wished this guy would take off. He was interfering with my getting the hot blond into the sack.

Carroll asked "Can I go?"

By this time I was getting annoyed, and I replied "It's a free country. You can go wherever you want."

Carroll was persistent, and I wound up telling him that I knew a guy named David Cook who was trying to arrange a room for me at Sturgis and that maybe David could find a room for him too. David wound up getting each of us a room, but not at the Bullock Hotel. All we could get was a Friday and Saturday night at a Best Western on the edge of town in Deadwood.

The Deacons of Deadwood Motorcycle Club

Carroll and I shipped our bikes to Rapid City, South Dakota, and flew up to get them. During our two days in Sturgis we rode with David Cook and the Houston contingent to see Mount Rushmore and through Custer Park and the Needles Highway. At night we drank whiskey and played poker. On Sunday morning, Carroll and I got on our bikes and started riding back to Houston.

For us, this was a pretty big adventure. I had been riding my Road King for less than six months, and Carroll's bike was an ancient Ultra-Classic that leaked oil as fast as it could be poured in. The goal on the first day was to make it to Billings, Montana, and on the next day, over Bear Tooth Pass into Yellowstone and then on to Jackson Hole. From Jackson Hole we planned to ride through Wyoming, Colorado, New Mexico and back to Texas.

The ride from Deadwood to Billings was brutal. There was a crosswind so strong that Carroll and I had to ride on the shoulder of the road and lean our bikes into the wind to avoid being blown over. The windshield on my bike actually blew off.

The ride the next day was even rougher. It was August, but it was snowing on the top of Bear Tooth Pass. Carroll and I stopped and had our picture taken in a snow drift.

When coming off of Bear Tooth Pass, we came to Silvergate, Montana, which was only about a mile outside of Yellowstone. Carroll and I were so cold we didn't think about continuing on to Jackson Hole. Instead, we checked into the Range Rider Lodge, which was a large log building that once had been a gambling hall and whorehouse. Guests would stay in the whores' old rooms, which still had their names on the doors. The rate was $38 payable in cash.

When we were checking in, we noticed a bar that was about 40 feet in back of a locked gate at the entrance way of the Lodge. I asked what time the bar opened and the attendant said it usually opened at 5:00, but he would open it for us right away.

Carroll Kelly and me atop Bear Tooth Pass on our first ride to Sturgis.

Carroll and I made it to Jackson Hole and stayed two days then headed toward Cheyenne. About halfway there we stopped at a service station that had about 30 Hells Angels gassing up. There was no more outgoing guy than Carroll Kelly. He strode up to one of the Angels and asked whether the AJs were going to Jackson Hole.

The AJ said "We ain't going to Jackson Hole."

Carroll persisted, telling the guy that Jackson was a great place just down the road, and that the Angles should check it out. The Angels made it clear that they were not going to Jackson Fucking Hole, and that Carroll had better Shut the Fuck Up and leave the Angels the Fuck alone, which he did.

It had been another windy day, and by the time Carroll and I got to Pueblo, Colorado, we were exhausted. I fell asleep with my jacket and chaps on.

The next morning, I got a call from my office, and found I was going to have to spend a half a day working before I could leave. Carroll said he didn't have time to wait around and that he was heading home. Carroll was no Elza Smith.

Carroll rode that leaky Ultra all the way back to Texas, with a stop in Tombstone, Arizona.

Years later, Carroll wrote an account of this trip and posted it on the Club's website. Carroll's recollections about our meeting and that first ride are not quite the same as mine, but they are close. It was a lovely article that I value deeply. It is attached in an Appendix to this book.

Then there was John Aubrey and John Talbot, who later became known as "The Two Johns."

John Aubrey had come to Houston 30 years previously with $300 he had borrowed from his parents. He got a job with George R. Brown and eventually became Mr. Brown's business manager. Mr. Brown would allow John to make small side-by-side investments with him and John did well. He eventually owned many rental properties throughout Houston and started his own oil and gas company that occupied one of the top floors in the tallest office building in downtown Houston. John was engaged to the love of his life Amy for nine years before they married because he didn't want to marry her until he could afford to offer her the life he believed she merited.

I met John Aubrey through Joe "Cruz" Valdez, who was a Bandido with whom I had opened a motorcycle custom and repair shop in David's space after David had closed Luxury Cycles. John Aubrey was one of our first customers.

John had bought a Harley-Davidson Dyna Wide Glide for Cruz to customize. Cruz built the bike then rebuilt it and rebuilt it again. The bike eventually was sent to Carl's Speed Shop for custom engine work and then was sent to Arizona for a custom paint job. All in all, John spent nearly $100,000 on the bike, and it was gorgeous. The only problem was that it wouldn't run. It was always exciting to watch John try to fire the bike up, usually with disappointing results. At least no one could steal it.

Sam Allen

What John wound up with was a $100,000 lawn ornament. He eventually got $9,500 on the bike as a trade in for a new Harley from Corpus Christie Harley-Davidson, which is owned by Deacon member Preston Douglass. Preston eventually gave the bike to the president of the Corpus Christi chapter of the Bandidos.

Riding motorcycles with John Aubrey and his wife Amy was an adventure. Amy loves to ride and told John she would ride anywhere he wanted to go, but they had to wear helmets. And wear them they did. John and Amy are the only couple known to pack four helmets on one bike when traveling across the country. Sometimes they would wear no helmets at all. Sometimes they wanted a full face helmet. Other times a half helmet would do. No matter what they needed, they were by God prepared.

John and Amy packed more stuff onto an Ultra Classic than seemed possible. Just packing the four helmets was a trick. When traveling with John and Amy we always would leave an hour late because that's how long it took them to pack their stuff.

John Talbot was John Aubrey's best friend and in many ways was John Aubrey's opposite. While John Aubrey had grown up in nice but fairly modest means, John Talbot's father owned a successful oil drill pipe company that Talbot eventually took over. John was a rambunctious youth and was in and out of several schools until he was finally packed away to a military academy with the hope of injecting some discipline into his disorderly, but antics-filled life.

Talbot had been married once before and the stories of his marital adventures are legendary. He once brought a woman to his house when his wife was out of town. When his wife got back, she found the woman's girdle stuffed down at the end of their bed. When she confronted Talbot with this damning evidence and asked whose girdle it was, John feigned anger and said it was his own. He claimed he used it to sweat off pounds when he was running, and in that he was going to head out for a run right then. He squeezed into the girdle and headed out for a jog.

The Deacons of Deadwood Motorcycle Club

Weeks later his wife was overheard at a party telling her friends how vane men were, and used as an example John's wearing a girdle to hide his belly when he was working out.

Another time he had a date in a duck blind for a hunt (you know he is a Coonass; who takes a chick to a duck blind?). As much as he quacked his call, no ducks would come. So, he decided he might as well go for some duck-blind pussy.

He got the chick's coveralls to her ankles and had her bent over the side of the blind to do the wild thing in the wild. Abruptly, he told the Madonna of the Bayou to be still. She said "OK, think about baseball," thinking he was about to have a pre-mature e-quack-u-la-tion. He slowly reached for his shotgun, rested his elbow on the chick's back, and started firing at some ducks.

John says he only got one of the ducks.

When it came to Talbot's second wife, he was as cautious as John Aubrey had been with his first (and only), but for different reasons. Talbot loved his long-time girlfriend Pat; he just didn't want to get married.

Pat got tired of Talbot's recalcitrance and gave him a date certain by which they had to get married or she was going to leave. Talbot used excuse after excuse to postpone the big day, including injuries he had suffered after hitting a deer at over 80 miles an hour on his motorcycle on the way to Big Bend (that's how he got the nickname the "Deerslayer"). Pat held firm and they got married on the appointed date. When the minister asked if Talbot promised to "forswear all others," Talbot reportedly said "I do, but only while I'm in Houston," which shocked the minister. The only laugh came from Pat, who knew better.

When Talbot first started riding with our group, everyone noticed he was tentative on his bike. He did not like to ride fast and often would hang back. As it turned out, Talbot was hanging back because he didn't know how to ride a motorcycle.

Sam Allen

Talbot got his first motorcycle through his association with John Aubrey. Talbot had never met Aubrey, so he had a mutual friend arrange an appointment for him with Aubrey to try to drum up business for his pipe company. A friend of Talbot's had told him to bring up Harley-Davidson's because Aubrey loved riding them. Talbot brought up Harley-Davidson's, and the next thing he knew, he was at a Harley dealership with Aubrey.

Talbot wound up buying a motorcycle that day, and the plan was to take it to Cruz to get it chromed out. Talbot insisted that Aubrey ride the bike to Cruz's shop, but he didn't tell Aubrey the reason was that he didn't know how to ride a motorcycle. During the couple of weeks it took Cruz to trick it up, Talbot went to motorcycle driving school and he never let on that he simply didn't know how to ride a motorcycle.

John Aubrey introduced John Talbot to me at a fundraiser I sponsored in 2001 benefiting Prevent Blindness. The model was based on David Cook's Ride to Fuad's. The whole gang was there. David Cook came with his girlfriend Janice (as opposed to his girlfriend Marva or his girlfriend Lynn). Ricky Cook was there, as well as Ted Ricketson and Carroll Kelly.

The best thing about this party was the girls. A bunch of them started dancing with each other on the bar. Later they started making out with each other. There were bunches of beaver and boob shots.

Carroll Kelly was outraged at this conduct and said that had he known it was going to be that kind of event he never would have come. That was quite a remark for someone who was attending with his girlfriend instead of his wife.

Even though the Prevent Blindness benefit was put on six months before the Club was founded, many of the early members viewed this event as the first real Deacons Ball. All of the future founders of the Deacons of Deadwood were there, other than my brother Tolly, who was living in Philadelphia. The party became a model for our early Balls.

The Deacons of Deadwood Motorcycle Club

In about 2000, David Cook was diagnosed with terminal pancreatic cancer. He was given only a few months to live, but true to form, David beat the odds, and lasted over a year. David was afraid, but faced his disease with bravery. He would say "I'm not afraid of dying, I'm afraid of not living." That probably was true. David didn't want to miss out on anything. He would joke that he had sold his soul to the devil, but he still hadn't delivered the title and he planned to be in heaven before the devil figured things out.

David had been living with one woman for over 20 years, had been dating Marva for the same 20 years, and during the previous few years he had a third woman he was seeing. They knew each other and would visit David at the hospital, sometimes at the same time. Only David Cook could fade that.

David died on October 14, 2001. He didn't have a formal funeral. Instead, he was cremated and there was a memorial service for him at the Hoffbrau Restaurant, which had a bar David and all of his friends frequented. Hundreds of people attended, and the David Cook stories abounded. This was a celebration of life and no one has lived a life quite like David Cook's.

At one point, some woman who none of us knew was going on and on and on with a eulogy. I was standing with Ricky Cook and a friend of ours named Brett, and I whispered "Who is this broad? This eulogy is longer than JFK's."

Brett said, "Yeah, and he fucked Marilyn Monroe."

Such was the atmosphere.

David used to say that he wanted his ashes spread in River Oaks. He said he always wanted to live on the rich side of town and that some time when we were riding our motorcycles through there, if we got a cinder in our eyes, we might think it was Old Cooksie saying hello.

All of this formed the background for the founding of the Deacons of Deadwood and the establishment of many of our traditions.

Sam Allen

Some claim that David Cook was the inspiration for forming the Deacons. That is not true, but David had a profound influence on the Club. We got our name from an offhanded remark David Cook made one time in Deadwood, South Dakota. The Deacons' Charity Ball is a direct descendent of David's "Ride to Fuad's." The Deacons' annual ride to Big Bend started with a ride David organized. The Hill Country Ride started with a ride organized by Sam Douglass and his son Preston, each of whom were friends of David's who became founding members of the Deacons. All of the Club's founders met through David Cook in one way or another and many future Deacons had known and ridden with David long before the Deacons was founded. All of these people, rides and events mixed to create the Deacons of Deadwood Motorcycle Club.

CHAPTER 2

FOUNDING THE DEACONS OF DEADWOOD

"...and God said 'let there be light,' and there was light, and God saw the light was good."

— *Genesis*

Stelter's closed sometime around the year 2000. The land upon which Stelter's was situated was in an area of downtown Houston that was being redeveloped. The value of the land had increased substantially, so Bubba sold it and moved to Las Vegas. Nobody picked up the slack for Thursday night riding in Houston. David Cook was gone, so even the gatherings at his place were over.

Thursday night riding in Houston was grim. There was plenty going on, but there was no organization about it. Ricky Cook and I started joking that we should start our own motorcycle club and that it would be named The Deacons of Deadwood. Other than this general idea, there is a lot of confusion concerning how the Deacons of Deadwood was founded. There are different versions of the story and the real story probably is a combination of the variations.

There were two groups talking with Ricky and me about forming a motorcycle club. One group was a crowd that had been hanging around Luxury Cycles and David Cook for years. The other group hung around

Big John's Icehouse. That group included an informal riding club called the Mag 7. Of that group, Monte (the "Full Monty") Jones, Erick ("ER") Robertson, Bob (the "Torch") Mitchell, Dwayne ("Cadillac") Tuttle and Ronnie Northcut, all became Deacons.

No matter which group was involved, all discussions about forming a motorcycle club involved a lot of alcohol. As much fun as all the drinking and pontificating about forming a motorcycle club had been, the real catalyst for the founding of the Club came during a period of relative sobriety.

I had for years been driving up and down Route 66 during Thanksgiving week. I would take this trip solo and looked forward to the solitude of driving through the west. Thanksgiving week in 2001 was only a few weeks after David Cook had died and I contemplated asking Ricky to join me on the trip. I thought hard about this because I didn't want it to change from the peacefulness I usually enjoyed during this time into a drunken ramble across the country. But in the end, Ricky was my best friend, so I invited him to come along.

Ricky suggested that we trailer our bikes out west. I gave Ricky the 411 and told him it would be cold as hell out there. Ricky persisted but I won out on this one. Three days later we pulled into Gallup, New Mexico. It was 7° and snowing.

We turned out to be good traveling buddies. I liked to listen to talk radio and Ricky liked to listen to Eminem. Ricky hated talk radio and I hated Eminem. So, we settled on audio books and listened to some good ones about the Civil War, including one about the Battle of Antietam and another about how Robert E. Lee convinced the Confederacy not to commence a guerilla war after Lee's surrender at Appomattox.

We could stay quiet for hours without feeling the need for small talk, but when we talked, it often was about forming a motorcycle club. We started outlining the structure of the Club, what the name would be, who its founders might be, the goals the Club might have, the Club's patches and all the other details that go into forming a motorcycle club.

The name was easy. It would be the Deacons of Deadwood after the remark Ricky's father made during the Sturgis rally that there were so many of his group up there that they should be called the Deacons of Deadwood.

No particular founders were mentioned; we just assumed it would be all of our friends who rode motorcycles. The only real rule would be that there would be no rules, because if rules existed they would have to be enforced and how in the world would we do that?

From the outset, we thought that the Club would conduct only one charity event a year, and it would be first-class. We didn't want any part of swap meets, events held at icehouses or other biker joints or anything else of which we would not be proud. The thought was to sponsor something akin to David's old Ride to Fuad's, but on a larger scale and with honest accounting.

Coming up with the patches was the most fun. We agreed that the Club's patches would be centered around the "Dead Man's Hand." The Dead Man's Hand got its name from the poker hand Wild Bill Hickok was holding when he was killed by Jack McCall in Saloon No. 10 in Deadwood, South Dakota. Everybody agrees that Wild Bill was holding black aces and black eights. The fifth card is the subject of controversy. Some local newspapers reported that the fifth card was either a red queen or a red Jack. Other accounts claimed it was the nine of diamonds. We settled on the nine of diamonds because that is the card in the Dead Man's Hand that Saloon No. 10 uses in its logo.

We decided that the Dead Man's Hand would be on a green background the shade the felt used on poker tables at casinos. Ricky thought that the Dead Man's Hand should be held by bony skeletal fingers. I thought that would look too cartoonish, but Ricky held the day and he was right. Later on when I was writing the lore behind the

Deacons of Deadwood's patches, I asked Ricky if it would be offensive to claim that the skeletal fingers represented David Cook's bony hand holding the cards to our lives from the grave. Ricky got a laugh out of that and claimed that the real worry should be David's other hand, which probably would be on our wallets from the grave.

The Deacon's patch was copyrighted in 2003 and was trademarked in 2011.

44%ers at an icehouse.

We also decided upon a "Nine of Diamonds" patch representing the nine of diamonds in Wild Bills' Dead Man's Hand. Only the first nine members of the Club were to receive this patch.

Like all motorcycle clubs, the Deacons would have an "MC" patch designating that it was a motorcycle club.

Then there was the 44% patch.

In the 1950s, an article appeared in the magazine of the American Motorcycle Association claiming that 99% of all motorcycle riders were good citizens and it was the remaining 1% that gave bikers a bad name. The Hells Angels immediately adopted a 1%er patch to tell the world that they were part of the 1%.

The Deacons of Deadwood Motorcycle Club

Many bars, especially in the west, will not allow bikers to wear their patches. The idea is to avoid fights between rival clubs. Some clubs came up with codes to let everyone know their affiliations without having to wear their patches. For instance, if you see someone in a bar with a T-shirt that says "81", you know that person is a Hells Angels affiliate because H is the eighth letter of the alphabet and A is the first letter of the alphabet; thus 81 equals HA, which equals Hells Angels.

The Deacons' 44% patch is a hybrid of these two concepts. Each 4 stands for the fourth letter of the alphabet, so 44 equals DD, which equals Deacons of Deadwood. The % was added on to make clear that the Deacons were not quite halfway bad ass. This is the only patch about which the Deacons are questioned on a regular basis.

Other than the patch signifying that the Deacons were from Houston, Texas, and patches identifying the president, directors and officers, these were the only original Deacons patches. Unlike some clubs, Deacons would be allowed to wear non-club related patches, such as patches from motorcycle rallies and military insignias; however, no patches supporting other motorcycle clubs were permitted.

Ricky Cook and his Deacons patches

When we returned from our trip discussions about forming a motorcycle club began in earnest. We found lots of enthusiasm from our riding friends and we welcomed input from them. I found an outfit called Ideal Embroidered Patch out of Florida that specialized in custom patches, including patches for motorcycle clubs. Maggie Miner of Ideal Embroidered Patch came up with artwork for the original Deacons' patches based on descriptions that Ricky and I provided. The artwork went through several renditions before final patterns were approved. Maggie still makes all of the official Deacons' patches.

In the meantime, other issues on forming a motorcycle club were addressed. The Bandidos MC dominates motorcycle riding in Texas. The Deacons were going to have to get the Bandidos' blessing to form the Club. I called up Cruz, my partner in Bayou City Cycles, for help. Cruz was a Bandido who owed me something north of $30,000 from Bayou City Cycles' losses, and I doubted I would ever get repaid. I told Cruz that if he could square things between the Deacons and the Bandidos, I would forgive the debt. Cruz agreed to that deal and promised me that the Deacons would not get any trouble from the Bandidos. Cruz came through, and from the outset Deacons have had cordial, but distant, relations with the Bandidos.

Cruz now is suffering from Lou Gehrig's disease. He remains a good friend.

Despite Cruz's help, we had some trouble with our main patch. We originally ordered a three-piece patch, the center of which was the Dead Man's Hand held by the skeletal bony fingers on a green circle. The top rocker was the word "Deacons" and the bottom rocker was the word "Deadwood." The Bandidos were not big on the Deacons having a three-piece patch. So patches were reordered with the top and bottom rockers attached to the center circle. Although it wasn't intentional, from a distance it looks like a three-piece patch.

Only a few of the original three-piece patches survived. Ricky and I each have one. The circular Dead Man's Hand portions of the three-piece patch were handed out to wives, girlfriends and other Deacons' supporters. The top and bottom rockers never were used.

The Deacons of Deadwood Motorcycle Club

Everything was coming together, and the Deacons of Deadwood Motorcycle Club was founded on April 29, 2002, as a Texas not-for-profit corporation through the filing of Articles of Incorporation with the Texas Secretary of State. The Articles of Incorporation named John Aubrey, Elza Smith and me as the initial directors.

The Deacons organizational meeting was held on April 30, 2002, at my apartment in downtown Houston. At that meeting, it was resolved that the initial members of the Deacons of Deadwood were:

David Cook	Ricky Cook	Sam Allen
John Aubrey	John Talbot	Tolly Allen
Elza Smith	Carroll Kelly	Ted Ricketson

So, as originally envisioned, the Deacons of Deadwood had nine founding members who received the Nine of Diamonds patch.

The initial officers were:

Sam Allen ....President
Elza Smith ....Vice President, Road Captain and Sargent at Arms
John Aubrey................Vice President; Keeper of the Exchequer
Ricky Cook ....Vice President
John Talbot ....Vice President
Tolly Allen ....Vice President
Ted Ricketson ....Vice President

Sometime between April 30 and May 10, 2002, the new one piece patches arrived. They came on a Saturday afternoon to my office in downtown Houston. I couldn't wait to get mine sewn onto a vest, so I pulled out the Yellow Pages (that's right; back then the internet was not what it is today) and started looking for someone who could do it right away. I found Hollywood Tailors on Travis Street, which was within walking distance from my office. Hollywood Tailors was in the process of being transformed from a tailor shop into the Char Bar, but tailoring services still were available. I dropped my vest and patches off, went back to work, and picked up my brand-new set of Deacons Colors later that afternoon. Today, the Char Bar is one of the most popular bars in downtown Houston, and you can still order a tailor made suit from there.

We had our second meeting on May 10, 2002. It was scheduled to be held at Cabo's on Richmond Avenue. Cabo's at that time was a popular spot in Houston that featured a 40 foot tall sculpture of a saxophone. When we arrived, it was loud and the crowd was horrible so we moved to Sam's Boat just down the street. Everyone was excited about this meeting because the patches were being handed out.

In the small period of time between the Deacons' organizational meeting and our second meeting, the membership had increased substantially. Although the Deacons' records are sketchy on this point, new members included Sam and Preston Douglass, Fred Farner, Fred Haas, Bob Mitchell, Eric Robertson, Monte Jones and Mike Callaghan.

Sam Douglass had known David Cook for years. Sam made millions as an entrepreneur, most notably through SCI, which was the largest funeral directing company in the country, and through Equus, which was a private equity fund specializing in investing in small and mid-size companies. Coincidentally, I had met Sam Douglass years previously when I was on the legal team representing Merrill Lynch in some of SCI's public financings.

Preston is Sam's son. At one time he was the district attorney in Kerrville, Texas. That worked out great for Sam the night he was arrested for drunk driving there. The case never went to trial. Preston now owns Harley-Davidson dealerships in Corpus Christi and Laredo, Texas.

Sam, Preston and Fred founded the Hill Country Ride that has become so popular with the Deacons of Deadwood.

The Deacons of Deadwood Motorcycle Club

Fred Haas is one of the largest car dealers in the United States. He also was part of David Cook's Fuad's bunch and went on the first Hill Country Ride. When I called Fred to tell him about the Deacons of Deadwood, I explained that this was not going to be a ragtag bunch of guys, but that it would be an upscale motorcycle club with quality members. Fred responded that he knew that any club I founded would be top-notch and said he would be glad to join. Although Fred was as close to being a founding member as he could be, he never actually attended a meeting. Nonetheless he remains a good friend of many Deacons and he was kept on our membership rolls for years.

Bob Mitchell, Eric Robertson and Monte Jones all were part of the Mag 7 that hung around at Big John's Icehouse. They had been my friends for years before I bought a motorcycle.

Mike Callaghan was a Big John's guy, but he didn't ride with the Mag 7. He was a hard core rider who was perfect for the Deacons.

The first order of business at the May 10 meeting was the distribution of patches. When I passed them out, Ted Ricketson's wife, the Fly, asked where the women's patches were. I replied that the women were not getting patches. The Fly asked why not, and Sam Douglass interjected by saying it was because we were a motorcycle club and motorcycle clubs don't have women.

That did not go over well with the Fly. She made Ted drop out of the Club, which was unfortunate, because Ted was sporting his new Deacons of Deadwood tattoo. So, Ted Ricketson has the distinction of being a founding member, the first member with a Deacons tattoo and the first member to resign, all in less than two weeks.

Monthly dues of $15 per month were established, as was an initiation fee of $130, for which each member would receive a set of patches and two T shirts. The dues and initiation fee were low intentionally because we did not want money to be an impediment to attracting the members we sought. That philosophy remains today, and although there is a rumor around Houston that the Deacons' initiation fee is $10,000, the dues and initiation fee have never been raised, although we now have a $25 application fee.

At that meeting, we also discussed becoming a 501(c)(3) charity, starting a website and planning the First Annual Deacons of Deadwood Leather and Lace Ball. The location had already been fixed as Rockefeller Hall, and Fuzzy Side up had been selected as the band. There were discussions about putting together a budget, designating a charity, finding corporate sponsors, setting ticket prices, rounding up door prizes and auction items, media exposure and potential celebrity participation.

Fuzzy Side Up at the first Charity Ball

There were additional discussions about new member recruiting, ordering hats, T-shirts and other apparel and whether the Club should have monthly or weekly meetings. No records exist as to the details of the discussions on these matters, but clearly, the agenda indicates that the Deacons of Deadwood had a vision.

CHAPTER 3

THE EARLY YEARS

"If chaos is a necessary step in the organization of one's universe, then I was well on my way."
Wendelin Van Draanen – *Flipped*

Records of Deacons' activities in our first year are sparse. The first meeting was held in my apartment. Later, meetings were held on the back deck of Blanco's Bar, then at the Lofts at the Ballpark apartments, where Carroll Kelly lived. Dana Linton was the concierge there, and her husband Matt Linton soon became a Deacon. On May 4, 2004, the meetings were moved to the Hoffbrau (which became the Saltgrass) and we have held our monthly meetings there ever since.

Bikes at the monthly Deacons' meeting.

Sam Allen

Early on, everybody was trying to figure out how to run a motorcycle club. Even though there were articles of incorporation, bylaws and a board of directors, there were not many rules. The members tried to put together rides, but attendance generally was sparse; after all we started with only nine members.

Even though we were not as organized as we are today, the blocks laid during the early years were the corner stones upon which the Deacons' current organization was built. One of the first matters was the establishment of a sound financial system.

John Aubrey was our first Keeper of the Exchequer (a fancy word for treasurer) and the father of the excellent accounting system we enjoy today.

John insisted that the Club's books and records be reviewed and audited by BKD, which was John's personal accounting firm and the seventh largest accounting firm in the United States. It was not easy for John to convince the Club to hire BKD, the biggest objection being the likely expense. However, John won on this issue, mainly because he refused to act as treasurer unless we agreed. It turned out to be one of the soundest institutional decisions we made in the early years.

We believed that financial transparency and the willingness to show our charity partners and contributors an organized set of audited books and records would help us establish a reputation of integrity. That was especially important because we did not want to inherit David Cook's reputation of being liberal in charging personal expenses to the charity account of his annual Ride to Fuad's. If any charity or donor wanted to ask how the funds we raised were spent, we would be able to demonstrate that all expenses were *bona fide* expenses of the charitable effort and that all of the net proceeds were being donated to the intended beneficiaries with nothing going to the Club or its members.

Although John created an excellent financial system, he managed that system by dumping all of the underlying bookkeeping and related work on BKD. So, we were surprised to receive an unexpected invoice from BKD of over $20,000 at the end of our first year. Fortunately, John was an excellent BKD client in his personal capacity and was able to convince Blake Randolph, who was the BKD partner that John used, to charge the Deacons an annual flat fee of $3,500 for accounting work. That fee included auditing our books and preparing our tax returns. However, we would have to do all of the underlying bookkeeping functions. Ann McCall, who worked for Blake Randolph at BKD, generously donated hours of her personal time to help with our bookkeeping.

Blake and Ann are no longer at BKD. Blake left because he butted up against a mandatory retirement age. Ann left to work for one of BKD's clients. However, Ann still volunteers her time to help keep our books and records complete and up-to-date, and BKD still audits our books and prepares our tax returns at a discounted rate. The Deacons owe a debt of gratitude to BKD in general and to Blake Randolph and Ann McCall in particular. Without them, our financial system would not be as sound as it is today.

We also went tech savvy early. George Bogle owned an Internet related business and was named as the Club's first technology chairman. George developed our first website, the basic structure of which remained for nearly a decade.

We had growing pains. Membership grew quickly, over doubling to in excess of 25 within a few months. There were virtually no procedures for admitting new members. Existing members simply would introduce their friends to the rest of Club and they would be admitted. It became evident pretty quickly that such a haphazard membership procedure could result in accidentally admitting people who we would regret having around. So procedures were established to help screen candidates.

The first procedures required an existing member to nominate a candidate for admission and to submit that nomination to a membership chairman, the first of which was Carroll Kelly. The membership chairman would then give a membership application to the candidate. That application would be circulated to all members of the Club. Any member could veto the candidate on a one blackball basis. This system worked well procedurally, but it really didn't provide for meaningful screening of candidates. We relied on the idea that our existing members would not nominate assholes.

There was a worry that we were expanding so rapidly that in short order new members would be able to take the Club over from its founders. To address this issue, we came up with the concept of voting and nonvoting members.

To be a voting member, the member had to attend five meetings in any trailing 12 month period. Any member who failed to attend five meetings in any trailing 12 month period was a nonvoting member. Voting members could vote on any matter coming before the Club. Nonvoting members could vote on anything except amending the articles of incorporation or bylaws, electing directors or making financial assessments against the members. So for instance, a nonvoting member would have the right to veto the application of a candidate for admission, but would not have the right to vote on raising dues.

All members at the time of the adoption of this rule were grandfathered in as voting members; however, voting member status had to be earned each year, so if a founder failed to attend five meetings in a trailing 12 month period he would lose his voting member status and it would have to be re-earned.

The founders recognized that that this system still could result in newer members being able to control the Club. However, the founders believed that the Club should be run by those participating in its events, and if the founders could not demonstrate the leadership qualities needed to attract votes for election to the board they should be replaced, and if the founders were too lazy to attend five meetings, then they should lose their power to vote. This is still the system and philosophy we use today.

The Deacons of Deadwood Motorcycle Club

The Mad Doctor was one of our early friends. Doc is the head photographer for *Outlaw Biker* magazine and has been a member of the 1%er MC the Invaders for 50 years.

Doc would hang out at Sam's Boat on Richmond Avenue and attend every biker event around Houston. He could talk the clothes off of any chick, and often would take nude pictures of them inside bars or in parking lots. He could get shots of single women, girl on girl shots, sister shots, mother and daughter shots, boob shots, beaver shots and total nudity shots. He could talk married women into getting naked in front of their husbands or daughters. Anywhere where you could find motorcycles and women you could find Doc and nudity.

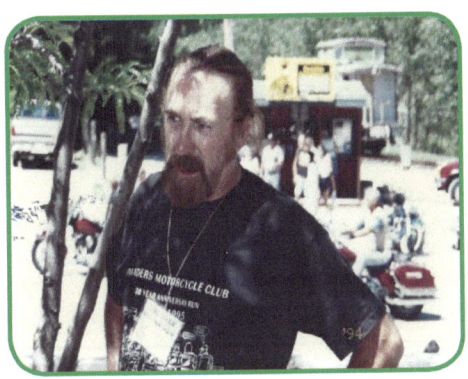

The Mad Doctor.

Doc has been a guest at many Deacons' Charity Balls and he has talked many of our guests into baring more than they would like to see on someone's Facebook page.

One Saturday afternoon at Sam's Boat, the Mad Doctor introduced me to Al Arfsten. Al was an ex-Marine who loved to ride motorcycles. He became the first member admitted to the Deacons of Deadwood outside Ricky's and my immediate circles. The Club would not get another "outside" member until 2004.

Sam Allen

Seguin Al Arfsten.

The Mad Doctor was influential in the acceptance of the Deacons of Deadwood into the Houston motorcycle community. During our first year, Doc had a heart problem and needed some help. A fundraiser was held at a bar on Westheimer Avenue in Houston. We thought it was important to attend; however, no one knew who we were and we had never had a fully attended Club ride flying our Colors. No one knew what to expect from the Bandidos or anyone else. We recognized that we were going to have to go out in public flying Colors sooner or later and that this event might as well be the time.

We showed up about 20 members strong during the middle of the party. There was no trouble with the Bandidos. Because of Doc, the Bandidos knew who we were and welcomed us. We reached into our pockets and donated over $1,000, which made our donation the largest of any motorcycle club in attendance. Both the Mad Doctor and the president of the Bandidos made an announcement to that effect and thanked us. Our attendance and generosity at this event went a long way toward peaceful relations with the Bandidos for years and the Mad Doctor remains our good friend

The Deacons of Deadwood Motorcycle Club

Other than riding, searching for new members, and watching Doc take nude photos, the biggest activity during the first year was organizing the first annual Deacons of Deadwood Charity Ball. We had decided we would sponsor one charitable event a year benefitting children in the Houston area. The plan was to partner with a well-known charity that would give the Deacons credibility in our fundraising efforts. Partnering with a major charity also was important because we would need to piggy-back on the charity's tax-free status so donations to our event would be tax deductible.

Many motorcycle club-sponsored benefits are at an icehouse or other rundown venue with crappy music and hot beer. They usually have a silent auction with a bunch of junk and a 50/50 raffle in which the winner might get a couple of hundred dollars. While these are events are fun and result in a lot of good for folks for whom a little help can make a big difference, that's not what we wanted to do. We wanted a first-class event with gourmet food, top shelf liquor and well-dressed guests. We wanted the event to be so much fun that folks would look forward to coming in subsequent years.

The attire was to be "biker formal." For the men, blue jeans were allowed, but no T-shirts, tank tops or ratty biker attire. Men might wear tuxedo shirts with the sleeves cut off so they could show their tattoos. Women were encouraged toward leather and lace type outfits that would show as much tits and ass as possible. It was sort of a grown up biker leather and lace "dress up" type of thing designed to allow the guests to have a more risqué time than their usual social circles would allow.

One year, a chick showed up with skin tight leather jeans on the bottom. On top, she had nothing on except having her body painted like a tuxedo. From a few feet away, it looked like a tuxedo, but up close, her nipples popping through the latex paint gave her away. That's biker formal.

Getting a reputable charity to support the Ball turned out to be harder than anticipated. Charities were leery of participating in a fundraiser with a motorcycle club (even a 44%er club). They were afraid that their association with a motorcycle club might sully their own reputations. Make-a-Wish Foundation ultimately agreed to participate.

One of the biggest problems in organizing the first Ball, or for that matter organizing anything else in the early years, was accommodating all of the strong personalities in the Club. Most of our initial members were businessmen or professionals who were used to running things. They were successful because they ran things well. This caused considerable friction within the Club and resulted in many members questioning the Club's foundations. For the first time, the question arose as to whether we were a charity or motorcycle club. Mike Callaghan tried to resolve the issue by proclaiming: "We aren't either one; we're a drinking club that rides."

Mike the "Hooligan" Callaghan.

Either way, the clash of so many "Type A" members made putting on the Ball difficult. As John Aubrey said, "This is not fun."

This discussion has continued with varying degrees of intensity for the last 12 years. Today, we have the luxury of putting on the premier motorcycle-based charity event in Houston while at the same time having enough members that any Deacon can find somebody to ride with virtually at will. That was not the case in the early years. We had fewer members than today, so there were fewer people to share the burdens of putting on the Ball. It also was harder to round up people to go on motorcycle rides. So, the discussion of whether we were a charity or motorcycle club had much more meaning in the early years than it does today.

Despite all the angst, the Ball was a success. We raised $22,500, all of which was donated to Make-a-Wish. The first Ball was followed up with another event for the benefit of Make-a-Wish in 2003, at which $59,000 was raised, $50,000 of which was donated to Make-a-Wish, with the rest being donated to smaller charities. In 2004, $65,000 was raised, $50,000 of which was donated to Camp for All and $5,000 of which was donated to Make-a-Wish. Again, the rest was donated to charities for which a small donation could make a big difference.

The beginning of 2003 brought three new directors to the Club: Bob Mitchell, Mike Callaghan and Steve Lamb. Bob and Mike were Nine of Diamonds Patch holders.

Bob was part of the Big John's Icehouse crowd that road with the Mag 7. He had a Road King, but he never rode it far. Once when someone asked why Bob never went with us to Big Bend, Mike Callaghan responded "It's 525 miles too far west of Big John's Icehouse."

Bob's nickname was the "Torch." He got that nickname when we were drinking Flaming Dr. Pepper's. Bob caught his thumb on fire when he was about to drink one, but he downed the drink before blowing out the fire on his thumb. He said "I was like a beacon in the night. From now on I'm the Torch."

Mike Callaghan originally is from Coventry, England, but he has lived in the United States for decades. His British accent is still so pronounced that it's sometimes hard to figure out what he saying. When the *Son's of Anarchy* came out and everyone was talking about it, Mike asked "Who the hell is Snarkey?" He is a hard-core rider of the old-school variety. Ricky Cook gave him the nickname the "Hooligan" because he looks like one.

Sam Allen

Steve Lamb had been introduced to the Club by Make-a-Wish. Steve had been doing volunteer work there while we were putting on the first Ball. He attended the Ball and was impressed with the Deacons' style and its ability to raise significant charity funds through a motorcycle club. A month or so after the Ball he ran into some Deacons at a biker bar. He asked about joining and was admitted within a couple of weeks. Steve went on to serve as a director for a total of seven years and as president for three years, making him the longest serving member of the Deacons' management.

Once the first Ball was over, we tried to focus more on riding. The Club's original vision was to gather a pool of riders that could be tapped to ride on an impromptu basis. Although it was a great idea, it did not work out well. The problem was we did not have the critical mass of members needed to get significant participation on short notice. Many of the members were professionals who often were busy at work or out of town on business when calls for rides came. So, we decided to initiate a program of organized rides.

The idea of mandatory rides was suggested, but then rejected, because of the reality that there was no mechanism to enforce participation. Instead, we decided to appoint a ride chairman who would be in charge of organizing a ride after each Club meeting on the first Thursday of every month, and organizing a ride on the third weekend of every month. We reasoned that no matter how busy a member might be, he likely could schedule rides for those two times.

The ride chairman was different than a road captain. We really didn't understand the concept of what the duties of a road captain might be. To our mind, the road captain was somebody who would be in charge of safety and similar matters during actual rides. Alternatively, the ride chairman would be somebody who set the time, place and routes for the newly designated post-meeting and monthly rides.

In June 2003, John Talbot was appointed as the first ride chairman to serve for June, July, August and September 2003, and Ricky Cook was named to succeed Talbot for the months of October, November and December 2003. The first organized Sunday ride was held on June 21, 2003, and it was to Elza Smith's beach house on Trinity Bay.

Although we now had a structure in place to have some organized rides, it did not work out well in practice. Club meetings on the first Thursday of every month generally were well attended and the members almost always would ride to some bar following the meeting. But the rides scheduled for the third Sunday of every month often were sparsely attended and sometimes only the ride chairman would show up. That was discouraging for the membership, but even more discouraging for the ride chairmen, who would go to a lot of trouble to plan fun rides only to have an apathetic reception. Things would improve over time, but it took years before we were able to muster the kind of participation in riding that we hoped to have from the outset.

Despite the tepid enthusiasm for local rides, from early on, Deacons were not shy about longer rides. Even though the Ball exhausted lots of everybody's time, many members found the time to go on the Hill Country and Big Bend Rides that David Cook had started years previously, but this time flying our Colors. Most of us went to Sturgis and stayed at the Bullock Hotel.

The Iron Butt Association has designated different long mileage rides for which awards are available. The easiest of these rides is the *Saddle Sore 1,000*, which requires riders to travel 1,000 miles in 24 hours. The *Bun Burner* is 1,500 miles in 36 hours. It is possible to complete both rides in a single trip and that's what we planned to do.

The first organized Deacons Iron Butt ride took place on June 14 and 15, 2004. The first day's ride was 750 miles from Houston to El Paso, and then back 250 miles to the Gage Hotel in Marathon, Texas, to complete the *Saddle Sore 1,000*. The second day was 500 miles back to Houston to complete the *Bun Burner*. Everybody who started completed both rides in the allotted time and ultimately received commemorative patches from the Iron Butt Association.

In July 2004, the Club experienced its first serious injury to one of its members. Duke Nunn got drunk one Sunday morning and sped down Kirkwood Avenue at over 80 miles an hour. He went down between Memorial and Briar Forrest sometime before noon and sustained a serious head injury from which he would never fully recover.

Duke used to go to Big John's Icehouse on Sunday mornings for breakfast and try to work the New York Times crossword puzzle. If you looked over Duke's shoulder, it was easy to see that he would have half the words filled in wrong. If the clue was "Three letter word for canine," he would write in "cat.

On the morning of the wreck, Duke had been on a 24 hour bender. He called Sally Gracia to go to lunch, but Sally couldn't go, so he called Marilyn Hartley (a.k.a. Marilyn Manson) to ask if she wanted to go riding. When she showed up, she told Duke he was too drunk to ride and she didn't go. That turned out to be a wise choice.

Duke's injuries were severe and he was not expected to live. He was in a coma for a month. His family wanted to terminate attempts to revive him. However, Duke had dated Sally off and on for years and he had given Sally a medical power of attorney. Sally had Duke put on a respirator and it saved his life.

Duke was a roofer by trade. He never had much money and he certainly didn't have any medical insurance. So to help Duke out, we had a "Dollars for Duke" fundraiser on August 24, 2004, at Big John's Icehouse. I donated a tattoo of the Deacons' Dead Man's Hand that had to be purchased by a woman with no previous tattoos, who would agree to get the tattoo on her breast. I agreed to match the top bid and to pay for the tattoo. Tickets to watch the winner get the tattoo would be sold for $100 each.

I never thought anyone actually would purchase this item. However Adrian Hoph bought it and a few weeks later she and several Deacons went to Shaw's Tattoo Studio to watch her get her tits inked. That Adrian would not be shy about all this was not surprising since she lived at The Live Oak Nudist Resort. She was given the number "LOR 1," which was tattooed below the Dead Man's Hand.

The Dollars for Duke Benefit netted over $15,000 for our fallen brother.

Duke lived for another seven years, but he needed assisted living for the rest of his life. At first, Sally took care of Duke. His family members refused to help. He was in and out of facilities that invariably would kick him out because he could not control violent episodes he often would have. Duke eventually told Sally she should have let him die. This broke Sally's will. Soon after that, Sally turned Duke's care over to the State.

Adrian's tattooed tit.

Duke was sort of forgotten over the years. He would show up at Big John's or other places from time to time, but he didn't look like we remembered him. He would always give a smile of recognition when he ran into any of his Brothers.

Duke finally died in 2011.

The Deacons of Deadwood did not do right by Duke. We should have made a better effort to keep up with and care for him. I hope we have learned something from this.

As 2004 began to wind down, it was time for the Club to begin considering the election of its president and directors for 2005. By this point, I had been president for almost three years and had led the Club to some impressive progress. Membership had grown from nine founding members to over 50 members. Three successful Charity Balls had been conducted with net proceeds of over $140,000. Our financials were sound. The monthly meetings were well attended. Participation in the designated rides held on the third Sunday of every month had increased, and our members had been on several Iron Butt and other out of town rides. The Club was strong and for the most part the members were having fun.

I thought I had been a reasonably popular president, especially among those who joined in the first year. Those members had seen firsthand the confusion that had to be sorted out and the strong personalities that had to be accommodated for the Club to achieve its goals. This was not an easy process and I made many unilateral decisions. Some of those decisions were not well received, but most members understood that I made the decisions I believed were in the Club's best interest. In all likelihood some decisions were good and others were bad, but that's the nature of leading.

I was ambivalent about running for another term. I enjoyed being president, but those encouraging me to remain in office had little knowledge of the burdens involved. Running the Club took many hours every week, and as the Ball approached each year, it took dozens more hours every week. Although committees had been established to help share the burdens, those committees did not always function well and I often had to do most of the work myself (or it seemed that way to me).

In addition, being president could be hurtful on a personal level. I had been accused of stealing from the Club treasury, taking kickbacks from the caterer and other vendors at the Charity Balls, lying to the membership on a variety of topics, and in general of being overbearing autocrat. And those accusations were from my best friends.

Some of the newer members thought I controlled the Club in a secretive and dishonest way. They thought that all decisions were made in some kind of smoke-filled backroom with the Club's other founders without regard to the general desires of the membership as a whole.

The Deacons of Deadwood Motorcycle Club

The fact is that I had been autocratic and had run the Club with bit of a heavy hand. I believed then, and I continue to believe, that many of the decisions I was making were not for the expediency of the moment; they were essential for the Club's survival. Only our oldest members can recall how close an issue survival was in the early years.

I was confident that I could be reelected. Even so, I had doubts as to whether that would be wise. The results of my decisions generally had been good, but I knew my popularity would not last forever and that perhaps it would be better if I stepped down.

Many of the older members encouraged me to run for a fourth term of office. Some even suggested that I should be elected president for life. These members believed that the Club had not matured sufficiently to operate without my acting as a benevolent dictator.

Carroll Kelly, in his usual blunt and forthright way, brought the issue to a head. He said that it was time that the Deacons found out whether this was "Sam's Club" or whether it was a "real club." Carroll recognized that I had put in lots of hard work and even admitted that my autocratic style had been necessary from time to time. But, he argued, although it would be easy for our membership to continue to rely on my hard work, the more sound way for the Club to face the future would be through new leadership to see whether there really was a Club at all.

The more I thought about this the more I believed Carroll was right. I decided not to run for a fourth term as president. I sent the membership a William Tecumseh Sherman letter stating that I was not running for president, that if nominated I would not accept, and if elected I would not serve. I also told the membership that I would not run for director. I knew my personality and understood that if I was on the new board, a risk would exist that I would unintentionally overshadow the new president. I simply thought it was time to step aside.

Sam Allen

Here is the letter that I sent to the membership:

October 15, 2004

Deacons of Deadwood Motorcycle Club:
Dear Deacons:

   I have decided that I'm not going to seek reelection as president or run for director of the Club next year, and through this letter, I am requesting Carroll Kelly to be sure my name is not included on the ballots for either of those elections. We have built a stable infrastructure that to a large extent will help the Club to be self-sustaining. We have many able members capable of doing a fine job and I encourage an active debate on the selection of our next president and board.

   I have long said that one of my main goals for the Deacons of Deadwood was for the Club to get strong enough that I no longer have to be president. We have reached that moment. We have come a remarkably long way since 12 of us founded this Club two and half years ago. In the last year we have:

- Doubled our membership;
- implemented and streamlined procedures for electing new members;
- established a good set of books and records;
- amended our articles of incorporation and bylaws to streamline the election process and implement a structure that will ensure continuity in Club operations from year to year, including a mechanism to ensure more Club members can participate in the Club's management;
- implemented a much improved rides program;
- established a first-rate website;
- dramatically increased our visibility in the community;
- founded the Deaconess Chapter;

- established a first-rate system of billing Club members for their Ball tickets, dues, T-shirt purchases and other items;
- solidified our relationship with our Corpus Christi members;
- attracted a motorcycle club from Austin to be a potential chapter of the Deacons of Deadwood;
- established a turnkey formula for running our Charity Ball that has both greatly improved the party from our guests' point of view and greatly reduced the administrative burdens from the Club's point of view; and
- increased our net charitable proceeds by 50% over the previous year.

That is quite a laundry list of accomplishments for one year and I am proud to have been a part of this growth in the maturity of our Club.

I still plan on being active in Club affairs. I'll be glad to assist the new president and board in any way I can, including showing them how past administrations have gone about general Club business, running the Ball, accounting for funds and similar matters. Ultimately, however, the new president and board must be free to implement their own policies. That is why I have decided not to serve on the board next year. The new president and board should not have to look over their shoulders to me when managing the Club.

One of the reasons I've decided not to run for office next year is I believe I can serve the Club better as a general member. For instance:
- Becoming a charitable organization for IRS purposes has been on our agenda for the last two years. Those charged with that duty simply have not performed.
- George has established a first-rate website, but it can only be as good as the content we provide him.
- I have long thought that a Deacons of Deadwood newsletter would be a great opportunity for the Club.

Sam Allen

These are all things I am willing to do but would not have time to do if I had all the day-to-day tasks the president must address.

Some members have indicated that if my name does not appear on the ballot for president, they will mount a write in campaign for my reelection. Others have encouraged me to run one more year and make it clear that this will be my last. We had that conversation last year, and I suspect that if I serve as president 2005, will be having that same discussion this time next year. It is simply time I step aside and let some new blood into the management of this Club.

Once again, I am proud of all the accomplishments we have made together the last two and half years, especially our accomplishments in 2004. Thank you to everybody who helped make this Club what it is today.

Very truly yours
Samuel N. Allen

So, my reign as the leader of the Deacons came to an end, but I believed I had left a strong and healthy Club for the next president and board. It turned out things were not as healthy as I had thought.

Ten years after founding the Deacons.

CHAPTER 4

RICKY'S TURN

They're changing the guard at Buckingham Palace.
Christopher Robin went down with Alice.
They've great big parties inside the grounds.
I wouldn't be King for a hundred pounds.

– A.A. Milne

The Deacons always nominate candidates for president and directors at the December meeting and the election takes place at the following January meeting. At the December 2004 meeting, John Talbot told me he assumed Dan Bezborn was going to be the next president.

Dan had been the Club's most effective ride chairman. He was a likable guy with a hot British girlfriend, and he was able to generate more participation in the designated monthly rides than had any previous ride chairman. Dan also exhibited the kind of leadership qualities necessary to be a successful president. Everybody knew he wanted to be nominated.

Ricky Cook as our second president.

Sam Allen

I told Talbot I intended to nominate Ricky Cook. That caused a stir because Bezborn had been lobbying the membership and he believed he would be running unopposed. Having to run against another candidate, let alone one of the Club's founders, had not been in Dan's plan.

Although the Club had over 50 members, there were only 28 voting members eligible to vote for the election of the president and directors. Being the Machiavellian I always have been accused of being, I made a preliminary count of likely votes and found that there were 12 votes solidly backing Dan and eight votes solidly backing Ricky. So, Dan would need only three additional votes to get elected, but Ricky would need seven. Eight uncommitted votes were up for grabs, but it looked like Dan had an edge.

Then something extraordinary happened. Dan sent out a series of e-mails generally asserting that the Club was a corrupt and disorganized organization. His e-mails included personal attacks on Ricky Cook, Carroll Kelly and several of the members, including me. Dan claimed that only through his guidance could the Club be led out of the darkness into the light.

This was not just one e-mail. Dan sent out a series of them, each with more invective than the previous one. Ricky asked me how he should respond to these *ad hominem* attacks. I advised Ricky not to say a word and Ricky followed that advice.

Ricky was elected president by receiving votes from 19 of the 28 voting members. It was surprising Dan got any votes at all. His conduct was so odd because before his failed presidential campaign he never had acted in such a harsh and mean spirited way, and if he had kept his mouth shut, he likely would have been elected.

Dan's relationship to the Club and its members was never the same, and although Ricky re-appointed Dan as road captain, his interest in the Club waned. He dropped out a few months later. That probably was for the best because although he seemed to be a great guy at first, he turned out to be an asshole. We would encounter bigger assholes down the road, but none of them were considerate enough to resign and go away like Dan did.

The election of directors was conducted under a new procedure that had been approved at the December, 2004, meeting. During 2004, the Club's membership grew to over 50. Many of the members had been admitted in 2004 and they had not attended the five regularly scheduled monthly meetings required to be eligible to vote for the Club's president and directors. However, in short order, these new members would become voting members and would theoretically have the power to elect an entirely new board. That in itself was not necessarily a bad thing; however the longer standing members were concerned that a complete replacement of the board could result in a loss of continuity in the Club's management.

To address this concern, our bylaws were amended to create a staggered board consisting of three classes of directors plus the president. Under the new system, directors would be elected for a three-year term and would rotate off the board at the end of that term. The initial staggered board would consist of two Class A directors that would serve for a three-year term; two Class B directors that would serve for a two-year term; and two Class C directors that would serve for a one-year term. In elections in subsequent years, two new directors would be elected to replace the directors whose terms were to expire. Outgoing directors would not be eligible for reelection until one year after the expiration of their previous term of office. Through this mechanism, only two directors could be replaced in any election, thus assuring continuity in the Club's board. This is the same board structure we have today.

In spite of my declaration that I would not run for director, I was persuaded to run, and I was elected as one of the Class A directors to serve for a three-year term. I received 27 of the 28 possible votes, with Bezborn being the only member not to vote for me. John Talbot was elected as the other Class A director. Carroll Kelly and Steve Lamb were elected as Class B directors to serve two-year terms. Bob Mitchell and Joe Kilchrist were elected Class C directors to serve one-year terms.

Ricky took over at a tough time. There was constant bickering, and almost all of it originated from a small group of people. Few days would go by without one group of members being pitted against another group on whatever the controversial issue of the day might be. One of the most persistent complaints was that the board was doing things secretly without getting the approval of the membership as a whole. The members making this complaint apparently did not understand the purpose of having a board of directors. To quell this criticism, Ricky started opening board meetings to the membership at large on the condition that they were there to listen and observe rather than to actually participate in the board's decision-making process.

New member David Lee was one of the first to take advantage of this policy. David showed up at one of the board meetings held at Bubba's Sports Bar. The board was discussing some controversial matter when Carroll Kelly invited David's views on the topic. Carroll was reminded that although members were permitted to attend the board meetings, they were not supposed to participate. Carroll was insistent on the matter and David got to speak.

David went on and on and on and on and on. The longer he talked, the more animated he became, and the more animated he became the more vitriolic he became. No one could get him to shut up. Carroll finally interrupted David and said "Who cares what you have to say anyway? Who asked for your opinion?"

The meeting erupted in laughter even before David could shout out "You did!"

This was classic David Lee and classic Carroll Kelly. As to David, he never lacked for an opinion and he could never express one concisely. He also had a problem making his points in a civil manner and he was to become one of the biggest troublemakers in the Club. As to Carroll, it was a good example of his "Ready – Fire – Aim" approach to life that often had unintended consequences.

Rancor in the Club was so dominant a problem that there was extensive discussion concerning limiting the kinds of e-mails and other forms of communication that would be permitted among the members. The minutes of the April 2005 meeting include the following passage:

> "It was further agreed that the 'BS' stop, that the rhetoric subside, that derogatory e-mails between the members cease-and-desist, and that our members move toward camaraderie, fellowship on rides, and fun that are and must be the overriding purposes of our Club's existence."

This resolution must not have made much of a difference because it was reintroduced and once again included in the minutes of the September 2005 meeting.

Other policies were tried. Those who engaged in disruptive communications were threatened with sanctions, monetary fines and potential expulsion. The discussions about prohibiting vitriolic communications were filled with vitriol. Even Dan Bezborn, who was one of the biggest troublemakers, had had enough, and he resigned from the Club in August 2005. Slinging shit to the end, his letter of resignation was full of invective. Unfortunately, Dan's resignation letter has been lost, but its contents were so mean-spirited that a note was made to that effect in the minutes of the September 2005 meeting.

Worse was yet to come.

In March 2006, Bruce McDonald made a motion to amend the bylaws to reduce the size of the board from six to three members and that the board be reorganized to consist of the president and those three directors. Ted Faleski seconded the motion. Their purpose was to kick Ricky out as president and kick me off of the board.

Sam Allen

It's hard to figure out how McDonald though he was going to get away with this. The motion was not on the agenda for the meeting. There was no general feeling that Ricky and the existing board did not enjoy the overwhelming support of our members. So, the only way this motion would have had a chance of passing would have been if McDonald and his ilk had secretly rounded up enough votes for its passage. They did not do that and the motion failed with a vote of four votes in favor and 15 votes against. Despite this loss at the ballot box, Bruce kept on like the Energizer Bunny.

A couple of months before the 2006 Ball, Carroll Kelly sent an e-mail to me instructing me to present myself before the board of directors to explain why I had authorized the use of pornographic material in promoting the Ball. I called Carroll to find out what he was talking about. Carroll told me that the photographer for the Ball, who I had hired, had an advertisement on his website promoting the Ball that was accompanied by a pornographic photograph of me and some others. I went to the website and saw the promotional tag, but I didn't see any suggestive photographs.

I saw Carroll the next night at the regularly scheduled monthly meeting and told Carroll that I had looked at the website, had seen the promotion, but had not seen any inappropriate photograph. Carroll replied that he had seen the photograph and I called Carroll a flat out liar. After quizzing Carroll about the accusation, Carroll finally admitted that he had not seen any inappropriate photograph, but Bruce McDonald had seen it and had reported it to Carroll.

The photograph in question turned out to be on a "Members Only" section of the website that made no mention of the Deacons of Deadwood or our Ball. McDonald was a member on that website and had seen the photograph in the Members Only section. Rather than giving an accurate account to Carroll, McDonald reported that the promotional tag and the photograph were used together to promote the Ball. That simply wasn't true.

It also wasn't true that I had authorized anything with respect to promoting the Ball on the photographer's website. The photographer put out the promo as a favor to the Deacons without asking permission. Moreover, I had no idea what the picture in question was. When I finally saw it, I remembered the picture. It was hardly pornographic. Although it could be loosely described as erotica, there was nothing lewd about it.

That's the kind of guy Bruce McDonald was. Instead of just giving me call about the situation he decided to kick up shit with the board of directors. The result was a brouhaha that never should have occurred and the near destruction of the close friendship that Carroll and I had enjoyed. Carroll was so stubborn he would never admit that he should have called me to resolve the issue without turning it into a public matter. I was so pissed off I barely talked to Carroll for six months.

The porno promo.

It was suggested that the root of the discontent among some members was that different groups of members had joined the Club for different purposes. For instance, some had joined primarily to ride motorcycles and others had joined because of our charitable works

To help resolve this problem, Ricky appointed George Bogle and me to draft a Club Statement that would embody the principles upon which the Club was based and the goals that the Club was trying to achieve. Once drafted, the Club Statement would be open for discussion by the membership to be sure that in its final form it reflected the broadest possible viewpoint. Prospective members would be expected to read and execute a copy of the Club Statement so that they would understand both the benefits and obligations of being in the Deacons of Deadwood.

As adopted, the Club Statement first set out a brief history of the Deacons. It then stated that the Club's purposes were to form new friendships, ride motorcycles with those friends, and to help others.

The procedures for admission were set out in detail. The Club Statement emphasized that the Deacons was a brotherhood in which every member was unanimously accepted into the Club. As being part of a brotherhood, every Deacon was expected to support every other Deacon whenever possible.

The problem of inappropriate e-mails was addressed by making clear that every Deacon had a right to voice any concern he might have, but the expression of those concerns should be done in a reasonable and honorable manner.

Lastly, the Club Statement told prospective members that it was up to them to make most out of their experience as a Deacon, and that each member is under personal control of how much to give to and get out of the Club.

The Club Statement technically still reflects the Club's guiding principles; however, it has long been forgotten.

The Club was facing problems in collecting dues from its members. The dues were only $15 per month, so there really was no financial burden on anyone, and the failure to receive dues from a few members did not pose any financial risk to the Club. Even so, it was embarrassing for the treasurer and other officers to have to repeatedly call members to get them to pay their dues. Perhaps not coincidentally, those most delinquent in payment of their dues were the malcontents who seemed to bitch about everything.

The collection of dues became such a problem that Ricky and his board amended our bylaws to provide sanctions for nonpayment. Those amendments generally provided that a member would stay in good standing until the expiration of 60 days after notice from the secretary that the member was in arrears. If the dues in arrears were not paid within five days after the 60 day period, the member would be deemed to be not in good standing, and would be subject to expulsion by majority vote of the board. If the dues were in arrears for more than 120 days, then the member would be automatically expelled without further action. A variation of this rule remains in our current bylaws.

In September 2005, the IRS issued a Determination Letter declaring the Deacons to be a 501(c)(3) tax-exempt charity retroactive to the date of the founding of the Club. The Determination Letter was signed by, of all people, Lois Lerner, who is embroiled in the IRS scandal in which the IRS targeted conservative groups for special scrutiny in their applications to become tax-exempt entities.

Becoming a 501(c)(3) gave us a new legitimacy and the ability to hold ourselves out as a charity in our own right. We no longer would need to piggyback on the tax-exempt status of our charity partners. It also would allow persons who made donations directly to the Deacons to deduct those donations.

In 2005, we solidified our relationship with Camp for All. Joe Kilchrist had introduced the Club to Camp for All in 2004. Camp for All representatives met with Ricky and our board seeking a $1,000 donation, and the board was so impressed it recommended a $5,000 donation in 2004 and another $5,000 donation in 2005. The Club liked Camp for All so much it voted to split 75% of the net proceeds from the 2005 Ball between Camp for All and Boys and Girls Country. That was a problem because we had already promised that we would give 75% of the proceeds from the 2005 Ball exclusively to Boys and Girls Country.

Nobody (except Ricky and me) seemed to have much of a problem with the Club having broken its word. It wasn't even popular with the charities we sponsored because they were hesitant to participate in an event that was benefitting another organization. In 2006, we went back to our model of giving 75% of our net proceeds to a single charity.

One of the reasons Camp for All became so popular with the Club so quickly was that there was a riding element involved. Camp for All sponsored an annual bicycle ride that was a warm-up for the MS 150, which is a bicycle ride between Houston and Austin that raises money for multiple sclerosis research. We had been asked to ride around Camp for All's bicycle course to assist cyclists that might have broken down, crashed or otherwise needed assistance. This was viewed as something that not only would assist a quality charitable organization benefiting children, but would be a great Club ride.

The first of these rides in which we participated was on April 2, 2005. We would continue to assist Camp for All in each of these rides until they were discontinued in 2013.

Deacons' bikes at Camp for All.

In 2005, Tommy Cason organized the Deacons' first trip to the Houston Livestock Show and Rodeo. The Deacons rented a double suite that would hold about 100 guests. For a $100 ticket, attendees were guaranteed all of the food they could eat and all of the booze they could drink. We attended the Rodeo for years, and over that time, this turned out to be a great deal for the Deacons and a bad deal for the Rodeo because we drank them dry year after year.

The Deacons of Deadwood Motorcycle Club

Yippi Ky Yo Ky Yay.

In 2005 we held our Charity Ball at the Decorative Center, which was a huge facility that had ample space for the band, the silent auction and plenty of bars. There was a futuristic looking main bar that looked like something out of *The Jetsons*. The only problem with that Decorative Center was with the acoustics, but even that turned out to work out just fine. We donated $54,000 to Camp for All and Boys and Girls Country.

The 2006 Ball also was held at the Decorative Center. We had reserved a block of rooms at the Doubletree on Westheimer and everybody went to an after party held in a suite that the Doubletree had donated to us. Apparently, John Talbot had an excellent time. He passed out in the elevator and rode up and down with the hotel's guests for several hours until someone woke him up the next morning.

We donated $70,000 to the charities we sponsored.

Ricky always was big on holding a portion of our Ball proceeds back to be used on an *ad hoc* basis in case someone needed help on short notice. That policy was put to good use in 2006.

One of my partners' daughters had moved to Las Vegas, and she had a daughter who had been diagnosed with an aggressive bone cancer. One of our members was able to get her admitted to MD Anderson. The family had medical insurance that covered some of the treatment, but it did not cover all expenses. By using our saved funds, we were able to pay for transportation and lodging for the entire family's trip to Houston to get the daughter admitted to the hospital and get her treatment going. That kind of donation is somehow more satisfying than simply writing a large check to an established institution.

The end of 2006 brought the Club two sad events.

The first one was that one of our founding members, Carroll Kelly, was diagnosed with kidney cancer. He was not sure how serious it might be, but he knew any cancer was serious. He faced it with uncanny courage. Other than letting some of the members know the diagnosis, he rarely talked about it, and nothing changed in his day-to-day life. This cancer ultimately would take Carroll from us, but he was with the Deacons for several more years before that happened. We made a substantial donation in his name to MD Anderson.

John Aubrey (center) and Carroll Kelly (right).

The other sad event was the first death on a Deacons ride. On November 26, 2006, we were riding to Boys and Girls Country to present them with a $50,000 donation. Two of the guests on that ride were Tommy Cason's friends, Richard Van Aukin and his wife Lovinia, who were riding at the end of the pack with John Talbot and Debbie Little, who was on her own bike. At the junction of Highway 105 and Highway 149, Richard failed to negotiate a turn and hit a culvert, throwing Richard and his wife off their bike.

Debbie Little ran to Lovinia and Talbot ran to Richard. Richard was badly injured and calling out to his wife. Debbie's look to Talbot told the story: Lovinia had been killed.

Debbie stayed with Lovinia until a black station wagon arrived to take her away. Richard was taken to a hospital and did not find out that Lovinia had been killed until the next day.

John and Debbie showed their mettle that day.

Richard was made an honorary Deacon and he participated in Club events for a while, but he eventually dropped out of the Club.

As 2006 wound down, the Club was in pretty good shape, but the acrimony stirred up by guys like Dan Bezborn and Bruce McDonald continued, and they were aided by new member David Lee with some older malcontents like Dick Tate and Elza Smith.

Nonetheless, membership had remained stable and we had sponsored two more successful Charity Balls. In conducting those Balls, we had retreated from our failed attempt in splitting Ball proceeds between multiple major recipients, and once again had returned to our model of giving 75% of our net proceeds to a single charity. The ride program had been improved with greater Club-wide participation. In addition, a solid relationship had been built with Camp for All based on both the quality of that organization and our opportunities to help them while riding motorcycles. Everybody anticipated the Club continuing to grow stronger.

CHAPTER 5

THE ROCKET LAUNCHES

"Launching a start-up is like firing off a rocket ship, then trying to hold it together with duct tape. Simply surviving feels like a success."
– Shane Snow

President Rocket John Aubrey.

"Rocket" John Aubrey was a founding member of the Deacons of Deadwood. He was on our first board and was our first Keeper of the Exchequer, which is the third most thankless job a Deacon can have. Nonetheless, he served in that capacity for five years, and during that time, he established the sophisticated bookkeeping and accounting system that we still use.

John also had been in charge of the raffle of the motorcycle given away at each Ball. That is the second most thankless job a Deacon can have. It was an organizational monster, mostly because back in those days, we couldn't count on our members to sell the tickets, keep track of the money for the tickets they sold, or even keep track of the tickets themselves. Members who could not sell their tickets would leave them with girlfriends or bartenders to sell. Invariably, the girlfriends or bartenders would lose the tickets. Other times one member would give his tickets to other members, and then the members to whom the tickets had been given would claim that they never had received them. As bad as all this sounds, it really was worse, but over time John was able to set up procedures that resolved most of these problems.

Eventually John was tricked into running the Ball's silent auction, which is the most thankless job. Talbot asked Aubrey if he would run the raffle again and Aubrey replied not just no, but Hell No! He said he would take any other job, and Talbot said "Great, you are the new silent auction chairman".

When Ricky Cook's second term of office was winding down several members approached John about being the next president. John had held every other significant post in the Club and felt it was his turn to step up. He also thought it was a good time for him to do it because by having served as raffle chairman and auction chairman, he had run the most difficult features of the Ball during the previous two years.

The meeting at which John was nominated to be president was held at La Griglia. I nominated John. Elza Smith nominated himself. I pointed out that under Roberts Rules of Order, a person cannot nominate himself to an office and I also pointed out that no one had seconded Elza's nomination. With that issue resolved John ran unopposed and eventually was unanimously elected as our third president. Mike Callaghan was elected to the board for the second time, this time for a three year term.

Callahan had turned out to be one of our most colorful members. During our first Iron Butt ride to Sturgis, Mike Iron Butted it to Deadwood, slept overnight on the floor of Carroll Kelly's hotel room, then Iron Butted it back to Houston the next morning. He went on a 1,500 miles in 24 hours *Bun Burger Gold* ride to Washington DC with

Carroll Kelly, a couple of other guys and me. He later did both the *Border to Border* and *Coast-To-Coast* Iron Butt rides.

Mike's solution to every problem with a troublesome member was to kick him out. When the board was discussing kicking out members who hadn't" paid their dues," Mike piped up and in his heavy English accent we heard "Yeah, get rid of the Jews," but what he actually said was "Yeah, get rid of the dues." He would get a chance to kick some troublemakers out of the Club in just a few weeks.

John's biggest goal was to make the Club more fun. In the early years, John had been among the crowd that thought the Ball took up too much time and energy and caused dissension among the members. He was all for having the Ball, he just didn't want it at the expense of everyone being miserable. So, John established a more sophisticated set of committees to run the Club and the Ball than previously had been in place.

He also set up a set of checks and balances in the Club's procurement procedures. Under this structure, no single person was authorized to create an account, approve payments with respect to that account and write checks on the account. For instance, if one member came up with an idea for a new T-shirt, he could approach the person in charge of purchasing T-shirts for approval. The person in charge of purchasing T-shirts could approve the purchase but could not write the check for the purchase. The check writing authority resided in the president and treasurer. All of this was smart fiscal practice.

John wanted to establish the Ball as a significant social event. The first five Charity Balls all had been successful, but John wanted to expand the pool of potential attendees by switching the focus from being a biker party to more of a biker themed party that might attract a wider audience. He thought that some of Houston's big charitable donors who might be hesitant about attending an event put on by a motorcycle club might find it fun to get to dress up in biker gear for a motorcycle themed charity event. John did a great job in this effort by simultaneously satisfying the bikers and also attracting some of the "River Oaks Crowd."

But what John really wanted to do was to be a leader. He believed that the rank-and-file members of any organization are not only willing to be led, but they are glad to be led by someone who will give them direction and guide them toward personal excellence and the prosperity of the entity as a whole. That philosophy had worked well in John's businesses and he believed it would work with the Deacons of Deadwood. His ability to lead was to be tested early on.

David Lee was becoming an increasing source of discord within the membership. Understanding how Lee became so dissatisfied requires some background.

David joined the Deacons in 2005, and came in full of enthusiasm. He went on all the organized rides and wanted to organize rides himself. He knew how to repair bikes and was of great help if anybody got into trouble on the road. Carroll Kelly nicknamed him "MacGyver," after the guy on the TV show who could escape from any trouble by building escape tools out of anything that happened to be at hand. Within a few months of being admitted, he was appointed road captain, and there was talk of him being elected to the board.

David ran for the board at the end of his first year in the Club and was defeated by a single vote. He ran again the following year and thought he had garnered sufficient pledges to be elected; however, by that time his star had faded, and many of those who had pledged to vote for David voted for someone else. It was not a close call; he did not have near the votes to be elected. He demanded to see the ballots so he could identify those who had pledged to vote for him but had voted for someone else. He became bitter.

David seemed to have a genetic need to lead, but the members did not want his leadership. So instead, he became the leader of the malcontents. Bruce McDonald had seemed to be a nice enough guy, but he soon came under David's wing and turned out to be an asshole of Homeric proportions. Dick Tate and Elza Smith had always been sanctimonious complainers and they also fell in within David's sphere. There were half a dozen other whiners who were a pain in the ass, but not as troublesome as David, Bruce, Dick and Elza.

During the month before the April meeting, David and Bruce conducted an e-mail campaign condemning pretty much everything about our management. These divisive e-mails were making everyone miserable. Some members avoided coming to meetings because they were so rancorous. Almost all of the complaints substantively were trivial but were intentionally caustic in their presentation.

For instance, by examining the Club's financials, David and Bruce claimed to have found an apparent discrepancy in the number of new members that had been admitted in the previous year and the amount dues and initiation fees that had been collected. They questioned why monthly dues had not been collected in full and why the names of those in arrears were not published to the whole Club. They questioned why out-of-town members were not required to pay annual dues. In addition, certain debts owed by members to the Club had been written off, inappropriately in their view. David and Bruce claimed all this was done under a cloak of secrecy.

They also complained about several minor administrative matters, such as updating our website to show which members had participated in certain rides, displaying newly authorized patches, spelling Wild Bill Hickok's name correctly, posting information about the previous year's Ball, and similar matters.

John had many calls with David and Bruce and told them that their strident e-mails were unacceptable. He reminded them of Club policies on inappropriate invective and of the consequences of violating those policies. Nothing worked.

Sam Allen

I was treasurer at the time and I responded to all of David's and Bruce's e-mails in writing. I pointed out that during my presidency and my tenure as treasurer, I sent monthly financial statements to the entire membership. I also pointed out that BKD reviewed our books and records on a monthly basis, and both audited our financial statements and prepared our tax return each year. To my view, these were a pretty transparent set of procedures.

I also responded to their specific inquiries.

First of all, the amount of money at issue was under $300. I pointed out that the reason for the discrepancy in the number of new members and the amount of dues that had been collected was because there were people who were members at the beginning of the year who resigned during the course of the year and were entitled to refunds. There also were members who came in during the course of the year who did not have to pay dues for the entire year. I told them that it had long been Club policy not to charge out-of-town members any dues or require them to buy Ball tickets. That was especially *apropos* to Preston Douglass, who despite living in Corpus Christi bought a VIP table at each year's Ball even though he couldn't attend. It would have been little unseemly to collect $5,000 from him for his VIP table and then bust his ass for $180 of dues that out-of-town members were not required to pay anyway.

As to write offs, they all were done with full board approval, and all involved legitimate disputes between the Club and certain members who believed that the Club's calculation of what they owed was incorrect. In each case, the board had determined that the amounts at issue were so small that it was worth writing them off rather than creating controversy within the membership.

All of this generated lots of e-mail correspondence among the members. Although there were a handful of members who supported David and Bruce, most of the members were tired of their bullshit and wanted them to stop causing trouble. Jim McConnell's response to one of Bruce's e-mails said it well:

> "The last time I checked, the Deacons have elections every year. We have a Treasurer that is in charge of money, we have a President that it sets the agenda for meetings, we have a member that is in charge of the website and who designates and delegates who writes articles and when and if they are due. I suggest you contact these people personally rather than "calling them out" in your e-mails. No one has to answer to you. You don't make the agendas for the meetings; you're not charge of collecting dues or any other monies I am aware of; you don't pay attention when things are discussed at meetings, as you keep bringing them up over and over."

Reviewing the Club correspondence that has survived concerning these matters reveals just how "small ball" all of this was. None of the issues raised were significant and there were reasonable responses to all of the concerns. There was no reason for the acrimony that these guys caused, and they caused it relentlessly.

All of this came to a head at the April 2007 meeting. Although John Aubrey was president, he could not attend, so I conducted the meeting. It was a melee. David, Bruce, Dick Tate, Elza and their ilk were in full attack mode, and those who opposed them attacked right back.

After the meeting, several members asked to see me privately. They told me that they were fed up with David and Bruce and that they intended to resign unless prompt action was taken to resolve the problems they were causing.

This was the first meeting that Bob Cavnar attended. He asked me if the meetings were always so contentious. He said he didn't need all the drama and he just wanted to ride motorcycles. I told Bob that the meetings often were worse, but by the next meeting the problem would be resolved, and it was.

I called John and told him about this mini revolution. John remembers that when he got the call he was tending a clothes line at his house in Aiken, South Carolina. John told me "This Club has asked its management to lead and that's exactly what I'm going to do."

When John got back to town, he immediately met with his board to determine how best to handle things. We had never faced the potential expulsion of a member and our bylaws did not address the issue. However, the board had the authority to amend the bylaws without consent of the membership as a whole. A plan was formed for the board to amend the bylaws to establish procedures to expel members under appropriate circumstances and then to implement the amended bylaws to expel David Lee, Bruce McDonald and possibly Elza Smith.

On Tuesday, April 10, 2007, the board amended the bylaws to provide that any member could be expelled upon a unanimous vote for expulsion by the board of directors followed by a vote for expulsion by two thirds of the voting members.

The next day, the board held a special meeting to vote on the expulsion of David Lee and Bruce McDonald. Elza barely escaped. Although there was significant support for expelling Elza, I made the pitch that although Elza certainly was a troublemaker, he was a founding member and should be given another chance. The board ultimately agreed, but Elza was told that the board in the future would take a zero tolerance policy towards his conduct. Elza responded that he could not promise to change. He was told that no promise was needed, but if he kicked up anymore shit he was gone.

John met with David and Bruce and discussed the issues with them for a last time. They were invited to attend the board meeting to make their case on why they should not be expelled. The board had determined to allow David and Bruce to make their statements without interruption.

The Deacons of Deadwood Motorcycle Club

We wanted them to have a chance to make their best defense and not do anything that would give our members the impression that the outcome was predetermined.

Bruce made a polite presentation claiming that he never had any intention of causing trouble and that all of his actions and inquiries were designed to better the Club. He claimed that he was an accountant by trade and had questions about the Club's financial statements for the routine kinds of things that any accountant might notice. He said that he would try not to be as caustic in the future, that he liked being a Deacon and that he hoped the board would not vote to kick him out.

David Lee was a different story. He was loud and aggressive, and the longer he spoke, the louder and more aggressive he became. He went on and on asking the board to justify a whole list of actions it had taken with which he had taken issue.

After about half an hour of this, Mike Callahan had had enough. In his usual blunt manner and strong British accent, Mike interrupted and said "David, you're not here to quiz the board. You're here to resign."

The other board members quieted Mike down and reminded him that all had agreed that David and Bruce would be allowed to make their presentations uninterrupted. Mike quieted down for a while, but in the end his patience was exhausted. He said "David, you're ruining our Club. No one likes you. Leave your Colors and go."

The rest of the board members once again were able to quiet Mike down and David gave the rest of his presentation without interruption.

Of course, as Bruce had feared, the decisions were clear. There was nothing that David or Bruce could have said that would have prevented the board from voting to expel them, and they so voted immediately after David and Bruce left. The day after the board meeting, John sent the following Notice:

Sam Allen

"All Members of the Deacons of Deadwood:

"Over the past months there has been an inordinate amount of batch e-mailing, e-mail bantering and offensive message board postings among a few Members that has been controversial, and grown burdensome and bothersome to a large number of the Members. Numerous Members complained to the Board, and several Members complained to me directly – even stating that they were going to quit the club if these actions continued. Unfortunately, after reading a recent series of batch e-mails, one new prospective member asked that his application be placed on hold.

This sort of incident became prevalent several years ago and we had a similar outcry, and a policy was put into place to deter offensive e-mails, but no teeth were attached to the policy. Clearly the Club told the Board last week that it needed to act. To that end, the Board had several conversations last week and met for over an hour and a half yesterday to amend the Bylaws to expel Members by a vote of two thirds of the Voting Members, to define offensive e-mails, to put teeth into the policy and to address the Club Members' concerns.

The Directors, through the Club Members and their comments noted that David Lee and Bruce McDonald were central to the situation and with input from a large number of Members of the Club decided to implement the newly adopted Bylaws.

To that end, a Special Members Meeting of the Deacons of Deadwood will be held on April 20, 2007 at 7:30 PM at the Hoffbrau Restaurant. The record date will be April 11, 2007. Voting Members as of that date will be allowed to vote at that Meeting. Under separate cover, the Club Secretary will e-mail the list of Voting Members as of the Record Date to all

The Deacons of Deadwood Motorcycle Club

Members. The purpose of the meeting will be to discuss and vote on the motion to expel David Lee and Bruce McDonald from the Club. All Members are encouraged to attend and the Voting Members are encouraged to be present or to vote *via* proxy. This is a serious issue and your thoughtful input is appreciated."

John C. Aubrey
President

Dick Tate took up the cause for the David and Bruce crowd in a letter to Club secretary Carroll Kelly:

"I'm diametrically opposed to this action. It is clear to me that this would never have been an issue if Sam had opened the books and shown both David and Bruce what was what. It appears to me that Sam has elected to get rid of those who are asking the embarrassing questions rather than comply with the simple request. I'm sure he has proxies from many who give them to him at his asking Carta blank (*sic*). This should be considered my proxy to you voting against this action.

Had I been Sam, I would've said to hell with it a long ago and turned the bookkeeping over to those who were asking the questions. 'Think you can do it better...here' type of logic. However, he has brought the club to a point where the division line is being drawn, and he is in effect saying "this is Sam's club," and all of you had better support me, those who don't will be tossed out."

Dick's letter had a modicum of truth. I was not saying that "This is my club, and if you don't agree with me I'll kick you out"; however, I was glad to join John Aubrey and most of the rest of the Club in kicking David and Bruce out, and I worked hard toward that end.

On the morning of the meeting, I called both David and Bruce and told them that they should not require the Club to expel them. I told them that they would be better off resigning on their own terms. That way they could tell the world what a bunch of assholes the Deacons were and no mention would have to be made publicly that they were so disliked that they were booted out.

Bruce responded in a polite way and told me that he would rather let the process take its course and wait to see how the vote came out. David Lee, true form, was aggressive. He told me to fuck myself and that the Club would never kick him out.

I told David they were going to lose by a vote of 19 to seven. That startled David and shut him up for a heartbeat, but he regrouped and asked me how I knew that. I told David I could count the votes, and that I would never let a vote happen if I didn't know how it was going to come out.

The meeting was short. David Lee showed up and was his usual asshole self. Before the vote was taken, a loaded pistol fell out of his pocket and clattered across the floor.

The Club had a roll-call vote and expelled David and Bruce by a vote of 20 to six. Rusty Drake had changed his vote at the last minute from against expulsion to in favor of expulsion.

I had taken David's and Bruce's attacks personally, as was fitting since most of their attacks were directed at me personally. I wanted to make a statement. I got the proxy of every member voting to expel David and Bruce. David and Bruce heard me cast 20 roll-call votes to kick them out.

The sentiment of the Club was even more graphic. Only voting members were allowed to vote on the expulsion. If non-voting members had been allowed to weigh in, there would have been another 20 votes to boot them out.

The Deacons of Deadwood Motorcycle Club

So, it was only six days from the date members had demanded the expulsion of David Lee and Bruce McDonald to the day the board amended the bylaws to set up expulsion procedures. The day after that, the board unanimously voted to expel them and a week after that they were gone. Dick Tate and Ken Carr resigned in protest.

There was no doubt that when it came time to lead John Aubrey had led.

A few weeks later Rocket John got to preside over a happier gathering. On April 26, 2007, the Club celebrated its fifth anniversary on the back deck at Blanco's. The Deacons had met there during the early years and we went back there to reminisce.

Justin "The Kid" Dossett on the night he became a Deacon.

The meeting was well attended, and many older members we had not seen in a while showed up. The only order of business was to pass out commemorative gold stars with a green "5" to all of the members who had been in the Club for the whole five years since it had been founded. Those Members were Ricky Cook, Tolly Allen, John Aubrey, John Talbot, Elza Smith, Carroll Kelly and me. Other than Ted Ricketson, whose wife, the Fly, made him drop out after she found out she was not going to get a patch, all of the founding members remained in the Club.

Sam Allen

John Aubrey made a nice presentation of these five-year stars. He said that some of the members might not appreciate the significance of receiving them, but to put it in perspective, Justin Dossett was being admitted to the Club on that night, and he would not get his five year star until 2012. I told Justin that in five years I would cut the five-year star I was receiving off of my vest and would present it to him on the day he earned his five-year star. Five years later I did just that.

Things got better socially after David Lee and Bruce McDonald were kicked out of the Club and Dick Tate had resigned. Although there was less friction, there was a feeling among some members that action was needed to better unify the Club. Part of the problem was that most of the founding members lived inside the Loop or nearby on the west side of Houston. But a substantial number of the newer members lived south of town. Al Arfsten (an inside the Loop guy), came up with the idea of having a monthly "South Side Social" in which once a month the members who lived inside the Loop or on the west side of town would travel to the south side for an informal get-together.

It was a good idea that was implemented for six months or so. Johnny Bish, who owns a carpeting and flooring company in Pasadena, was charged with setting up the socials. These events eventually faded out, but the program demonstrated the kinds of things that we tried in the hope of bringing the membership closer together.

John put on two Charity Balls, both in the Decorative Center. The 2007 Ball set a new record for attendance with over 450 guests. Joe Kilchrist sold over $100,000 of VIP tables and for the first time, we raised over $100,000 net to the charities. Camp for All was our primary beneficiary.

John wanted to upgrade our silent auction, so he brought in a company that specialized in running those events and that brought in a bunch of high end items that we never would have been able to offer on our own. But John brought in some great offerings himself, including a trip to the Masters and a trip to Oakmont Country Club, which has hosted more US Opens than any other golf club.

In 2008, John put on the Ball in the face of Hurricane Ike, which was the biggest natural disaster to hit Houston in half a century. Power was out all over Houston and we worried that it would not be restored by the date of the Ball. John had to rent tents and generators in case we had to go it alone. Power was restored in time, but our bottom line was affected by the cost of renting the equipment that ultimately did not need to be used.

In 2008, Boys and Girls Country gave the Deacons their Friends of Children Award, which is given annually to Boys and Girls Country's most significant sponsor. By 2008, we had donated over $200,000.

By the middle of 2008, Carroll Kelly's cancer was coming to a head. Outwardly, he looked good and he did not talk about his health issues; however, some of his closest friends knew that his doctors had informed him that he had weeks, rather than months or years to live. John Aubrey organized a motorcycle ride from Seattle back to Houston that many suspected was likely to be Carroll's last long ride.

The ride started on June 8. John and Amy Aubrey, Elza and Beverly Smith, Jim McConnell, Carroll and his girlfriend Ann Emory and I shipped our bikes to Seattle for this ride.

Jim McConnell was an interesting guy who had never before gone on any long trips with the Club. He had made millions as an oil and gas land man and was living off of royalties he accumulated over 30 years. Jim didn't have to work anymore so he was spending his time promoting, of all things, hip-hop singers. He wasn't making any money at it, but he was having fun and getting a lot of black poontang. Jim came along on the ride because he had a daughter he wanted to visit in Reno. Then he wanted to break away and go to Las Vegas for some of his hip-hop business.

John planned a great route. We stayed on the Pacific Coast Highway as much as possible until just north of San Francisco, then we cut over the mountains to Reno, Nevada. From Reno, we rode 325 miles across Nevada's Highway 50, known as the "Loneliest Road in America." From Ely, Nevada, the ride was across northern Utah to Grand Junction, Colorado, then followed the mountains south to Cuchara, which is an old town in a defunct ski resort in southern Colorado near the New Mexico border. From Cuchara, it was to Amarillo, Fort Worth and back to Houston.

The Pacific Northwest often is cold and rainy and it was no exception during this ride. The first couple of days were chilly, windy and misty, but the ride went through some magnificent countryside and along beautiful coastline. Early one evening we came across a large herd of elk in the middle of a redwood forest. The elk were right next to the road and were not scared of us.

During this ride, Tiger Woods was fighting it out with Rocco Mediate for golf's U.S. Open title at Torey Pines. John, Carroll and I all followed the tournament during the ride home. We made it to the Stockyards Hotel Bar in Fort Worth in time to watch the Sunday round. At the end of the round Tiger and Rocco were tied, which meant the next day they would have to play 18 additional holes in a playoff.

Monday morning everyone headed for home. I was listening to the U.S. Open playoff on the radio on my Ultra Classic. That's what all the bad ass bikers were listening to on their satellite radios that day. Carroll was leading the group and just south of Dallas, he unexpectedly crossed about three lanes of traffic and exited I-45. I knew I couldn't get over in time so I kept riding as I watched Carroll go down the exit ramp. It was the last time I saw Carroll on a motorcycle.

Carroll died on September 6, 2008. He had just finished playing golf with friends and was on his way to watch his grandson play little league football. He felt a little lightheaded and stopped in to a drugstore for some medication. A few minutes later he was found dead beside his car. Carroll lived his life doing what he wanted to do right up until the moment he died.

The Deacons of Deadwood Motorcycle Club

Carroll was the first Deacon to pass away and it shook us, especially our older members. We were unsure how to react. Some of the members knew Carroll only through his affiliation with the Deacons. The older members knew that as much as Carroll loved the Deacons, the Club was only a small part of his life. Carroll had been a lawyer and businessman who traveled in lofty circles. Carroll knew everybody. He had known every Texas governor and senator for the last 40 years. He played golf with Willie Nelson and Darrell Royal. He recruited Vince Young for the Texas Longhorns.

Some members thought the old school thing to do would be for the Deacons to wear our patches to Carroll's funeral. Others thought that would be disrespectful to Carroll, his family and his lifelong friends who didn't know anything about the Deacons. Carroll's family bailed us out and requested that we come with our patches.

We had virtually 100% attendance. Several former members who had dropped out of the Club were there. A separate section in the church where the service was conducted was reserved for the Deacons. Someone remarked at how thoughtful that was of Carroll's family. Others wondered whether they just wanted to keep us away from the nice people. John Aubrey was one of the pallbearers.

Riding to Carroll Kelly's funeral.

Eulogies were given by Carroll's best friend from law school and one of his sons. Then a video of Carroll's life was presented. When the video got to Carroll's life with the Deacons, many tears were shed. Although Carroll could say and do infuriating things, he was one of the most respected Deacons and was truly loved.

After the funeral, the Deacons rode in a procession to the original Ninfa's restaurant on Navigation Street just outside downtown Houston. I had reserved the room where Carroll had introduced himself to me nearly a decade earlier. Carroll loved nachos, and I ordered all the nachos, beer and margaritas the members could eat and drink. I also distributed framed copies of the photo that had been taken of Carroll and me in the snow drift atop Bear Tooth Pass in Montana on our first trip to Sturgis.

Everyone got drunk as hell, but the question Carroll had once asked of whether we really had a Club had been answered.

As John's presidency wound down, there was a lot for which he could be proud. He had led the Club when asked to rid itself of some long-standing troublemakers, and as a result, the membership's camaraderie was at its highest. John had presided over two Charity Balls, one of which netted us over $100,000 for the first time, and the other of which was held in the aftermath of Hurricane Ike. The Club's Membership exceeded 60 for the first time. Most importantly, John had made being a Deacon more fun than it ever had been.

CHAPTER 6

THE REIGN OF KING JAY I

"And do you know another thing Arthur? Life is too bitter already, without territories and wars and noble feuds."
— T. H. White, *The Once and Future King*

Jay McKendree met the Deacons of Deadwood through Elza Smith. Jay was practicing law as an associate at a personal injury law firm and he represented Elza and his wife Beverly in a lawsuit arising out of an accident they had when they ran over a sunken manhole cover on downtown Houston streets that were under construction. Jay lost the case, but Elza introduced Jay to the Deacons.

Jay had never met a Deacon other than Elza before being admitted to the Club. The first meeting he attended was in January 2003, at which officers and directors were being elected. Jay was admitted at that meeting. Back in those days we did not have voting members and nonvoting members, so Jay got to vote for the president and directors without knowing any of the candidates.

Jay enjoyed the Club from the outset, and especially liked the rides scheduled for the third Sunday of each month. The first of these rides in which Jay participated was led by Carroll Kelly and Dan Bezborn.

Jay's soft-spoken manner commanded respect from the outset. Early in his tenure he was named to the Club's first charity committee, and soon thereafter he was appointed treasurer. It was thought that his diligent nature and even temper made him suitable for the job. What really helped was that his wife Angie knew how to use the accounting software that the Club used so he could rely on her in making the necessary bookkeeping entries and keeping the financial statements straight.

As treasurer, Jay would attend the board meetings and give financial reports. He also took notes of the meetings and prepared the minutes, so he also was the *de facto* Club secretary. He remembers those meetings as kind of mini Deacons' chapter meetings. Formal rules of conducting meetings were not followed, but everybody seemed to arrive at a consensus on important issues.

When John Aubrey's term as president was winding down, some of the Club's leaders met to figure out who a good successor might be. Jay had done such a good job as treasurer that everybody agreed he would be a great candidate to succeed John. John and some others approached Jay to ask him if he would be interested in serving. He was surprised that he was being considered for the position and thought that there must be others more qualified. It took some persuasion, but he agreed.

Jay was elected unanimously and he became the only Deacon to serve as president without first having served on the board. Justin Dossett and Orlando Sanchez were elected to three year terms on the board.

Justin was our youngest member and because of that he was dubbed "The Kid." He had the innocence and energy of a puppy dog (he still does). His enthusiasm for the Deacons and his participation in all our activities garnered the respect of the membership.

Orlando Sanchez had been prominent in Houston's Republican political circles. He had served on the City Council as one of its only conservative members. He later ran for mayor and was defeated by a thin margin, but only after the Clintons sent in their henchmen Terry

McAuliffe at the last minute to rally the Democratic troops. Orlando eventually was elected Harris County Treasurer, which is a post he still holds. Orlando turned out to be an enthusiastic rider. He took over organizing the Club's Big Bend rides and he founded the Fort Clark ride.

The meeting at which Jay was elected is noteworthy for a couple of reasons. First, it had the largest attendance in the Club's history. Second, Noah Latham was admitted as an honorary Deacon.

Noah was the nine-year-old son of my girlfriend Melanie. Melanie had been killed in an altercation involving a former boyfriend and a gun. Noah's father was nowhere to be found. Melanie had been married twice: once to Noah's father and once to Trent Marbs, who is the father of Melanie's other son. Trent had no obligation to take Noah in, but he did, and Noah lived with him for several years until his biological father resurfaced. He turned out to be a good guy.

A young Noah "Wildhog" Latham the night he became a Deacon.

Ricky and I had a special vest made for Noah out of the Dead Man's Hand from one of the old three peace patches that had been abandoned. Ricky also gave Noah a comb that looked like a switchblade. Ricky joked that if he wore the patch and took the comb to school he would be called down to the principal's office, and when asked to explain himself Noah would say "We only care about three things: whiskey, women and violence."

With Noah's mother gone and his father missing, Ricky and I wanted the Deacons to take Noah under the Club's wing. He was unanimously elected as honorary Deacon, and the vest Ricky and I had given him was replaced with a full set of Deacons' colors. He came to almost all the meetings after that. I would pick him up on my motorcycle and Trent would pick him up after the meetings to drive him home.

Young as he was, he became one of us. A year or so after Noah had been admitted as a Deacon, my date tried to take care of him at one of our meetings. Noah told her "Don't worry about me, I know all these people."

At the January 2014 meeting Noah received a gold five-year star. Our member Ben Thompson gave Noah a job for the summer of 2014. Someday he will be the oldest Deacon.

An older Noah and his birthday cake.

From the beginning of Jay's administration, he decided that he wanted to preside over a strong board that would take a leadership role in making Club decisions. His philosophy was that the board was elected to do the hard work, and by doing so, the rest of the membership would have more free time for fun.

Jay also set up a succession plan so that each significant office in the Club had a back-up who could step into the shoes of a current office holder if need be. For instance, Jay knew that if something happened to the treasurer, he had the experience step in until a new treasurer was selected. Jay didn't tell anybody about this plan. It was just part of the competent leadership that Jay quietly provided.

Jay's first term in office saw the rise of the Princess of Darkness, a.k.a. the "POD." She was Ricky Cook's squeeze and she started coming to Deacons' meetings and other functions. Everybody who met her had an initial impression that she was an attractive and bright woman, which she sometimes was. But after a drink or two, or after virtually any provocation, her Dr. Jekyll would turn into Mrs. Hyde.

I was the Club's secretary during Jay's first term of office, and I first mentioned the Princess in the minutes of our meeting on December 3, 2008, which was our Christmas Party held at the Palm Restaurant. The menu included filet mignon, veal parmesan and salmon. The minutes reflect:

> "Since it was the Christmas party, many wives and dates were in attendance, the most notable of which was the Princess of Darkness. She arrived a bit late because there was no valet parking for her broom, and her flying monkeys were denied admission due to the lack of proper attire. Once she arrived, however, she looked stunning in a black cocktail dress she keeps in a special cave in her castle."

Later, the minutes from that meeting provide:

> "While the drinking was carried on, the POD got doggie bags to take all the leftover steak and veal home. Apparently, flying monkeys don't like salmon."

I started to include a Princess of Darkness update in the minutes of all our meetings. If a set of minutes did not have a POD update, members would be disappointed, and they encouraged me to make up things to report. There was no need. The Princess provided plenty of material.

John Aubrey was president at the next meeting, which was the meeting at which Jay was elected. The minutes record:

> "President 'Rocket John' Aubrey postponed calling the meeting to order because he feared that if he started before the Princess of Darkness arrived, she would put a hex on the Club that would result in his being elected for a third term in office, a risk he was wisely unwilling to take. However Ricky (the "Flying Monkey") Cook let him know that the POD would not be attending the meeting so those fears were unfounded. That being the case, Rocket John called the meeting to order at 7:35."

After the meeting, we went to watch the BCS championship game between Oklahoma and Florida. There was an addendum to the minutes:

> "We went to Champs, but it was so crowded, we all left for the Wet Spot. As we were leaving Champs, the POD was just getting there, and our adjournment to a different venue was not met with her pleasure. Fortunately, the noise from our motors was loud enough to drown out the wrath of the POD. She eventually met us at the Wet Spot, and as she entered, a pall fell across the land. The TV screens dimmed, and Florida lost the ball on a fumble at the Oklahoma goal line. Nonetheless, after a few libations, she seemed to temper her malevolence. All was once again joyful in Bikerland, and Florida went on to win the National Championship."
>
> "On a serious note, the POD was mugged on her way to her car. Her bag was stolen, and she suffered some injuries,

which fortunately were not serious. We wish the POD well. We also have sympathy for the guy who mugged her. He knows not what he has wrought upon himself!"

We always take a ride to a local bar after our regularly scheduled monthly meetings. Despite having been mugged at the February, 2009, meeting, the Princess came along on the ride after the March meeting. The minutes report:

"After adjournment, everybody rode to the Cedar Creek Bar, and then to the Big Star Bar. It was noticed that the Princess of Darkness was behaving in a particularly cordial manner. It was later revealed that it was because she was having a visit from her "friend", and she was suffering from toxic shock syndrome. Since the meeting, she reverted to her dark ways, and has in the past few days electrocuted Ricky's dog and nearly killed a horse."

There is some truth in that story; however, enough of the Princess of Darkness for now.

Like all of the previous presidents, Jay had to contend with members who were habitually tardy in paying their dues and buying their Ball tickets. Jay also had to contend with several ornery members who would resign from the Club every time something happened with which they disagreed.

To combat these problems, Jay and his board amended our bylaws to add rules concerning resigning from the Club and to add material consequences for the failure to pay dues or buy the required two Ball tickets on time.

The rules concerning resignation were referred to as the "Cadillac Joe Amendment," because "Cadillac Joe" Blount was constantly resigning from the Club then coming back once his temper had cooled. The new rule provided that a member giving an oral resignation had five days to reconsider. We did not want to enforce a resignation unless the member really wanted to resign.

As to paying dues and buying Ball tickets on time, the amendments in essence provided that:

- New members were required to pay their initiation fee, one year of dues and buy their two Ball tickets before being admitted to the Club. That amendment essentially was a codification of the policies in effect at that time.
- Existing members would have to pay their dues in full by January 15 of each year and pay for their Ball tickets by February 15 of each year.
- A member who was in arrears for 60 days would be subject to expulsion from the Club by action of the board.
- A member who was in arrears for 120 days would be expelled from the Club automatically without further action of the board or its membership.
- Despite the foregoing, any member in financial distress could enter into a confidential payment plan with the treasurer, and that member would not be in arrears along as he fulfilled his obligations under the payment plan.

These amendments met some resistance, especially among those who were habitually late in making the required payments. The biggest arguments against the amendments were:

- No other Club does this;
- The board can't do that; and
- That's bullshit.

The Deacons of Deadwood Motorcycle Club

Elza Smith was the biggest proponent of the "That's bullshit" argument. He thought the louder he said it, the more cogent the argument would be, because he made his argument at increasingly higher decibel levels. He claimed that these rules were something I did behind closed doors and claimed that the board had no right to amend the bylaws without approval from the members. He was wrong on both counts. I had nothing to do with passing those amendments, and the bylaws always provided for amendment by the board without Club approval. Elza must have forgotten that was exactly what the board did when David Lee Bruce and McDonald were kicked out.

Elza had to speak loudly to drown out the objections made by Cadillac Joe. Joe argued that no other club had rules that required their members to pay dues on time. He then resigned from the Club and said he was going to return his colors when he felt like it, but before turning them in, he was going to burn them upside down in a trashcan at a Bandidos meeting. It became evident that no one in the Club was much concerned about that indignity. Therefore, Jay instructed the sergeant at arms to escort Cadillac Joe from the meeting. Since Cadillac Joe was in fact the sergeant at arms, he had to escort himself out.

That was Joe's fourth resignation from the Club, thus breaking the previous record of three resignations held by Elza Smith. Joe and Elza had resigned and came back so many times that the Club thought about creating a new class of membership called the "temporary member," designed for members who spend as much time resigned from the Club as they spend as active members.

David Youngblood had been admitted as a member at that meeting, and when Cadillac Joe resigned, David's wife cheerfully reminded him that he had five days to reconsider his resignation. Elza Smith, in his usual well thought out and diplomatic fashion, told her to "Shut the fuck up," because women have no place at Deacons meetings.

Youngblood in turn told Elza to fuck himself, resigned from the Club and left the meeting with his wife. That broke Cadillac Joe's previous record for the quickest resignation after admission to the Club. He had to escort himself out because after Joe resigned, we were without a sergeant at arms so there was no one left to do the escorting.

Treasurer Ricky Cook announced that in light of the fact that David Youngblood had resigned on the day he was admitted to the Club, he would only have to pay the initiation fee and the yearly dues would be waived. Fortunately, David availed himself of the newly adopted five-day Cadillac Joe rule and came back to the Club.

As Jay settled in, it was evident that he was a capable and firm president. Jay had no problem taking action on his own initiative or through the board without discussion among the membership as a whole. Jay would simply announce what we were going to do. He was able to do this in a way that projected leadership without raising the hackles of the members, who as a rule, liked to participate in all significant decisions. A good bit of the reason that Jay could lead in this way was that he would seek consensus on important issues before presenting his plan of action to his board or the Club.

I started teasing Jay about his management style as early as Jay's second meeting as president, where I referred to him in the minutes as Jay "Dr. House" McKendree, because he broke his ankle when he dropped his bike while parking at Warren's Bar in downtown Houston and was walking around with a cane. More than one Deacon (including me) has done that at Warren's, and breaking a bone after dropping a bike at Warren's now is known as "Pulling a McKendree."

In March, he became Jay "Ahab" McKendree because although he was without the cane, he was hobbling around with an orthopedic boot and he walked like Captain Ahab of *Moby Dick* fame. In April, he became Jay "il Duce" McKendree after Benito Mussolini. By May, Jay was "der Furher." In July, he became a more modern dictator when he was named Jay "Kim il Sung" McKendree. By December, he was "el Hefe." At the beginning of the next year he was coronated as King Jay I.

All of this was in good fun. Jay was a very good and much liked President.

Jay was up for reelection at the January 14, 2010, meeting. The Princess of Darkness had not surfaced for a while, but she had recently reappeared. The minutes provide:

> "A foul weather had swept the land before this most important of meetings; the annual meeting where our King and new Knights are elected. A cold rain and hard wind swept through the bleak night as our brethren arrived in cars rather than the thunderous iron steeds for which they are known hither and yon. Never before had these glorious modern day Knights assembled under such a ghastly cloud of gloom. Although no one dared utter the words, all knew that there could be only one cause for the curse upon our despoiled surroundings: the Princess of Darkness was afoot, unseen, but unmistakably among us. All silently prayed for the strength and guidance needed to carry us through the unknown, but certainly hazardous, challenges before us."

> "With great trepidation, but also with the grace of God and a strong force of will, King Jay I called the meeting to order."

Jay was unanimously reelected as president, and Bob Bulian and Peter Sommer were elected as directors for three year terms.

Ricky Cook introduced Bob to the Club. He is one of our two members from the Black Hills of South Dakota. He went to Rapid City high school, as did Jim Row, although they were not there at the same time.

Sam Allen

Peter Sommer had been an executive for Chevron and had spent most of his professional life traveling the world with his wife Ellen. When Peter got ready to retire he renewed his friendship with Steve Lamb, who he had known when they lived near each other in Sugar Land in the early 1990s. He and Steve had ridden with David Cook in those days, and Peter remembers David being just as crooked and likeable as all the rest of us remember him.

Peter's first ride with the Deacons was to Big Bend. Steve Lamb had invited him to go, but Lambo didn't show up so Peter went on the ride without knowing any of us. He saw the Deacons as a serious riding club, and he knew that by joining he would get a chance to travel the United States, which is something he hadn't been able to do because of his professional life. Peter has now seen the country on two wheels, and is one of only three Deacons who has earned a "Map of America" patch by riding to all of the 48 contiguous states.

In late 2009, Matt Linton and George Bogle approached me about a plan that they had to start a new motorcycle club to be centered in the Clear Lake, Friendswood, and Galveston areas.

Both Matt and George had been Deacons since 2003. George had served as our first technology chairman, and had developed and maintained our website. George also had served as a director and ran for president twice. He went on our first Iron Butt ride. Although he tended to align himself with some of the Club's naysayers, George was a well-liked and well-respected Deacon. He believed strongly in the brotherhood of our Club and worked hard to strengthen that brotherhood. His nickname was the "Ambassador" because of his efforts to bridge gaps among different groups within the Club.

Matt is a soft-spoken and gentle guy. His nickname was the "Comrade" because he had a beard like Vladimir Lennin's. He's a professional photographer who teaches photography classes at the University of Houston in Clear Lake. He had been around motorcycles all his life and owned a

The Deacons of Deadwood Motorcycle Club

Knucklehead. When his daughters Camera and Xaiden were born, we passed a resolution designating them as the "Littlest Deacons." He was the first Deacon to be awarded a "Map of America" patch. Matt was one of the members who told me in 2008 that unless David Lee and Bruce McDonald were kicked out of the Club, he and a bunch of his friends would quit.

Matt and George said that they loved the Deacons of Deadwood and wanted to remain members; however, they claimed that a few existing Deacons and some other bikers they knew wanted to form a separate club with the existing Deacons being in both clubs.

Under their proposal, they would wear their Deacons' patches to all Deacons meetings and functions, but would wear the patch for the new club when riding on the south side of town at non-Deacons' functions. In addition, they would continue to fulfill all the requirements of being a Deacon, including attending five meetings to be voting members, paying dues and buying Ball tickets. They even would be willing to wear a "Deacons Supporter" patch.

I told Matt and George that I didn't have a particular problem with their idea, but it would have to be passed on by the entire Club, and there could be no assurance that the proposal would be acceptable to the membership at large.

Matt and George eventually presented their plan to Jay. Jay knew it was coming because I had given him a heads up.

In retrospect, Jay believes he handled things poorly. His first reaction was that he had no problem with their plan and he told Matt and George that he would support it. Jay had many late-night calls with George discussing the two-club proposal and how it would be implemented. Over the course of these conversations and with input from some of the Deacons, Jay changed his mind and concluded that a two club system would not likely be met with approval by the rest of the Deacons. He decided he could not support Matt and George's plan; however, he agreed to let them make their pitch at the next Club meeting.

By the time that meeting came around, word of Matt and George's plan had spread. That the idea leaked out before they were able to make their presentations really pissed George off. George wanted it both ways; he was actively recruiting our members to join his club, but he denied he was doing so. He had told us that there were several Deacons who already had agreed to join his club, but he wouldn't tell us who they were. At the same time, he expected confidentiality about his secret activities.

When the meeting came, Matt spoke first. He started his presentation by saying that he loved the Deacons of Deadwood and he would never do anything that would harm the Club. Mike Callaghan interrupted and said "Nobody ever harmed the Club by resigning." That remark set the tenor of the rest of the evening.

Matt's presentation was polite and respectful, and then it was George's turn. George also was polite and respectful, but his presentation went badly.

He started off by saying that the Deacons were not a real "MC", but were more of a social club. He pointed out that unlike all the "real" motorcycle clubs in Houston, the Deacons were not a member of the Confederacy of Clubs. He said that the Deacons did not participate in functions put on by other Houston area motorcycle clubs, and as a result the Deacons were not recognized as a true part of the "MC Community." He also said that a real MC would have a three-piece patch and would not have the cartoonish designations, such as being 44%ers, that the Deacons had.

George's message was that the Deacons had a place among social motorcycle riders but had no place in the MC world. He and his followers wanted to remain Deacons and continue to wear a Deacons patch, but they also wanted to be part of a more traditional motorcycle club with all that that entailed. George conceded that a real MC would not allow a member to be a patch holder in two separate clubs, but since the Deacons was not a real MC, he argued that should not be a problem either for the Deacons or his new club.

The Deacons of Deadwood Motorcycle Club

Whatever chance George might have had to convince the Deacons to allow him to form a new club and still wear a Deacons' patch was lost the moment he said that the Deacons was not a real motorcycle club. Everything George had said about the differences between the Deacons and more traditional MCs probably was true, but that did not detract from the fact that the Deacons believed that they were indeed a motorcycle club.

The Deacons considered Matt and George's proposal at the next meeting. The membership was offended at George's assertion that we were not a motorcycle club. That resulted in a lot of *ad hominem* remarks about those who were leaving. Others pointed out that they were our friends, and although we might not be willing to let them remain Deacons while being a member of another club, there was no reason that the friendships should not remain.

It was not a close call. The Deacons rejected Matt and George's proposal. Within 48 hours, the board amended the bylaws to prohibit a Deacon from being a patch holder in two motorcycle clubs.

I had heard a rumor that Bob Cavnar had decided to join the new club. I did not believe the rumor.

Bob was president of a fairly large oil and gas exploration company in Houston and had once been the CFO of El Paso Gas. He was president of the Houston Opera. He was elected to the board during his first year in the Club. He came up with the idea of having Club rings and designed the rings we ultimately approved. Bob also had been the most vocal negative voice on the board with respect to prohibiting Deacons from wearing patches of other clubs, and he had been an integral part of drafting the bylaw amendments prohibiting Deacons from doing so.

I called Bob to let him know about the rumor. Bob was quiet for a few seconds, and then he told me that it was true. He gave me no good reason for his decision other than that the new club offered to make him a founding member. When I told Jay about Bob's decision, Jay was both dumbfounded and incensed.

So, George and Matt resigned from the Deacons in short order to found the Sovereign Souls Motorcycle Club. Elza Smith, Mike Marlowe, Mike Poperszky, Froggy Castellano, Rusty Drake and Bob Cavnar left with them.

George was really chapped at the Deacons' decision not to support his two-club proposal. He claimed then, and has claimed for years, that Jay and I screwed him over because we failed to support him after initially telling him we had no particular problem with his plan. Apparently, George believes Jay and I should have supported his new club at the cost of going against the overwhelming views of our members. We did what we had to do.

There also is the question of just who was doing the screwing. After all, George had been secretly recruiting Deacons to join his new club. If he could have, he would have taken every single Deacon with him.

To hear George tell it today, he claims he was forced to resign from the Deacons. That is not true. He was forced to decide whether he wanted to remain a Deacon or whether he wanted to form the new club. He chose to leave the Deacons and form the new club.

Soon after the Sovereign Souls were formed, they offered to come to a Deacons meeting to formally turn in their Deacons' patches. That offer was made in good faith. They believed that was proper MC protocol. Their idea was to turn in their patches, have a beer with their former brothers and everybody would leave as friends.

Jay told them not to come. There was some real acrimony against the guys who left. Most of that acrimony came from the Deacons' newer members who had not been friends with Matt, George and the others for so many years. Jay and I told our members that those who left to form the Sovereign Souls were our friends and should remain our friends. The Sovereign Souls certainly wanted to remain friends of ours.

The Deacons of Deadwood Motorcycle Club

The departure of those eight guys was a blessing to both the Deacons and the Sovereign Souls. They wanted something out of a motorcycle club that we never would be able to provide. Alternatively, the last of malcontents had left the Deacons, and as a result, the contentiousness that had followed the Deacons for so many years left with them. The Saturday after the Sovereign Souls left the Deacons, we had the best attended ride in our history.

A few words about George and Matt are in order. They were not trouble makers like David Lee and Bruce McDonald had been. They brought their two club proposal to us in a respectful way and in good faith. The acrimony from their departure mostly was from relatively new Deacons who had not been brothers with George and Matt for the previous nine years. Almost immediately after they left, some Deacons started referring to the Sovereign Souls as the "Soul Sisters." The Deacons who were not around back then seemed to think this nickname as was a pejorative. That was not the intent; it was good natured ass busting. Matt and George were good guys and they remain our friends.

The departure of the Sovereign Souls left the Deacons with some technical problems. George had been the head of our technology committee and hosted our website through his own Internet business. After George left, we needed to move our website to a new host. Jay had to not only take on moving the website to a new host, but had to build a brand-new website himself. Jay had no experience in website construction, but he taught himself how to do it, and within one week, we had a new website with a new host.

Jay was able to save some of the content that had been on the website that George had hosted. Included in this content was a series of articles that Club members had written about their experiences as Deacons. Some of these articles survive and are attached as an Appendix to this book. Both Matt and George wrote articles, and it is interesting to compare what they had to say about the Deacons when writing the articles and what they had to say about the Deacons when founding the Sovereign Souls.

Jay remembers dealing with the Sovereign Souls and creating the new website as the toughest matters he encountered as president.

In addition to having to deal with members who were constantly resigning, getting people to pay their dues, and dealing with the Sovereign Souls, Jay had to preside over all of the other traditional Club functions including putting on two Charity Balls. When Jay took office, the country was in bit of an economic decline, and there was concern about how that decline would affect our fundraising efforts.

The Balls in the three years before Jay took office had been held at the Decorative Center, which is a beautiful but extravagant venue. Jay decided to take the Club in a different direction.

Jay and his board looked at several spots and eventually settled on la Colombe D'or. This unique venue has a Grand Ballroom with oak panels originally carved in 1715 that were installed in an estate outside of Paris in 1891. They did not require a site fee and they gave us favorable pricing on food and alcohol.

Both of Jay's Balls (that doesn't sound right, does it?) were a success both socially and financially.

Jay also had a healthy emphasis on riding. In 2010, he founded the Hot Springs Ride, which was made over the Fourth of July weekend. Everyone stayed at the Arlington Hotel, which was an Al Capone haunt. Then there were daily rides through the Ozarks. This ride has become a Club favorite for which a patch is awarded for participation.

Jay remembers his favorite ride as being the ride Orlando Sanchez organized to Fort Clark in Bracketville, Texas. Fort Clark was an old U.S. Army post used to protect travelers against Indian attacks. Much of the Fort remains and everybody on the ride stayed in the soldiers' barracks. There is a spring fed swimming pool that's probably 100 yards long. Everyone had golf clubs sent in so they could tee it up while at the Fort.

The Deacons of Deadwood Motorcycle Club

Six Deacons went on the first of Fort Clark ride, and they were awarded a "Six of Clubs" patch (as in golf clubs, get it?) in recognition of the six Deacons who participated. No more Six of Clubs patches will be awarded.

Jay's biggest disappointment was that we failed to get our own clubhouse. When the idea was first brought up, Jay had thought it impractical. After more consideration, he thought there was no reason why we should not have one. Jay, Steve Lamb, Ricky Cook, Ben Thompson, Geoff Seaman, Al Arfsten and I were appointed to a clubhouse committee to explore the idea. The clubhouse committee sought out potential venues and analyzed the costs that would be involved. We found a spot on Main Street in downtown Houston that had a storefront and its own bar. We could have rented it for $0.50 a square foot.

The project never gained traction. Some pointed out that there were parking problems. Others worried about the police presence downtown. Still others worried about liabilities arising out of accidents that might happen after people had been drinking at the clubhouse.

In retrospect, Jay believes that these and any other objections could have been overcome had we just simply made the decision that we were going to have a clubhouse rather than setting up a committee to determine the feasibility of having one.

Getting a new clubhouse remains one of Jay's priorities in 2014.

Jay had been skeptical of becoming our president for his first term. Because of all the acrimony with which he had to deal he did not want to serve a second term. It took the persuasive powers of his board and others to convince him to continue in office. Then immediately upon the start of his second term he had to face the whole Sovereign Souls problem and rebuild our website. Jay says that by the time his second term was completed "I had aged."

Still, Jay found it hard stepping down. Leaving office was easy, but setting aside feelings of responsibility and duty was not so easy. All of the previous presidents had similar experiences. No matter how much help a president might receive from his board and the other members, ultimate responsibility for the Club's well-being resides in its president. After a couple of years serving as president, it's hard to relinquish the reins and avoid the gut feeling that the successor president may not be quite up to the task. But they always have been.

Jay had presided over a tumultuous period in our history, but he left the Club stronger than it was when he had taken office. Despite having a group leave to form a new club, our membership had grown. We no longer had any habitual troublemakers, so our members were looking forward to, rather than dreading, attending Club meetings. The monthly rides were better attended and new annual rides were established that have become Deacons' traditions. Systemic problems in collecting dues and getting members to pay for their Ball tickets in a timely fashion had been resolved, so we were on a more solid financial footing than we had been in years. The Deacons of Deadwood Motorcycle Club was the best it had ever been.

King Jay I in his Colors.

CHAPTER 7

STEVE LAMB AND THE *PAX DEACONA*

> *"I got good times*
> *No more bad times*
> *I got my girl*
> *Who could ask for anything more?"*
>
> – George and Ira Gershwin, *I got Rhythm*

The *Pax Romana* (Latin for "Roman Peace") was a period of relative peace in the Roman Empire that started with Caesar Augustus and lasted a little over 200 years. With the departure of the Sovereign Souls during the beginning of the second term of King Jay I, the Deacons began to experience a sort of *Pax Deacona* (fake Latin for "Deacons Peace"). Steve Lamb inherited that peace and was able to use it and our new found unity to expand the Club beyond previously contemplated limits.

Lambo presiding.

Sam Allen

Steve found out about the Deacons though Make-a-Wish. His son Shawn had been killed in a tragic accident in 1997 when Shawn was 22 years old. Shawn was born while Steve was still a teenager and Steve raised him as a single father. Of course, Shawn's death left Steve with a loss only a parent can experience. As time went on, he decided to dedicate at least a portion of his life to the memory of his son. Steve doesn't remember why he picked Make-a-Wish. He did not know much about them other than they did things to make children happy. He showed up at their door unannounced and offered to help in any way he could.

Terry Andrepont was the president of the local Make-a-Wish chapter. She knew that Steve rode motorcycles, told him about a motorcycle club that was putting on a benefit for Make-a-Wish, and suggested that he might want to attend. That turned out to be the first Deacons of Deadwood Charity Ball.

Steve had grown up around motorcycles and knew his way around the 1%er crowd. He had ridden with the Richmond Ruffians, which was an informal group that had many members who later turned out to be either Deacons or close friends of the Deacons. Through the Ruffians, Steve knew Jim Lang, a.k.a. "Sprocket," who was the international president of the Bandidos.

Steve had been using Columbia Cycles for his motorcycle repair work, but the owner of Columbia proved to be unreliable. One of the Richmond Ruffians (who later became a Deacon and then a Sovereign Soul) suggested he try David Cook's Luxury Cycles. He remembers Cook the way everybody else remembers him. Steve might take his bike in for an oil change and have a $400 chrome derby cover installed on the bike when he picked it up. Like everybody else, he found David Cook infectious.

Steve had been to David Cook's Ride to Fuad's and had his picture taken with my then girlfriend when she wore nothing but a white dinner jacket. I must have met Steve at that party, but neither Steve nor I have any recollection of the meeting. That just shows that Steve had his priorities right. Linda was Hot, Hot, Hot, and I was just another pencil dick in the crowd.

Steve knew enough about David Cook's Rides to Fuad's to have some expectation of what he might find at the Deacons' Ball. However, he was impressed that the Deacons wore tuxedos with our patch on the back. Steve thought the 44% patch was pretty ballsy in the context of motorcycle clubs in Houston, which were dominated by the Bandidos. I was the first Deacon that Steve met. I remember meeting Steve at that Ball but I don't remember much about our conversation other than Steve seemed interested in the Club and its style.

Mike Fisher and Johnny Williams styling in Deacons' Formalwear.

About a week after the Ball, Steve ran into several Deacons, including John Talbot and me, at the County Line Icehouse on Westheimer. He introduced himself and asked some details about the Deacons. When asked how to become a member, I told him to just come on some rides and if everybody liked him he was in. The first meeting he attended was at Carroll Kelly's place at the Loft's at the Ballpark, which had a nice in-house theater area where we used to meet. Steve became a Deacon in October 2002.

Steve was elected to the board in 2003, which was the first year he was eligible for the position. Steve would go on to serve on our board every year he was in the Club but one before being elected president. The only year Steve was not on the board was due to our term limits policy that prohibits a board member from succeeding himself in office for a period of one year after the expiration of a three-year term.

Steve's memories of his early years in the Deacons are not vivid. He remembers that the Club was bottom feeding in terms of admitting new members and that we took in people in those years who we never would have accepted later on. Letting those folks in gave rise to a lot of the dissension we experienced in our early and middle years. Moreover, we actually lost a few members who quit because they thought we were admitting people who did not meet the profile they expected from an upscale club.

Steve was on the board when David Lee and Bruce McDonald were booted out. He remembers David Lee in particular as becoming a troublemaker after Lee had run for the board twice without being elected and remembers Lee demanding a recount of the vote the second time he was defeated for office. He also remembers that a loaded gun fell out of Lee's pocket at the meeting when he was booted out of the Club.

Steve's memory of George Bogle's and Matt Linton's proposal to form a new club with a new patch while remaining Deacons also is sketchy. His most vivid recollection of these events was that the Deacons' vote against the proposal was overwhelming.

Toward the end of Jay McKendree's presidency, I approached Steve and asked if he would be willing to run for president. This wasn't just my idea. All of the past presidents and other Club leaders supported Steve's candidacy. Steve had served on the board for six of the seven years he had been in the Club. During most of those years, he sold more Ball and raffle tickets than any other Deacon. Everyone admired him and everybody liked him.

Steve was reluctant to accept. The Deacons' board was the first board of directors on which he had ever served. Plus, he had been a passive board member content to stay in the background and support whoever the president was at any particular time. Steve was concerned that he simply didn't have the skills to be president.

I assured Steve that he would be just fine. I told him that he was inheriting a Club that was on a sound footing and that all of the past presidents would be available to help him when he needed it. It was "Steve's Time." Steve wound up running for the presidency unopposed and was unopposed for two more terms in office.

Early on in his presidency, Steve sought out John Aubrey for guidance. Steve had been impressed with the way John had held Club and board meetings when John had been president. Unlike previous presidents, John conducted his meetings under Roberts Rules of Order. John counseled Steve to set goals to build on the legacy that he someday would have. Steve's goals were focused on three areas.

First, Steve wanted to make the Deacons fun. That was an important matter because although most of the troublemakers were gone by the end of Jay's presidency, we still had not completely shed their influence.

Second, Steve recognized that he needed to rebuild our membership. Steve remembers that there were 35 active members when he became president. He wanted to add quality members that did not involve the bottom feeding techniques that the Club previously had employed.

Third, Steve wanted to be successful in the Club's charity efforts. Steve had been introduced to the Club by Make-a-Wish and it was the Club's charitable efforts that first attracted Steve to us.

These were laudable goals, but before he had a chance to begin implementing them, Steve had to preside over two sad events during his first month in office. Eric "ER" Robertson and "Seguin Al" Arfsten died within a week of each other in January 2011.

ER technically was not a founding member of the Deacons, but he was one of the members who came in immediately after the founding. He was one of the Big John's Icehouse crowd who had ridden with the Mag 7. When membership numbers were assigned about six months after we were founded, ER had number 8 and was a Nine of Diamonds Patch holder.

ER and me remembering Carrol at Ninfa's.

ER was a little guy who loved drinking, Ohio State football, NASCAR, big-game hunting, fighting and his wife Gay Lynn. When ER drank, he would get ornery and pick fights. He would say "I'm not afraid" and smack some guy three times his size. Although he almost always got the shit kicked out of him, he surely was not afraid.

One night after a Club meeting everyone went to Champs to watch the last game of the American League Championship Series between the Yankees and the Red Sox. If the Yankees won, I had free tickets to the second World Series game to be played in New York City. The Yankees won, and ER and I left for New York in ER's truck that night.

ER had quite a time in New York. On Saturday afternoon, we went to Jeremy's Ale House in lower Manhattan (which has a Deacons patch on its wall), and ER snaked some guys' wife and banged her in the men's room.

The day of the game, we were at Stan's Sports Bar outside of Yankee Stadium. The Jets were playing the Texans that night and the game was on the TV inside Stan's. ER started mouthing off to a big black guy who was literally 6'8." ER was razzing him about being a Jets fan. I thought the big guy was going to smack ER, but I diffused the problem by buying everybody triple Jaeger shots.

After the game, ER and I went to PJ Clarke's Bar on 55th St. and 3rd Avenue. It's so old that the shiny stuff on the mirrors has fallen off so they look like frosted glass.

George Steinbrenner, owner of the Yankees, was having dinner in the main dining room with his family. When ER found this out he bolted back to the dining room. I followed trying to defuse what surely was going to be an embarrassing situation. By the time I got there ER was sitting next to George Steinbrenner with his arm around him and holding out a camera asking me to take a picture.

I told ER to leave the Boss alone and let him have dinner with his family in peace. Steinbrenner was a gentleman and told me to take the picture.

After I took it, ER told Steinbrenner that we had driven all the way from Texas to see the game. Steinbrenner responded that he loved fans like us and that if the Series came back to New York City the following weekend he would fly us to New York and give us seats in the owners' box. Steinbrenner was famous for that kind of thing. He gave ER his business card and said "Have your people call my people and they will take care of it."

ER replied "I don't have any people."

The Yankees got swept in the Series so it did not go back to New York City, and ER and I lost our chance to be George Steinbrenner's guests. As it also turned out, that was the last World Series game played in the old Yankee Stadium.

ER was at Woodrow's on Chimney Rock on a Saturday afternoon in mid-January 2011. His friends did not notice when he left. His wife found him face down in the garage at the condo where they lived. ER was declared brain-dead later that afternoon, but he kept breathing for nearly a week until he died. He had a beautiful funeral that all the Deacons attended. The photo that I had taken of ER and George Steinbrenner was prominently displayed at the service. Future Deacon, Ronnie Northcut gave the eulogy.

Al Arfsten was the first person admitted to the Deacons who was not in Ricky Cook's or my immediate social group. He was introduced to the Club through the Mad Doctor, who is the national head photographer for *Outlaw Biker* magazine.

Seguin Al Arfsten.

Although Al had not been riding long when he came to us, he was the most old school biker in the Deacons. He traveled in circles that included all of the local motorcycle clubs, including the Bandidos. He was the first Deacon to get to Sturgis wearing a Deacons patch. He made the ride solo on a Fat Boy. Doc took a picture of Al next to the "Deadwood City Limits" sign and published it in *Outlaw Biker*.

He became "Seguin Al" out of a ride he led through the rain on the way to Big Bend. A group left for San Antonio on a Thursday night to avoid rain that had been forecast for Friday morning. Another group was scheduled to leave Friday morning. Al sent a memo to the entire Club saying that he would be willing to lead those who had never experienced riding through the rain.

Sure enough, on Friday morning a hard rain was hitting Houston and San Antonio. Al led everybody as far as Seguin when he decided it was raining too hard, so he turned around and led everybody back to Houston. What Al didn't know was the weather in San Antonio had cleared, and if he had pushed on for half an hour he would have successfully led his group into the sun. So, he was given the name "Seguin Al." The Club even convinced the mayor of Seguin to issue a proclamation bestowing that name upon Al.

Al had a congenital health problem that would cause him to have hundreds of tiny mini strokes simultaneously. This syndrome had killed his father. Toward the end of Al's life, the problem became more acute. He would have episodes in which he would not know what he was doing. One time, he was so disoriented he went to House of Pies totally naked.

We had invited the Mad Doctor to our Christmas party in 2010, and Doc noticed that Al was not there. That was odd because Al never missed anything. The next morning, Doc tried to call Al at his home and got no answer. Doc called the police, who went to Al's house. They looked through the window and saw Al lying in the floor. They broke down the door and found Al unconscious, but alive.

Al was taken to St. Joseph hospital in Downtown Houston and was stabilized. He would come in and out of consciousness. When awake, he was lucid, but impaired. After a couple of weeks, he was moved to a facility in Spring Branch. He died there about a month later.

Al's service was old school. There was no funeral *per se*; instead there was a gathering at Sam's Boat, which is where Al had lunch with the Mad Doctor almost every day. It was under 30° the day of Al's service. The Deacons bundled up and rode their motorcycles to the Boat. The entire Sovereign Souls' membership showed up out of respect, and that went a good way toward patch-

Deacons and Sovereign Souls at Al Arfsten's send off.

ing some old wounds. The Bandidos, the Amigos and other clubs sent representatives.

The Mad Doctor said a few words about Al, as did several of Al's closest friends, including me. Things were opened up to allow anybody to speak. The tone was solemn and tears were shed. It was the kind of thing that Al would have liked.

After these sad events, Steve was able to turn to the business of being president.

The first Charity Ball that Steve organized was the 10th Ball. Early on, there was talk about doing something special for the 10th anniversary. It took some convincing, but the board agreed to give it a try despite worries that the financial risk was too great. The board made its decision based in large part on assurances from Camp for All that they would take a significant role in sales efforts.

The board selected the Verizon Center (now called he The Bayou City Center) as the venue. As for the band, I pressed for the Animals because not only were they in the proper price range, they had over 20 chart hits, and I thought they might be a good ticket draw.

Steve was not hip on the Animals. He had listened to some recent Eric Burdon performances and thought he sucked. Plus, Steve thought that a band like the Animals would be a draw only to the geriatric set.

Steve finally settled on Foghat, which was a 1970s rock band that had a few chart hits including *Slow Ride* and *I Just Want to Make Love to You*. To put an end to the controversy of which band would be hired, Steve hired Foghat and paid the band himself.

Foghat at the Deacons 10th Charity Ball.

Steve and his board were counting on Camp for All's help in selling tickets. When that help did not materialize,

Steve called Pat Sorrells, the head of Camp for All, and asked about the lack of support. She told Steve that Camp for All had a policy of not actively supporting sales efforts for third-party events held on their behalf, and that the Deacons should not expect significant help from Camp for All in selling tickets for the Ball.

This was a troubling piece of news. Steve's board never would have agreed to increase the size of the Ball had Camp for All not pledged its support early on. Rather than panic, Steve redoubled his own sales efforts and sold more tickets than he had ever sold before. By the night of the Ball, 550 tickets were sold, which was about 125 more tickets than the Deacons' previous record. We raised about $160,000, which was about 50% more than the net proceeds of the previously most successful Ball, and about 100% higher than the average net proceeds from previous Balls.

The 2011 Ball was so successful that Steve decided that we should change the way we distributed funds to the charities we supported. In previous years, 75% of the net proceeds would go to a single charity, with the remaining 25% being held back for *ad hoc* donations. That worked fine when the proceeds of the Ball were under $100,000. But with Ball proceeds exceeding $150,000, Steve felt that the Club could get significantly more community recognition by distributing the proceeds to a greater number of quality charities benefiting children in the Houston area.

Steve set up a revitalized charity committee to make recommendations on how Ball proceeds should be distributed and to identify the charities to be supported. Mike Fisher was the chairman. He and his committee vetted candidates for donations more carefully than we had done in the past and made recommendations as to the charities to which we would donate and the amounts of the various donations. Devereux Foundation was selected as the principal beneficiary with a donation of $72,000. Covenant House and Camp Quality each received $23,000. About $35,000 was donated to a variety of other local charities, and the remaining Ball proceeds were held over to fund the next year's Ball.

In addition to just writing checks to well-established charities, more visible donations were made. For instance, we gave 100 bicycles to the Kim Coleman Education Fund. We also teamed with LINC Houston to sponsor a Christmas party for children from 350 families who otherwise might not have received any Christmas gifts.

With one big event successfully completed, Steve organized an even bigger Ball for 2012. With the experience he and his board had gained in being profitable with the Foghat show, Steve and his board felt they could ratchet up the quality of the entertainment. They signed Blue Oyster Cult, another 1970s rock band that had chart hits with *Don't Fear the Reaper* and *I'm Burning for You*. About 620 guests attended, and for the first time net Ball proceeds exceeded $200,000.

Billy Gibbons and the Moving Sidewalks.

In 2013 we signed Steve's friend Billy Gibbons from ZZ Top, who had recently reunited with his old high school band, The Moving Sidewalks. This was a *coup* for the Deacons. It gave the Ball a national exposure that no previous Ball had experienced. Folks flew in from all over the country. Over 800 guests attended, and net profits approached $250,000.

In three years, Steve had organized Charity Balls that raised almost as much money as the Deacons raised in the previous nine Balls combined.

In planning these Balls, Steve was lucky to have the assistance of Steve Skelton. Steve had been elected a director the first year he was eligible to serve. He had been in the music industry his whole life. He had started as a disc jockey and later promoted many top recording artists as a representative of various record labels. Bands Steve promoted included Motley Crue, Kiss and Foreigner.

Steve later became a partner in Bill Young Productions, which is the world's premier concert advertising company. While at BYP, Steve has done promos for artists as varied as Paul McCartney, the Rolling Stones, Fleetwood Mac and George Strait. Steve is a pro who knows how to negotiate contracts with recording artists and with concert venues. His guidance was invaluable in Steve Lamb's negotiations with Foghat, Blue Oyster Cult and Billy Gibbons.

Steve Skelton introduces Lambo at the 10th Ball.

At least a part of Steve's success in expanding our Charity Ball was due to his success in expanding our membership in both size and quality. Under Steve's guidance, the board took a more proactive approach in admitting members. In the past it had been a haphazard process that had rules that often were not followed. Steve decided to establish and enforce rules for admission.

We had a long standing policy that a candidate for admission had to go on three Club rides, and that the rides after each regularly scheduled Club meeting counted. Steve's board changed this policy to provide that at least one of the rides had to be overnight so that the candidate and the Club could better get to know each other and to give the Club a chance to evaluate each candidate's riding ability.

Steve found that new members liked the benefits of being a Deacon, but did not like the responsibilities. Everybody loved the camaraderie and riding, but not many liked having to sell Ball and raffle tickets. Steve thought it was important to explain to new members that if they were going to become Deacons, they would be expected to actively participate in our fundraising efforts. Steve established application procedures designed to more carefully vet candidates and to be sure that each candidate knew what would be expected of him after being admitted to the Club.

Under the new procedures, a candidate had to submit a written application for admission and pay a $25 application fee. The candidate also needed a sponsor identified on the application. Once the application was submitted, the candidate was required to meet with the board on multiple occasions so that the board could explain to the candidate what the Club expected from him. The candidate would be told that upon admission to the Club he would have to pay his initiation fee and one year's dues, and he would have to pay for two Ball tickets. Furthermore, he would be informed that he would be expected to sell at least two books of raffle tickets and four Ball tickets. The candidate had to represent to the board that he understood these obligations and that if he did not believe he could fulfill them, he should join another club.

This did not work as well as Steve hoped. Many of the newer members were not fulfilling their obligations to sell Ball and raffle tickets. In many cases, new members who had sold two books of raffle tickets and four Ball tickets asked why further demands were being made on them. To their minds, they had met their obligations. Steve would explain to them that meeting the minimum obligation was not the point; the point was to be an active participant in the Club's fundraising activities.

The Deacons of Deadwood Motorcycle Club

Although the performance of some of the new members was disappointing, the membership was increasing in size, and most of the new members had great enthusiasm for the "fun" part of being a Deacon. We had more local riding than ever before, and there were an increasing number of out of town rides. Steve hosted three of them.

The first was the Presidents Ride, which Steve held the month after he was elected president. His idea was to go on a weekend long ride over the Presidents Day weekend so he could get to know the members better. The ride went from Houston to San Antonio, then to Austin and then back to Houston. To enhance the interactivity, wives and girlfriends did not go along. There were stops in Shiner and Luling. Twelve Deacons went on the ride

Steve also hosts an annual ride to Arkansas during Memorial Day weekend. The Arkansas ride goes through some of the most beautiful country in America. During the first of these rides, one of the participants wound up having a threesome with the bartenders (both female) at one of the spots they visited.

In 2011, Steve hosted the *Lonesome Dove* Ride. Steve has a house in Montana, and he invited as many Deacons as wanted to go to meet him in Missoula and then take a ride following the trail blazed by the cowboys in Larry McMurtry's book *Lonesome Dove*. They didn't go to a single place mentioned in *Lonesome Dove*, but the ride was an adventure.

Deacons at Rocket John's house in Jackson Hole.

On the way home through New Mexico, they encountered a grass fire that had shut down I-40. They came across a guy who knew a shortcut that wound up being an unpaved road with lots of sand. Geoff Seaman went down in the sand and broke his collarbone. That's how Geoff got the nickname "Sandman."

This is the ride where credit card roulette first was introduced. That's where everyone at a meal puts their credit card into a hat. A card is drawn and the unlucky loser has to pay the entire tab. Mike Fisher and John Lowery lost the most times, which was a tough deal, because some of the tabs exceeded $800.

This also is the ride were John Lowery was appointed drink captain one day and was stripped of his title the next day.

There have been no additional *Lonesome Dove* Rides.

The *Lonesome Dove* Ride patch.

These days, every Deacon seems to need a "road name." Things didn't used to be that way. Anybody with a nickname came about it naturally. Of the founding members, I have always been Sambo, Steve Lamb naturally fell into Lambo and Scott Tambourine became Tambo. Ricky Cook has always simply been Ricky. ER had that nickname long before he joined the Deacons. Tommy Cason became the "Snake" because he had snakeskin on his vest. Bob Mitchell became the "Torch" when we set him on fire one night while drinking Flaming Dr. Peppers. John Talbot became the "Deerslayer" when he hit a deer at 80 miles an hour on his motorcycle and lived to tell about it. Carroll Kelly never had a nickname at all.

The Deacons of Deadwood Motorcycle Club

Today, the nicknames are contrived and Steve Lamb and I played a big part in that trend. Steve had hosted a board meeting at his house and after the meeting everybody got liquored up. Steve and I got hold of a membership list and started assigning nicknames to members. We decided that we would assign the nicknames, then order patches with those nicknames on them and award them at a Club meeting.

Johnny Williams as "Fester" is perfect. Selly Chinnery as "Token" is in poor taste, but so far Selly hasn't complained too much. We had to explain why we named Coy Banta "Coytus." Jay Mckendree originally was "der Furher," but he persuaded us that it probably wasn't a good idea to have a past president named after Hitler. Justin Dossett became the "Kid" because he was our youngest member. He no longer is the youngest member, but the nickname will stick forever. Geoff Seaman originally was the "Pollywog" because the sperm in seamen look like pollywogs. He later became "Sandman" after going down in the sand during the *Lonesome Dove* Ride. Alan Parks became "Jailbait" because he was dating a stripper who might have been a minor. Mike Turner became "Triple L" because he got pissed off when Lamb Left him in Luchenbach. Russell Morgan became "Papillon" because he looks like Dustin Hoffman in that movie. Peter Sommer became the "Commodore" because his booming voice and precise enunciation makes him sound like one. Orlando's girlfriend Vanessa had to explain "Dirty" Sanchez to him.

In Steve's first year as president, he proposed that we retire Sam Douglass from the Deacons honorably. Sam had been in the Club from the beginning and was a Nine of Diamonds Patch holder. He was one of the originators of the Hill Country Ride.

Sam was pushing 80 years old and was in declining health. Steve thought the Club should show Sam the respect and love that the Deacons had for him in an appropriate way. The Club had a party for Sam at Capone's. Sam's son Preston came in from Corpus Christi for the ceremony. We wore our white dinner jackets and presented Sam a sterling silver tray from Tiffany's engraved with the Club's patch and Sam's initiation number representing his honorable retirement from the Club. Sam Douglass is the only Deacon who has been honored in this way.

In 2013, Camp for All told the Deacons that in appreciation for our many years of support, they were going to name a stage for the Deacons. The stage was being constructed inside an addition to their "Star Palace" building. The stage was completed in 2014 and the official naming came then.

Two Deacons passed away during Steve's last year as President.

Tommy Cason had joined Club in 2003. I had met Tommy at the Live Oak Resort. Tommy was a quiet and gentle man who looked sort of like a grown-up Opie Taylor. But he was the horniest human being alive.

One time we were at Camp for All delivering a donation check. Steve was telling some assembled members that a very small percentage of women were

Tommy the "Snake" Cason was with over 40 squirters.

"squirters" during sex. Steve gave everyone an approximation of the number of women he had been with and said that only three or four were squirters.

Someone called Tommy over to give us some squirters' info. When asked how many squirters Tommy had been with, he replied that he didn't really know, but it was probably between 40 and 50. Tommy then started educating everyone on how to make them squirt.

Everybody started laughing like hell and Tommy quietly added that "You have to understand, I've been to a lot of orgies."

Another time Tommy was talking to me on a Sunday morning at Live Oak. Live Oak has a place called the Miller House, named after family that once lived there. The Miller House is a party place where a lot of swinging goes on. Tommy told me without a hint of irony "Sambo, Friday night at the Miller House, I never fucked more women in one night in my life. Last night, I only fucked three or four of them."

Tommy and Ricky Cook brought a chick they called the "House Mouse" on a Big Bend Ride. No one ever saw the House Mouse except Tommy, Ricky, Scott Tambourine and Mike Callaghan. It turns out she was a squirter. One time she squirted on the concrete floor in Tommy's man cave. When Tommy saw the puddle, she said "Ricky made me do it!"

In about 2009, Tommy developed inoperable throat cancer. He went through many rounds of chemotherapy and was put on a heavy regimen of medicines to combat his illness. By 2013, Tommy found it difficult to walk for any appreciable distance. Steve found out about this and sent out an e-mail to the members soliciting donations to buy Tommy a mobile wheelchair. By the end of the day, enough money had been pledged to buy Tommy such a sophisticated chair that the salesman said he had never actually seen one. There was enough money left over to make a nice donation to help Tommy cover some of his expenses.

Tommy Cason and his hot rod chair.

The whole Club rode out to present Tommy with this hot rod. It had been tricked out with a flame paint job and a Deacons' patch logo. Everybody was in front of Tommy's place in Pasadena watching Tommy get used to operating his new ride when a couple of cop cars showed up. A neighbor of Tommy's had called the police to report that a motorcycle gang wielding automatic weapons had invaded the neighborhood. Rusty Drake, who is a judge in Pasadena, got the matter diffused and everyone had a big laugh about the report that the Deacons were so bad ass.

Sam Allen

I was in St. Louis on my motorcycle when I heard of Tommy's passing. I had been asked months before to help with funeral arrangements when the time came and to give the eulogy at Tommy's funeral. I rode 850 miles straight home without stopping.

When Tommy died, he was the fourth longest standing member of the Deacons. We had full attendance at Tommy's funeral. Both of Tommy's ex-wives were there. One of them still had a place at Live Oak.

Tommy was buried in his white Deacons dinner jacket and a Deacons' decal adorned his casket. With the exception of one close relative, all of the pallbearers were Deacons.

Unfortunately, Tommy was not our only loss in 2013.

In late November 2013, I got a tearful call from Steve, who had just heard that LaMark Bejer had been killed on a motorcycle. LaMark was the first Deacon in our 12 year history to be killed on a bike.

LaMark of Excellence.

LaMark had been introduced to the Deacons by John Lowery. John and LaMark liked to hang around the Alabama Icehouse, and John once brought several rag tag Alabama Icehouse folks to a Deacons meeting.

LaMark was bundled in with those guys, but Lowery set us straight and LaMark became Deacon No. 97.

LaMark logged thousands of miles with the Deacons. He went to Sturgis, Big Bend, the Hill Country, the Ozarks and on the *Lonesome Dove* Ride.

LaMark owned an art display company called "LaMark of Excellence." He hung artwork in many of Houston's museums as well as for many private art collectors, like Bob McNair, who owns the Houston Texans, and oilman JP Bryan, who owns the Gage Hotel in Marathon, Texas, that the Deacons have so frequently visited during the Big Bend ride. LaMark, hung all of the artwork at the Gage, including the striking white buffalo in the bar.

LaMark hung this White Buffalo at the Gage Hotel.

LaMark had been drinking the night he was killed. He was riding up I-45 and came upon an accident that was being worked by an EMS unit. He hit his brakes to avoid the accident scene and went down. A car following him too closely ran him over and LaMark was dead at the scene. He was not carrying identification and it was several days before we found out about LaMark having been killed.

Steve took charge of everything. He contacted LaMark's family and coordinated their trip to Houston. He helped to arrange the services. He coordinated with the police and other authorities to find out the facts surrounding LaMark's accident and passed the information on to the Club, and in doing so, helped hold us together. He even helped out LaMark's family financially.

LaMark did not have a formal funeral. Instead, there was a service at the Alabama Icehouse. It was a cold day, but most Deacons came on their bikes. Steve gave a eulogy, as did John Lowery, who was LaMark's best friend in the Club. LaMark's daughter also gave a moving testimonial. Jay McKendree showed a terrific video (set to Lynard Skynard's *Freebird*) about LaMark's life and his time with the Deacons.

    LaMark's death hit the Deacons hard. Although no one discussed it aloud, everyone thought that this could have happened to any one of us. Steve led the Club during this time with self-confidence and compassion. It was the last substantial event over which Steve had to preside before stepping down as president, and he did it like a president should.

    Steve believes his most significant achievement as president was improving the membership process and increasing the size of the Club. He added over 50 members in the three years of his presidency, and we approached 100 total members. Attendance at the monthly meetings increased substantially. We could no longer fit easily in the Saltgrass party room. Not a day would go by without several Club-wide e-mails going out by members seeking others to go on an impromptu ride.

Remembering our Brother LaMark.

    Steve also is proud of expanding the Deacons "brand." When Steve joined the Club, if someone mentioned the Bandidos, everyone knew who that person was talking about. Steve wanted the Deacons to be that way. By expanding the number of charities to which the Deacons now contribute and getting more involved in the charitable and motorcycle communities in Houston, the Deacons' are noticed everywhere.

Steve misses being president. The president knows everything about what's going on in the Club every day. Members come to the president with all their problems and complaints, big or small. Once somebody else takes over, those matters go to the new president. Steve knows that he was a good president, and that over half of the Club's members today have known no president other than himself, and now Kirk Lane. While all that results in his receiving substantial respect, it's just not the same as being the leader.

Steve believes that a big part of his success as president arose out of his not having an immediate family. Not having to devote time to family matters gave Steve more time to devote to the Club.

Steve is one of only two Deacons to serve three terms as president. He served as president or as a director every year he was in the Club except one. That makes him the longest-serving officer in our history. He believes he has been able to give so much to the Club because it has given so much back to him, and that each member should give as much as his heart tells him to give. Although he doesn't talk about it much, he decided years ago after his son died to devote part of his life to support charitable works benefiting children. Pursuit of that goal through Make-a-Wish led him to the Deacons of Deadwood, and he has given his heart to this Club.

CHAPTER 8

THE DEACONESS CHAPTER

"Why are women so uptight? They've got half the money and all the pussy."

– Gary Busey

The relationship between the Deacons and the wives and girlfriends of its members became an issue at the meeting that the Deacons' patches originally were distributed. Ted Ricketson's wife, the Fly, asked where the patches were for the wives and girlfriends. The response was that they were not getting patches because they were not part of the motorcycle club. That didn't sit well with the Fly and the next thing you knew Ted was out of the Club.

Soon after that meeting it became apparent that we would have to come to terms with our female associates. I got together with Sally Gracia (now Sally Leidal) to discuss how a women's adjunct to the Deacons could be organized.

Sally was a bawdy broad who rode a big Honda Valkyrie and didn't take much shit from anybody. She knew most of the Deacons and me from Big John's Icehouse. The Deacons had not been founded when we invited her to ride with us on one of the early Hill Country rides.

Sally Gracia at a Deacons Ball.

Sally and I came up with the idea of the Deaconess Chapter of the Deacons of Deadwood, which would be a sort of club within the Club. The wives and girlfriends would be entitled to join the Deaconess Chapter, which technically would be part of the Deacons, but at the same time would be autonomous with its own rules and regulations.

Sally came up with the name. She did some research and found that the term "Deaconess" applied to women in the early Christian Church who were ordained to the Order of Deacon. The term "deacon" is of Greek origin and means a servant or helper. The members of our Deaconess Chapter would be helpers to the Deacons of Deadwood.

The Deaconess patch.

Sally and I designed the Deaconess patch. It was shaped like a diamond and had a Dead Man's Hand with the queen of diamonds substituting for the nine of diamonds in the Deacons' patch. The patch was adorned with a yellow rose and a red rose to give it a feminine touch. The yellow rose was for the Yellow Rose of Texas, and the red rose was just because they were pretty, just like the Deaconess' members.

Founding members of the Deaconess Chapter received the Queen of Diamonds patch rather than the Nine of Diamonds patch awarded to the founders of the Deacons. Instead of being 44%ers, the Deaconess members were 44.5%ers because that was Sally's bra size.

Sally and I submitted a proposal to create the Deaconess Chapter at the November 2003, Deacons monthly meeting. Carroll Kelly and I were the primary proponents. The primary opponents were everybody else.

Carroll pointed out that the women who would be members of the Deaconess Chapter were either married to or were longtime companions of the Deacons' members. He argued that it would be silly not to form a support group like the Deaconess Chapter because they likely would do anything within reason that we asked them to do in support of our activities. Plus, if the Deaconess Chapter was not formed, the home front might not be pleasant.

The discussion must have been short, because the Deaconess Chapter was formally created at the December 2003 meeting. Our bylaws were amended to create the "women's auxiliary." Under those bylaws, the members of the Deaconess Chapter were recognized as members of the Deacons of Deadwood, but their chapter was to operate under bylaws, rules and regulations that they would create. The only oversight from the Deacons would be that if any member of the Deaconess Chapter divorced or split up from their Deacons' counterpart, then that Deaconess member would have to leave.

The women attending the first meeting of the Deaconess Chapter were:

Sally Gracia	Tracy Jackson
KC Cox	Brandy Jones
Lisa Talbot	Carmen Furrow

Sally was elected as the Deaconess Chapter's first president and Lisa Talbot was elected vice president

The Deaconess Chapter expanded quickly, and by the next meeting, they had added:

Amy Aubrey	Pat Brister	Julie Bogle
Sherry Gibbons	Lynnie Mattison	Angie McKendree
Tedi Banta	Melanie Point	Sylvia Chester

One of the reasons it was important for the Deaconess Chapter technically to be a part of the Deacons of Deadwood was that it planned on doing charitable works of its own, and it needed to piggyback off the Deacons' tax exempt status.

Sam Allen

The Deaconess Chapter did not waste time to get rolling.

Its first big function was to help with traffic control for the 2004 MS-150. The MS-150 is a charity-based bicycle ride from Houston to Austin, Texas, that raises money for multiple sclerosis research. The traffic control function that the Deaconess Chapter provided was different than the policing of the warm-up Hill Top Ride sponsored by Camp for All in which the Deacons later would participate. So, the Deaconess Chapter was involved in the MS-150 before the whole Club was involved.

In 2004, the Deaconess Chapter teamed up with Stubb's Cycles to sponsor a series of blood drives. The first of those blood drives was in May 2004, and they continued at least through the end of 2005. While at these events, the Deaconess Chapter members would sell our Ball and raffle tickets.

The Deaconess Chapter conducted a series of lunches they prepared for the Galveston Ronald McDonald House, which helped children who were burn victims. The group would combine the Ronald McDonald House events with weekend-long beach trips at the San Louis Hotel. On the first of these trips, Sally and Lisa Talbot traveled to Galveston together. They had just met and were getting to know each other on the trip. After checking in to the San Louis, they went out for the afternoon and left their patio door open to let in the sea air. When they returned, the wind coming through the windows had been so strong that the curtains were stuck to the ceiling, and the rest of the room had fared no better.

While they were out, Lisa complained that her new Deaconess vest was too stiff, so she and Sally took their vests off in the San Louis bar, wadded them up and trampled them in an attempt to break them in. Later on when they were walking around through town they were greeted with hoots to "The San Louis Girls!"

The Deaconess Chapter also donated gifts to the Santa Maria Hostel, which serves women in crisis, such as women with drug or alcohol problems or women military veterans experiencing post-traumatic stress syndrome and similar maladies.

They also have participated in helping to build houses in conjunction with Habitat for the Humanities.

The Deaconess Chapter found some less traditional ways to raise money. In July 2004, they put on a bike and dog wash at Big John's Icehouse. You could get your dog, your bike or both washed. Bike washes were for cash and dog washes were in exchange for dog food that was donated to the SPCA. That meshed nicely with the Deaconess' support for Scouts Honor Rescue, which is an organization that focuses on the placement of dogs and cats into nice homes in Houston.

As Carroll Kelly had predicted, the Deaconess Chapter helped us out in every way we asked. The most thankless job they took on was running the silent auction at our Charity Balls. They not only helped with organizational matters; they made substantial donations to the auction, such as an outdoor deck that KC Cox donated twice, and their famous Wheel Barrow of Booze, which always brought a hefty price. They also took charge of decorating the venues where our Charity Balls were held. They have continued to help in these and in many other roles.

Sally eventually left the Deaconess Chapter. She had increasing family obligations and was dating John Leidel, who she later married. John was being recruited to join the Deacons, but Sally was not keen on that idea. She looked at her association with the Deacons as her thing and didn't think John's participation would work out well.

After Sally left, the Deaconess Chapter gradually became rudderless and eventually disbanded for a while beginning in mid-2007. The disbanding partly was over a disagreement over the members' visions of the Deaconess Chapters' role. Some wanted the Deaconess Chapter to be a social group that would help the Deacons in traditional ways. Others wanted the Deaconess Chapter to be more autonomous and conduct its own fundraising activities for beneficiaries they would choose.

Sam Allen

The Deaconess Chapter was reconstituted in 2008 by Jay McKendree's wife Angie, who became the new president, and Coy Banta's wife Tedi, who became the new vice president. In order for Angie to assume the helm, Julie Bogle had to step down as president, and Julie then became treasurer.

Angie wound up leaving for personal reasons, primarily relating to raising her young son. Angie and Sally were honored by being named lifetime honorary members of the Deaconess Chapter. Angie came back to the Deaconess Chapter as a dues paying voting member in 2014.

By the beginning of 2014, the Deaconess Chapter again faced an identity issue. Some of the Deaconess' wanted it to have an exclusive membership that would have a one blackball system similar to the system the Deacons use. The problem with this system was that some wives and long-term girlfriends of Deacons' were denied admission. They employed the so called "Sam Allen-Ricky Cook rule" that prohibited a woman's admission to the Deaconess Chapter until the woman had been a Deacon's significant other for at least a year.

This issue was resolved in early 2014 when they adopted a rule that gave the right to any significant other of a Deacon to be admitted without regard to the length of the relationship. Alternatively, breaking up with or divorcing a Deacon results in immediate termination of membership.

The Deaconess Chapter now has over 30 members, and many believe it is the strongest and most fun it has ever been; however, some of the longer-standing members believe that they have been under appreciated. That is partially due to some shabby conduct by the Deacons, like charging some women to attend the Deacons' Christmas Party because they are not "with" a Deacon, despite their long standing support over many years. Hopefully the Deacons will abandon this short-sighted policy.

The 2014 Deaconess Chapter.

CHAPTER 9

RODEO

*"I rode on in to Dallas, feelin' kind of low.
Thought I'd pick me up some change at the Ro-dee-o."*
– Larry McMurtry, *Moving On*

Other than some folks calling bikers modern-day cowboys, there's not much relationship between a motorcycle club and a rodeo. But Tommy the "Snake" Cason thought otherwise and in 2005 he proposed that the Deacons get a suite at the Houston Livestock Show and Rodeo. The members may not have been all that interested in the Rodeo; however, they *were* interested in the prospect of all the food they could eat and all the booze they could drink for $100. So, Tommy's proposal was met with enthusiasm and the Deacons were rodeo bound.

The Rodeo turned out to be a first-class event. Most of the Deacons dressed up for it either in cowboy attire or in their biker formal Deacons wear. One hundred tickets had to be sold, so many of the guests were not Deacons, but were friends of Deacons who liked the Rodeo.

During the first couple of years, we would go to a Saturday afternoon

Tommy Cason and Captain Kirk.

matinee show. Over time, it was thought that we were losing some members who would like to have attended but couldn't due to family and other obligations on a Saturday afternoon. So the annual Deacons suite was switched to the first Thursday of the Rodeo season.

The deal was supposed to be all the food each guest could eat and all the booze each guest could drink. Food was never a problem. It was usually simple but good fare split between Mexican and American dishes. There was everything from fajitas and refried beans to meatloaf and mashed potatoes. It was tasty and there was plenty of it.

Booze was a different story. In each of the first couple of years, the booze ran out and more had to be brought in. This trend was meeting with increasing disapproval by the Rodeo's management, especially since we quickly were gaining the reputation as having the rowdiest suite at the Rodeo. We had the same head bartender every year. I was standing at the bar watching golf on the big screen TV during a Saturday afternoon matinee. I heard one of the bartender's helpers say "These guys aren't so wild." The bartender replied "They ain't all here yet!"

One year we were reputed to have downed 16 bottles of Petron tequila during a single Rodeo performance. While that was a great story to tell, it seemed apocryphal.

It turned out to be true. The next year, I was walking through the Strand in Galveston during the Lone Star Rally. Somebody tapped me on the back to say hello. I tried to be as polite as I could, but I simply didn't recognize the man. I apologized and asked who he was. It turned out it was the guy responsible for stocking our Rodeo suite with food and booze. Without being asked, he said "I couldn't believe it, but you guys drank 16 bottles of Petron last year!"

The next year, we ran out of Petron, and we contacted a Rodeo official to replenish the stock. The official said that we had been allocated only two bottles. A copy of our contract with the Rodeo was produced, and it said that we were entitled to an unlimited supply of all of the brands of alcohol we had ordered. The Rodeo official had to admit that was the deal, but he said that there was no more Petron because it had been distributed to other suite holders. I told Rodeo guy to go confiscate some from the other suites and bring it to us. The Rodeo guy couldn't do that, but he brought in a lot of other high-end tequila.

During the Deacons' second Rodeo, "Seguin Al" Arfsten earned a change in his nickname.

Al found three tall hot chicks who were on spring break from some college in Florida. He invited them into our Rodeo suite. One of them drank so much that she was taken out on a stretcher. It turned out she was only 19 years old. We thought this was hilarious. The Rodeo management didn't think it was so funny and threatened not to let us back the following year.

It was decided that Al had earned a new nickname. He was given the choice between "Rodeo Al" and "Al the Pimp." He begged us to go with Rodeo Al, and at the June 2006 meeting, the Club voted to change Al's nickname accordingly. But it never really took hold. He would always be Seguin Al to the Deacons.

The most drunken time we ever had at the Rodeo was in 2012. Several of the Deacons' guests that year were from the Live Oak Resort, which is a nudist place in Washington County, Texas. The LOR folks were having a particularly good time. When the Rodeo performance was over, everybody boarded the train and headed to Warren's Bar downtown. One of the LOR guys had snuck a bottle of Cuervo out of the Rodeo arena, and he passed it around on the train. Everybody made it to Warren's, but that's the last most folks remembered.

The next morning, I was in bed at my apartment in downtown Houston only a block and a half from Warren's. When I woke up at about 11:30, there was half a dozen of the LOR contingent in my apartment. They rousted me out of bed and proposed that everybody go across the street to the Hearsay Lounge for some lunch. I got out of bed, put on my salmon colored Pebble Beach bathrobe, and headed to the Hearsay with the crowd.

When we got to the Hearsay, Steve Skelton's squeeze Kim told a story about how she had rescued Doug Hupf from a mugger outside Warren's the night before. Kim had gone outside to smoke, and saw Doug being rolled by a downtown derelict. Kim said "I pulled the guy off of Doug and kicked him in the balls. He went down and I thought that that didn't hurt me a bit, so I kicked him in the balls two more times."

Kim became the "Notorious Boot on Groin" or the "NBOG" for short. Everyone piled into a cab to Shaw's Tattoo Studio in Montrose to get NBOG tattoos. I went dressed in nothing but my salmon colored bathrobe. Someone took a photo of me looking ridiculous while walking my girlfriend's Chihuahua in that robe.

Five people wound up getting tattoos. Steve Skelton and I got hot chicks with big tits. The three others got tattoos they thought were appropriate to the occasion. One of those three was the woman who years before had the Deacons' Dead Man's Hand tattooed on her breast after the fundraiser we had done for Duke Nunn, who was a Deacon who had injured severely himself in a motorcycle wreck. All five tattoos had "NBOG" at the bottom honoring Kim as the Notorious Boot on Groin and commemorating the occasion.

As time went on, the Rodeo tickets became increasingly expensive. Even though the Rodeo was in March, we had to pay for our Rodeo suite in full before the end of December. The problem was that most of the Deacons who wanted to go wouldn't pay for their tickets until the last minute in March, so the Club would front the money, and then reimburse itself when the tickets were paid for. That worked out fine until the amount the Club had to front exceeded $15,000. The Club was unable to advance that much money and the members were unwilling to pay for their tickets in a timely fashion, so the Rodeo suite was abandoned after 2011.

CHAPTER 10

RIDES

"We never even said a word; we just walked out and got on that bike. And we rode. And we rode clean out of sight."

– Bob Seger, *Roll me Away*

Getting Started

Although the Deacons have sponsored philanthropic activities from the beginning, the Club's primary purpose was to gather a group of people who wanted to ride together. Bubba Stelter had sold his place, so Thursday night rides to his joint in downtown Houston had been discontinued. David Cook was gone, so the gatherings at his house and the rides he organized also were gone. The Deacons were formed to fill these voids.

In the early years, riding was grim. We did not have the critical mass needed to have a large number of well attended rides. Part of the problem was that most of us were professionals with time-consuming jobs, so it was hard to get members to be able to commit to rides in advance. To remedy that problem, we set up a program under which we would ride after each regularly scheduled monthly meeting and also would ride on the third Sunday of every month. The idea was that even busy businessman would be able to plan to attend rides if there was certainty that they were going to be held on those days.

Elza Smith was the Club's first road captain. That was distinct from the rides chairman, who was in charge of organizing the rides.

Sam Allen

John Talbot was the Club's first ride chairman. The first of the Sunday monthly rides was on June 21, 2003, and it was to Elza Smith's beach house on Trinity Bay.

Participation in the rides scheduled for the third Sunday of every month was not as good as was hoped. From time to time, members would suggest remedying the problem by having mandatory rides. Of course, that couldn't work in a club like the Deacons, because there could be no mechanism for enforcing participation.

Eventually, we achieved the critical mass and enthusiasm to generate many impromptu rides, but that took years, As recently as three years ago, the road captain might be the only person to show up for a ride. Some road captains resigned the position because of the frustration of being unable to generate enthusiasm for riding.

Deacons Ride to Cat Springs.

Although local rides used to be hard to organize, the Deacons never had problems with organizing out of town rides. Here is a history of the Deacons traditional rides. Some are annual events and some were one time deals, but they all have been fun.

Big Bend

The Origin of the Tradition. The Big Bend Ride predates the founding of the Deacons of Deadwood by years. The first one was in the fall of 1996 when David Cook and his girlfriend Marva, Raymond Henry and his girlfriend Pam, Joe Hutchison and his wife Lindle and my girlfriend Linda and I trailered bikes to Marathon, Texas, to stay at the Gage Hotel and ride through Big Bend for a few days. It was so cold when we got there that we never took the bikes off the trailers. Instead, we rode cars through Big Bend for the weekend. It was the first time any of us had stayed at the Gage.

A few years later, David Cook had died, but I had continued taking trips to Big Bend. The year before we were founded, I took the Two Johns, Carroll Kelly and Elza Smith to Big Bend for the annual Halloween Party at the Gage Hotel. In 2003, John Talbot took first place at the Halloween Party, John Aubrey's wife Amy took second and Rocket John took third. We started making this an annual event and often would ship our costumes to the Gage so we would not have to pack them on the motorcycles.

Over time, the Gage started throwing the Halloween Party in a warehouse across the railroad tracks from the hotel. Everyone continued to go to, but it was never as much fun across the street.

In 2005, Dick Tate organized an alternate Big Bend ride early in the month of October rather than for Halloween. After that, two or three different groups might go to Big Bend at different times during October. Orlando Sanchez wound up organizing the official ride and he experienced increased participation each year. The Orlando years were particularly fun for John Talbot and me because we would break away a night early and zip over to Acuna for a little fun south of the border.

The Big Bend Ride remains one of the most popular of the Deacons annual rides, although there seem to be many splinter groups and the whole Club rarely goes as a single unit.

The Legend of the Deerslayer. Here's how John Talbot got the nickname the "Deerslayer."

In 2004, a group headed to Big Bend stopped to gas up in Sanderson, Texas, which is about 60 miles from Marathon and the

Deacons in Big Bend.

Gage Hotel. The Deacons being Deacons, they left the gas station at different times. John and Amy Aubrey were last to leave. It was no surprise to anyone that they were having some gear loading problems, and Rocket John told everybody to take off and he would catch up. He said he had the fastest bike anyway and he would pass them all in a while.

Talbot was in the lead and was hauling ass toward Marathon. Sure enough, Rocket John and Amy went screaming by a few minutes later and quickly disappeared ahead of us. All of a sudden, the folks in the back came up to Talbot, who had gone down hard. He had hit a deer. He slid over 400 feet and bike parts were all over the road. John was conscious and trying to tell everybody that he was just fine, but it was pretty evident he was in shock.

John and Amy had passed Talbot a few minutes before Talbot had gone down. Aubrey noticed that no one was in his rear view mirror, so he stopped to wait for everybody to catch up. When nobody did, he knew something was wrong and he turned around to see what had happened. When he saw that Talbot had gone down, his concern was so acute that he looked to be in almost as much shock as was Talbot.

Carroll Kelly said there is no way that Talbot had hit a deer because anybody who hit one going that fast would be killed. Talbot assured Carroll that he had indeed hit a deer. Unconvinced, Carroll walked up the road as a one man search party. He seemed more concerned in proving that Talbot had not hit a deer than he was with Talbot's injuries. Carroll came back 15 minutes later with a look of disbelief on his face saying that he had found the deer that Talbot had hit.

Talbot was lucky on that ride that Melanie Point was riding with me. Melanie was a nurse, and took charge of things both at the scene of the accident and at the hospital to which John was transported. The next morning she was in Talbot's room changing his bandages with obvious tenderness and care not to hurt him. John mumbled that it was a good thing he had two bikes. Melanie gained the respect of everyone who was there that weekend.

Remarkably, Talbot did not break a single bone, but he had some serious road rash and looked like the Mummy, which was appropriate because the group was on its way to the annual Halloween Party at the Gage Hotel.

Talbot's wife to be Pat was not on the ride. She was called and told that John had been in a wreck, but the seriousness of the injuries was

At Big John's on the way home from Talbot's deerslaying.

downplayed. When he got back to Houston a few days later everybody stopped at Big John's Ice House for some Flaming Dr. Peppers, which was a tradition for the Big Bend group. Pat came to meet Talbot at Big John's, which was where she saw how extensive John's bandages were; however, she had been prepped for the event and took things pretty well.

Picking Up Tabs. One year a bunch of us were in the White Buffalo Bar at the Gage. We had run up a huge bill and I happened to be the last one standing. I got the tab for the whole group, signed John Talbot's name, and left a big tip. The total was well over $1,000.

The next morning, Talbot was in the lobby when he heard a Gage employee say "I wonder who picked up that bar tab last night?" He was surprised to hear another Gage employee reply "Mr. Talbot did!"

I had done this as a joke and told John I would reimburse him, but Talbot would have none of it. He has been busting my ass in a good-natured way about that incident for years.

Another time on our way home from Big Bend we all stopped at Big John's Icehouse for some Flaming Dr. Peppers. Bob Cavnar inadvertently walked out on his tab. I told the bartender that I would settle Bob's bill. Cavnar realized his mistake and called Big John's to leave his credit card number so he could be charged. When I found out about this, I waited a few minutes and called the bartender at Big John's from my cell phone, told her I was Bob Cavnar, and to put all of the Deacons tabs on his card.

The bartender was standing only three feet away and I assumed she would see the joke I was playing. But she didn't, and she announced to the bar that all of our drinks were on Cavnar. We ran up a huge tab.

I told Bob about it the next day and told him that I would reimburse him for the amount we had charged to his card. Bob thought the story was hilarious and wouldn't take payment; however, he did let me buy him dinner at the Palm to make us even. He came out ahead.

Hill Country

Eight Guys in Kerrville. The Hill Country Ride predates the formation of the Deacons. The first one was in 1997 on the weekend before Memorial Day. It was organized by Sam and Preston Douglass and Fred Farner in celebration of Preston's birthday. The others who went were David Cook, John Beck (of Beck & Maston), Fred Hass (of Fred Haas Toyota), Daryl Bristow (head of the litigation department at Baker Botts) and me. This always has been a four day ride for Preston's birthday and has never been an official Deacons ride.

Everyone rides to Kerrville on Thursday. On Friday we ride the Three Sisters and go through places like Vanderpool, Leakey, and Medina. On Saturday we go to Cooper's Bar B Q in Llano. Everyone heads home on Sunday.

There always has been a stop in Bandera. During one of the early years, we were at an icehouse in Bandera called the Forge, which also was a working blacksmith shop that made custom branding irons. A little old lady came up to me and said "Sir, are you in some kind of motorcycle gang?" I replied, "Ma'am, it's even worse; I'm a partner in a law firm."

The Deacons of Deadwood Motorcycle Club

These rides have changed in format over the years to alternate the days we do the base rides. Sometimes a lunch is arranged along with a band to meet us. In recent years, Preston has rented out the 11th St. Bar in Bandera for the Saturday ride and has arranged a crawfish boil or similar lunch for us.

In the early years, we stayed at the YO Ranch Hotel in Kerrville. They have a great pool with a swim-up bar, but it doesn't open until Memorial Day weekend. They had it open for us on the very first ride, but after that, they never would make it available. They must hate money.

The Kid in Bandera.

After some dissatisfaction with the YO, we moved to the Inn in the Hills for a few years. This place has the advantage of having a bar with a live band on weekends. There was some local action to fire on, but the success rates were grim. One year, David Law and Doug Growdin went to the Kerrville police station after the bars closed. They rang the bell, and when the duty officer responded and asked what they needed, they told the officer that they couldn't find any pussy in Kerrville and asked whether there were any women that they could bond out for the night. The officer advised them to go home.

In the last couple of years we have been back to the YO.

Sturgis

Most of the Deacons had been to Sturgis long before the Club was formed. Many went with David Cook to stay in the Bullock Hotel in Deadwood.

After the Deacons was formed, Al Arfsten introduced the idea that having a substantive association with the town of Deadwood might benefit the Deacons. Casey Campbell, the long-time manager of Saloon

No. 10, was made an Honorary Deacon. In addition, the Deacons joined the Deadwood Chamber of Commerce and Casey was our local representative to the Chamber.

We eventually stopped renewing our Chamber membership, but at least a few of the older Deacons remain friends with Casey.

Seguin Al Gets to Sturgis First. Al Arfsten was the first Deacon to ride to the Sturgis Rally wearing his Deacons' patch. The Mad Doctor took a picture of Al next to the "Deadwood City Limits" sign and published it in *Outlaw Biker* magazine. Al and all the other Deacons who rode to Sturgis that year received an Ace of Spades patch.

Carroll Kelly, John Aubrey, John Talbot, my brother Tolly and I rode our bikes to Sturgis that year taking the long way. We went from Houston to Amarillo, and then followed I-40 to Gallup, New Mexico. From there we headed north to Denver, Cheyenne, and Jackson Hole. From Jackson we went through Yellowstone and stopped to see Old Faithful along the way.

Trying to keep this group together was impossible. People (*e.g.*, John Aubrey) would disappear to go on their own private tours without letting me know. This was worrisome because I would be afraid that those leaving the group might have encountered some trouble.

By the time we got to Old Faithful I was really annoyed. After we had parked our bikes and were walking to see the geyser, Aubrey asked my brother Tolly how long he thought it would be before the next eruption. Tolly pointed at me and told Aubrey it would be immediately if he left the group again.

We made it through Yellowstone and stopped for the night at the Range Rider Lodge in Silvergate, Montana. This is the same old log whorehouse at which Carroll Kelly and I had stayed after our ride over Bear Tooth Pass during our first Sturgis ride. It was just as ratty as it had been when Carroll and I had first stayed there. The first room Talbot tried was full of moths and he and his girlfriend Pat had to search for a better room. Tolly's date refused to stay there at all and they found another hotel a mile up the road in Cook City. The punishment fit the crime for them because their hotel did not have hot water.

Late that night after the bars closed, David Cook and his girlfriend Marva rolled in trailering David's bike. The bar reopened and we poured down a few with David.

The next morning, we all went to breakfast at a little restaurant in a log cabin across the street from the Range Rider. Everybody except John Aubrey was served quickly. John was looking forward to the trout and eggs he had ordered and was getting impatient about the service. After repeatedly asking where his breakfast was, the waitress told John that they had to catch the trout from the stream out back and it would be on the table in a few minutes. This restaurant is still there and is a favorite stopping point for Deacons on the way to Sturgis *via* Bear Tooth Pass.

Outside of the restaurant there was a guy with a spotting scope showing tourists wildlife in the mountains. It turned out to be Dan Hartman, who is the world's most renowned photographer of wolves. I became friends with Dan over the years, and when he came out with a book of Yellowstone wolf packs, he gave me one of the only 300 hardcover copies. He signed it "To my good friend Sam – the alpha male of the pack."

We all made it to Sturgis the next day after a stop at the Custer Battlefield just outside Billings, Montana.

Carroll has too much Pussy. Carroll Kelly got all he could handle the year he took his wife and his girlfriend to Sturgis at the same time.

Carroll had told everybody his wife was flying up and he would meet her there. When it was time to leave, Carroll showed up with his girlfriend Ann Emery. Someone asked Carroll what he was going to do with Ann once his wife showed up in Sturgis. Carroll said it was no problem. He had an extra room for Ann down the hall.

This gambit worked out predictably. Carroll's wife caught on immediately, especially since Ann did everything she could to make sure Carroll's wife knew what was going on. There even was a staged photograph with Ann and Carroll's wife arm in arm.

One afternoon a group was in the bar at the Bullock Hotel and my date Tonya was looking for her reading glasses so she could read the bar menu. She asked "Where are my cheaters?" At just that moment, Carroll was walking into the bar with Ann. Ricky pointed to them and said "There they are!"

Later in the week Preston Douglass was going to his room at the Bullock and saw Ann drunk and in tears in the hallway. Preston went to see if he could help her and she said she couldn't find her room key. About this time Carroll bee bopped through with his wife, who said "What's wrong Ann, can't find your keys?"

After Carroll and his wife passed by, Preston asked if Ann had looked in her back pocket for her key. Sure enough that's where it was. She thanked Preston and said "Preston, come into my room right now and fuck me." Preston replied that he could not do that and Ann said "Come on. It will only take 12 minutes." Preston said that he only had 10 minutes and left her in the hallway.

By the time Carroll got back to Houston divorce papers had been served.

Bad Ass Biker John Talbot. One year on the way to Sturgis, the usual cast of characters rode the Million Dollar Highway to Ouray (pronounced "Yoo-ray"), Colorado, and then on to Telluride.

The Million Dollar Highway is one of the most beautiful, yet most dangerous roads to ride motorcycles in America. There is some controversy as to how it got its name. The most common is that it cost $1 million to build in the 1930s. Another account is that an early traveler said "I would not go that way again if you paid me $1 million." Still others claim that the Million Dollar Highway got its name because the gravel used to build the road came from nearby gold and silver mines and was rich in ore estimated to be worth over $1 million.

The morning of that ride, the group had gone to Window Rock, Arizona, which is the most holy of Navajo places. It is a huge face of red sandstone with a large hole through the middle made from wind erosion. A Navajo woman was selling good luck talismans and everybody but Talbot bought one.

Later that afternoon, Talbot was proud of himself for having successfully negotiated the Million Dollar Highway. As he was parking his bike in Ouray, he missed his kickstand and tipped over into the street. A couple of little old ladies looked at him in disbelief. So much for looking like a bad ass biker, but I guess he deserved it for not having bought the good luck charm.

After picking up his bike and retaining whatever dignity he might have had left, he walked across the street to the Outlaw Saloon, which was reportedly an old John Wayne hang out. Everybody signed a shingle that still is displayed on the wall at that bar.

Sambo and the Commodore in Canada, eh? In 2009, Peter the "Commodore" Sommer and I decided to ride through the New England and Canada on our way to Sturgis. I had ridden my bike to Connecticut to see my mother. I then rode to Portland, Maine to meet the Commodore.

The Commodore.

Peter had shipped his bike to the local Harley dealership in Portland. When we picked up his bike, Peter found that he had brought the wrong keys and could not open the saddlebags. Fortunately, the ignition was on so he could start the bike.

Peter had packed two helmets in his bike that he could not access because he didn't have the key. So, he had to buy a third helmet, thus surpassing the Aubrey's two helmets per person inventory.

The first day we rode in a cool and persistent rain through some beautiful green mountains in Maine and New Hampshire until we got to the Canadian border. The Canadian customs officials asked if we had any contraband in our saddlebags.

The Commodore replied:

> "Unfortunately, I had my motorcycle delivered to Portland, Maine, and mistakenly brought the wrong set of keys; therefore, as much as I would like to comply with your request to examine the contents of my saddlebags, I regret that that will be impossible due to the obvious impediments to opening them."

> "I appreciate your indefatigable efforts to secure the border of your great nation from the havoc often wrought by members of motorcycle clubs of a less genteel pedigree than ours. Nonetheless, I can assure you on my word of honor as a former executive of the Chevron Corporation and as a member in good standing of the Deacons of Deadwood Motorcycle Club that my saddlebags do not contain any article or substance that would be prohibited from being transported into Canada, or that would pose any danger to any of its citizens, its wildlife or its environmental purity."

> "So kind Sirs, we will be on our way. Tally Ho!"

The customs official replied "You guys pull in over there."

The Canadian customs officials examining Peter's bike were pretty good guys. Rather than drilling out Peter's locks, they took some care in unbolting the hardware so they could examine the contents of the saddlebags without damaging the bike. The process took several hours, and when we were done, Peter and I presumed we could be on our way. That wasn't to be.

The Deacons of Deadwood Motorcycle Club

Earlier in the process, a female customs official asked for my vest, which of course had all of my Deacons patches. After the customs guys finished inspecting Peter's bike, I was escorted into a room that looked like something off of *Law and Order*. The room was stark, and I was in a chair that was bolted to the floor. The customs official said that before Peter and I would be allowed to leave, I would have to explain the meaning of each of my Deacons patches.

When she got to the 19 Patch, I said it was our most secret patch and that I would rather not explain its meaning. She was insistent. She asked whether it stood for having to kill 19 people before being patched in as a Deacon. I explained that the Deacons were lovers not fighters and that she should check out our website to verify that. In the end, I had to explain the meaning of the patch.

After Peter and I finally cleared the border, we rode through a large traffic jam in Montréal. It was still raining and getting dark. We stopped at a gas station and asked where the closest national chain hotel was. The gas station attendant said it was a long way away: probably seven or eight miles.

We made it to the hotel as it was getting dark. When we got there, it turned out there was a bagpipe convention going on. You really can't make this stuff up.

Anyway, we rode all the way around the Great Lakes and came back into the United States in Minnesota. We rode across Minnesota and North Dakota, then down through South Dakota into Deadwood. It was jackets and chaps the whole way. We met Justin Dossett, Justin's father Martin, Ken Carr and a few more Deacons in Deadwood, and then rode through the Black Hills for couple of days before heading back to Houston *via* Denver and the Brown Palace Hotel. All in all, the ride was over 4,500 miles in 10 days.

Stampede! In 2013, Geoff Seaman, Kirk Lane and Dorsey Parker were at Black Hills Harley Davidson in Rapid City and decided to ride up to Keystone, near Mt. Rushmore. Kirk was weaving through the thousands of bikes when he cut things close and went down. The Captain walked away unscathed, but his Indian was scalped. He had lost one of his mirrors and broke his hand brake lever so only two fingers could fit on it.

When they got to Keystone, they decided that a few drinks were in order. An attractive young lady came by and offered body shots she would serve while standing on her head. The Captain had a few just to see her unusual technique.

The day had worn on and they decided to take a 20 minute ride to the Crazy Horse Monument. They hopped on their bikes and made a U-turn in town. The Captain laid down a patch of rubber filling the air with thick white smoke into the face of the town sheriff, who pulled him over right away. The rest of the group figured that the next stage of their ride was going to be bailing the Captain out of the local jail.

The Sheriff let the Captain go and told him not to disrespect his town again. When the crowd saw that the Captain was not being arrested, thousands of on looking bikers went crazy with applauds and cheering.

About 40 minutes into the planned 20 minute ride they found that they were doing the Needles Highway in reverse with about an hour of daylight left. The "Tail of the Dragon" has nothing on this great riding road with all its turns and pigtails. The Crazy Horse Monument was nowhere in sight.

They went around a curve and standing in the middle of the road was a herd of about 30 buffalo. The mountain was so steep on the left that the buffalo could not go up and on the right was a guardrail protecting a 100 foot drop off. So the buffalo could only go up or down on the road. With darkness coming on, the Captain decided the only option was a buffalo drive down the mountainside, so he started revving his engine and moving forward. Before, they knew it the buffalo started running down the highway.

They went about 500 yards when they saw two motorcycles coming up the mountain from the opposite direction. Geoff could see in their eyes fear and amazement at this herd of buffalo stampeding straight toward them. About 10 yards from where their bikes had come to rest the buffalo found a path and jumped off the road and went up the mountain.

The Captain stampeding buffalos in the Needles.

Iron Butt Rides

An outfit called the Iron Butt Association sponsors extreme motorcycle rides, the easiest of which is the *Saddle Sore 1,000*, which requires a rider to go 1,000 miles in 24 hours. The *Bun Burner* requires a ride of 1,500 miles in 36 hours. The *Bun Burner Gold* is 1,500 miles in 24 hours. There also is a *Coast to Coast* ride in which a rider is allowed to go from one coast to the other in 50 hours, and a *Border to Border* ride from one US border to the other in 36 hours.

The Deacons' First Iron Butt Ride. The first Deacons' Iron Butt Ride was a combination *Saddle Sore 1,000* and *Bun Burner* taken on June 14-15, 2003. The participants were Carroll Kelly and his girlfriend Ann Emery, George Bogle, Mike Callahan, my then girlfriend Lynnie Matteson, and me. The first day of the ride was 750 miles from Houston to El Paso and 250 miles back to the Gage Hotel in Marathon, Texas, to complete the *Saddle Sore 1,000*. The next morning everyone rode 500 miles from Marathon, Texas, back to Houston to complete the 1,500 mile long *Bun Burner*.

Everybody made it.

The First Deacons Iron Butt to Sturgis. The first Deacons Iron Butt Ride to Sturgis was taken in August 2003. This also was a combination *Saddle Sore 1,000* and 1,500 mile *Bun Burner*. The participants were John and Amy Aubrey, Carroll Kelly and Ann Emery, and Mike Callaghan. The first day was from Houston, Texas to North Platte, Nebraska. The next day was 500 miles to Deadwood. Since the ride from North Platte to Deadwood is under 500 miles, a circuitous route was taken to get in the required mileage.

Everybody made it.

Once in Deadwood, Mike Callaghan slept overnight on the floor of Carroll Kelly's room at the Bullock Hotel. He got up the next morning without telling anybody and Iron Butted it back to Houston.

The First *Bun Burner Gold*. The *Bun Burner Gold* requires a 1,500 mile ride in under 24 hours. Carroll Kelly, Mike Callaghan, Dick Tate, a friend of Dick's named Norman Mumford, and I left Houston on May 28, 2004, to make it to Washington DC on Memorial Day weekend for the Ride to the Wall. The Ride to the Wall is an annual motorcycle ride through the Capitol Mall in Washington DC in honor of military veterans. In addition, the dedication of the World War II Memorial was that weekend and we wanted to attend.

Everybody made it.

Before leaving, I told the rest of the group that I thought they liked to ride a lot faster than I did and I was not going to try to keep up. I said I would meet everybody in Washington. It turned out to be a surrealistic ride. I would be in a gas station in a remote place in the middle of the foggy night and some or all of the rest of the group would be pulling in for gas. Other times, I would pass the rest of the group on the road.

When I got to Washington I checked into my hotel and started calling around to find everybody. No one had checked into their hotels and I couldn't raise anybody on their cell phones. I began to worry that there had been a problem. However, it turned out I was the first to arrive in DC and everybody was OK. Mike Callaghan called me and we headed to the Old Ebbit Grill for some beer and crab cakes.

When Carroll Kelly arrived, he called me and said "Pards, my Iron Buttin' days are over!"

We had planned to go on the Ride to the Wall; however, once we got there, we found out that we would have been required to assemble at the crack of dawn in the Pentagon parking lot and to wait for five hours to get to ride through DC. So we skipped that. In addition, security at the dedication of the WW II Memorial was so stringent that we were unable to get close, so we missed that too.

We had special T-shirts made up for the ride. The front of the T-shirt had the Deacons' Dead Man's Hand with chevrons saying "Ride to the Wall." The back of the shirt had the words "God Bless Those Who Served to Keep Us Free" underneath an American flag. Many veterans stopped to thank us for the patriotic thought. Of course, we were the ones who needed to be thankful to those veterans. Several veterans asked where they could get one of those T-shirts. We took orders and mailed them to all who asked.

The next morning Carroll left Washington DC in the rain and rode nearly 800 miles to Atlanta without stopping. Callaghan did an Iron Butt ride back to Houston. I headed west through Pennsylvania and Ohio to visit my brother in Cincinnati before heading back to Houston.

The Commodore and Wildman Go Hard Core. In 2010, Peter Sommer and Ben Thompson earned their Hard Core patches in style. They left Houston and rode nonstop to Jacksonville, Florida in the rain. They got up in Jacksonville at 4:00 am, and 36 hours after leaving home, Peter found himself two miles from his house in Houston. They zipped through Houston and wound up in Kerrville, which was almost 1,200 miles from Jacksonville.

They checked into a Best Western and slept for four hours. They were up again at 4:00 am and rode to Tucson, Arizona, where they had lunch with Peter's son. They jumped back on their bikes and made it to San Diego that night.

They took their time getting home, making stops in Las Vegas and Zion National Park.

These guys wound up doing Iron Butt rides that I've never heard of:

- 1500 miles in 36 hours.
- 2000 miles in 48 hours.
- 3000 miles in 72 hours.
- Coast-to-coast in 50 hours (they made it in 41 hours).

Border to Border. Mike Callaghan is the only Deacon to have completed this ride, and he did it solo. He rode from Laredo, Texas to Winnipeg in Canada.

Cruzin' to Cure

In 2004, Al Arfsten introduced the Deacons to Mark Hopkins of Cruzin' to Cure, which was a motorcycle-based organization that raised funds benefiting breast cancer research projects. Each year, Cruzin' to Cure sponsored a poker run to raise money for that cause. Following the poker run, there would be a live band, a silent auction and all the other stuff that normally is associated with motorcycle-based fundraising events. Mean Gene Kelton would play for free. Gene wound up getting killed by a drunk driver.

Cruzin' to Cure would award a specially painted motorcycle helmet in a trophy case to the motorcycle club that had the most attendees on the poker run. The Deacons won it several years in a row. We liked this organization so much that we would pay the entry fee

Accepting the Cruzin' to Cure Helmet.

for the poker run for each Deacon so the Club would get credit for all of those entries toward winning the helmet.

Cruzin' to Cure made a donation of $5,000 to the Deacons in 2004 and became our first institutional sponsor.

Mark Hopkins died unexpectedly. Debbie Little, who became a Deaconess, took the helm at Cruzin' to Cure, and kept its tradition of supporting the Deacons. Over time, Cruzin' to Cure's fundraising efforts were less successful, but they continued to support the Deacons. In some years, Cruzin' to Cure donated 100% of the funds it raised to the Deacons.

Cruzin' to Cure is not as active as it once was, but Debbie Little tried to remain a friend of the Deacons. However, she wound up being treated in a pretty shabby way when the Club charged her to come to our 2013 Christmas party on the theory that she was not married to or dating any Deacon. Obviously, this was an unacceptable insult to someone who had been such a superlative Deacons supporter for a decade. Hopefully, the current Deacons' management will read this account of the relationship between the Deacons and Debbie so that she will not be humiliated by our Club again.

Hilltop Ride

The first Deacons' Hilltop Ride was on April 2, 2005. The Hill Top Ride was an annual bicycle ride sponsored by Camp for All as a warm up for the MS-150, which is a charitable bicycle ride from Houston to Austin benefiting research for multiple sclerosis. There are three different bicycle routes on the Hilltop Ride. One is about 20 miles long; one is about 40 miles long; and one is about 66 miles long. The Deacons were asked to ride their motorcycles along these routes to help any bicyclists who might be in need of assistance.

Sam Allen

This rapidly became one of our favorite annual rides. We were sponsoring Camp for All's charitable activities as well as being able to contribute in the context of a beautiful motorcycle ride.

As time went on, the Deacons who participated in the Hill Top Ride focused more on drinking Change "then" to "than"beer at a little joint about 10 miles from Camp for All than they focused on helping the bicycle riders. In the early years, we would ride around the bicycle course a time or two before hitting the beer joint. Later on, many of us went straight to the joint.

Deacons neglecting their duties during the Hilltop Ride.

One morning a bunch of us were at this beer joint when somebody bought two kegs of Bud Light. Jimmy McConnell quipped that there must be a wedding going on.

The Deacons participated in the Hill Top Ride every year from 2005 through 2013. Camp for All did not sponsor the Hill Top Ride in 2014, so the future of this event is questionable.

President's Ride

Steve Lamb hosted the first Presidents Ride, which he held the month after he was elected president in 2011. His idea was to go on a weekend long ride over the Presidents Day weekend so he could get to know the members better. The ride went from Houston to San Antonio, then to Austin and then back to Houston. To enhance the interactivity, wives and girlfriends did not go along. There were stops in Shiner and Luling. Twelve Deacons went on the ride.

During the first Presidents' Ride, LaMark Bejer picked up a chick in the Menger Hotel Bar. LaMark, the Captain and Lambo were partying in the chick's room. She had her son with her in a separate room from hers. From time to time she had to check on him, and because of the juxtaposition of the rooms, it was easier for her to check by going out the window of LaMark's room and crossing the roof to her son's room. At some point, LaMark wound up on the roof, and it caved in and LaMark's leg got caught. The kid had a cool helmet, and one of the Deacons stole it. The helmet now is hanging on the ceiling of the 11th Street Bar in Bandera.

Two of the guys on the trip (who will remain nameless) called hookers who met them in the Menger Bar. They told the Commodore that the hookers were friends from college. One of the hookers left a vibrator in the hotel room, and it later was planted on John Asta's bike (he was not one of the guys who had imported the rent-a-pussy).

The President's Ride was so popular that it was repeated in 2012 and 2013 with ever increasing participation. In 2014, Captain Kirk kept the tradition going and 63 Deacons went. Clearly, this ride now is a Deacon tradition.

Hot Springs

The Hot Springs Ride traditionally has been taken over the Fourth of July weekend. Jay McKendree and his wife Angie had for years been traveling to Hot Springs that weekend to visit Angie's family. The first year that the Deacons went along was in 2008, when six Deacons made the ride. They were Jay McKendree, Preston Douglass, Orlando Sanchez, Nowery Smith, John Talbot and Brian Krause, who disappeared without telling anyone the morning after arriving in Hot Springs.

A few more Deacons went in 2009. The group rode into Oklahoma and got lost during a record high temperature of 117°.

Blackouts Motorcycle Cleaner sponsored the Deacons at a lake house that year. After dinner the group rode back to downtown Hot Springs to the Arlington Hotel in their swimsuits and boots.

The Hot Springs Ride is now an official Patch Ride of the Deacons of Deadwood.

Fort Clark

This ride traditionally has been taken in the late spring. It was founded by Orlando Sanchez in 2009 when he led Jay McKendree, Mike Marlowe, Peter Sommer, Justin Dossett and Ted Faleski to Fort Clark in Brackettville, Texas.

Fort Clark is a well-kept facility that features a 100 yard long spring fed swimming pool. It was an army outpost established in 1852 that saw service during the Civil War. It later garrisoned the second cavalry division, which protected travelers from hostile Indians. Much of the Fort remains intact. Everybody stayed in the soldiers' barracks.

Each year, Orlando's girlfriend Vanessa follows the riders in a truck and takes everybody's golf clubs along. The golf course at Fort Clark is horrible. The fairways are mostly rock and gravel. There are cactuses and rattlesnakes. The greens often are covered with deer shit. Still, playing that little track is a lot of fun.

John Wayne built a movie set in Brackettville for the filming of the movie *The Alamo*. Many other movies since have been made there.

Brackettville is only 60 miles from Del Rio. Orlando traditionally has led a group across the border for dinner. Ma Crosby's (now closed) has a Deacons Supporter sticker on the mirror in the bar. In 2010, everyone went to the largest bullfight in Del Rio. Sometimes, some of the Deacons would sneak off to the Sportsmen's Club for a little local fun.

The six participants in the first Fort Clark Ride received a Six of Clubs patch. No other Six of Clubs patches will be awarded; however, a Fort Clark Ride patch is awarded to those who make the ride.

The Deacons of Deadwood Motorcycle Club

Lonesome Dove Ride

In 2011, Steve Lamb hosted the *Lonesome Dove* Ride. Lambo, Captain Kirk, Geoff Seaman, Mike Fisher, LaMark Bejer, John Lowery, Peter Sommer and Ben Thompson went.

This ride was supposed to follow the trail blazed by the cowboys in Larry McMurtry's book *Lonesome Dove*. The ride started out in traditional Deacons' style. It began at a Harley dealership in Missoula Montana. Five Deacons started out ahead of the rest of the group and the rest were supposed to catch up a few minutes later. The first group took a wrong turn. The two groups were 120 miles apart before the mistake was discovered.

They didn't go to a single place mentioned in *Lonesome Dove*, but it was an adventure. This is the ride where the Club invented credit card roulette. That's where everyone at a meal puts their credit card into a hat. A card is drawn, and the unlucky loser has to pay the entire tab. This also is the ride were John Lowery was appointed drink captain one day and was stripped of his title the next day.

The group had ridden through the Rockies experiencing all four of the water groups, rain, sleet, hail and snow. Coming out of Santa Rosa, New Mexico, they hit grass fires on I-40 about 90 miles west of Amarillo. The freeway had been closed for hours and the bikes were reading over 120 degrees on the temperature gauges. They ran into a rancher who said he could get them out of the mess so they jumped the median and followed him down a dirt road that was like a washboard.

They went over a rise and hit about 100 yards of wind-blown fine sand that was about 10 inches deep. Some of the bikes made it

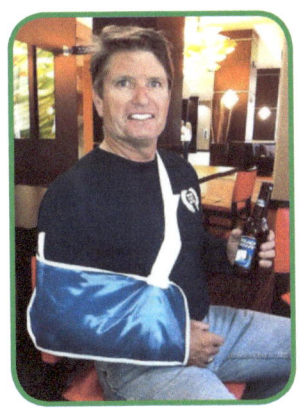

The Sandman in Amarillo.

through, but Geoff hit the sand and flew over his handle bars, landing on his shoulder and breaking his clavicle in three places. The Captain went down trying to avoid hitting Geoff. The Captain and Geoff picked up their bikes and muscled them through the rest of the sand to join their brothers who had made it through. Geoff got the nickname "Sandman" from this incident.

Geoff was sitting on the side of this dirt road in the middle of nowhere with seven of his brothers trying to figure out what to do. There were no emergency services because every emergency responder in the county was fighting the fire. The temperature was over 120 degrees. No one had any water.

A rancher, easily in his 80's, came down the road. The Deacons asked him if he had any beer or whiskey they could buy, but it turned out the rancher didn't drink. That's how the Deacons figured out he wasn't a Navajo or a Mexican. As a last resort, the Deacons asked if he had any water. He said he did, and pulled out two of the oldest, nastiest bottles imaginable, but no one was in a position to complain.

In a couple of hours, a wrecker showed up. After dropping off Geoff's bike at the H-D dealership in Amarillo, the wrecker took Geoff to the regional hospital, which was more like a vet clinic. While Geoff was waiting to get examined, he found a guy beside him who was in for a brown recluse spider bite.

After a long wait, a sling and a bunch of pain killers, Geoff walked out of the hospital to get a cab, and his new arachnid-loving buddy came out with his wife and offered Geoff a ride down town. He figured his luck was changing.

When they got to the parking lot, one car stood out in a mass of vehicles. It had no paint and it looked like it had been totally sandblasted. It had a windshield but no side windows. The springs were sticking through the seats. That wound up being his Geoff's ride downtown.

Geoff's clavicle was replaced on July 27th and he was released to ride in the Dead Man's Parade in September. It got rained out that year but he rode to Big Bend in October.

The Hooligan at the Indy 500

In 2005, the Hooligan, the Two Johns, Carroll Kelly, Ricky Cook and I went to the Indy 500. Everybody rode their bikes except Ricky, who trailered his bike up behind Melanie Point's truck. I had just started dating Melanie.

We stayed in Cincinnati at my brother's house. The morning of the race, we rode our bikes to Indianapolis, where I had arranged for a police escorted ride to the Speedway. That's a huge deal, because traffic is so bad at the Indy 500 that it would have taken several hours for us to ride in. Instead, it was under 15 minutes from the Hoosier Dome to parking at the track.

Everybody loved the race, but when we went back to our bikes, Callaghan's bike had been stolen. He thought that we were joking with him, but we were not. Fortunately, Ricky was there with Melanie's truck, so the Hooligan had a ride home.

Instead of heading back to Houston, I was headed to California for my law firm's annual partners' retreat. I had shipped appropriate attire and my golf clubs to the hotel in Laguna Niguel. In a move that would have made Carroll Kelly proud, I sent Melanie off back to Houston after the race, then headed to St. Louis where I picked up Connie Mahaffee at the airport. Connie claimed to be a full-blooded Chiricahua Apache. I had known Connie from Houston, but she had moved to California and had flown in from there to meet me. We had a great cross country ride and I dropped her off at her home on my way to the retreat. From there, it was 1,500 miles back to Houston on I-10, for total mileage of over 5,000 miles on the whole trip.

CHAPTER 11

THE DEACONS HAVE BIG BALLS

The girls are all happy
Cause the Big Ball's in town
Big Ball's in Cowtown
We will all go down

– Bob Wills, *A Big Ball in Cowtown*

Early on, we decided we would sponsor one charitable event per year benefitting children in the Houston area and that it would be an offshoot of David Cook's Ride to Fuad's. It was to be a first-class event with gourmet food, top shelf liquor and well-dressed guests. The attire was to be "biker formal," the meaning of which was left to the guests, but the point of which was to see as much tits and ass as possible. The hope was to host an event that would be so much fun that guests would look forward to coming in subsequent years.

Today, the Ball is the premier motorcycle-based charity event in Houston.

2002

The first Annual Deacons of Deadwood Charity Ball was held in October 5, 2002, at Rockefeller Hall in Houston. The band was Fuzzy Side Up, which was a 1970's music dance band. Their lead singer was a big black guy whose real name was James Brown. There were 218 guests who paid $125 a ticket. It was catered by Abuso Catering. The event raised $22,500, all of which was donated to Make-a-Wish.

Stubb's Cycles donated a Harley-Davidson Sportster that was raffled off through the sale of 150 tickets at 100 each. Sam Douglass won. That was a problem because Sam not only was a Deacon but he also owned the Corpus Christi Harley dealership. Everything had been done honestly, but given David Cook's reputation, some thought the raffle had been rigged. The rules were changed prohibiting a Deacon from winning the raffle.

In putting on our first event, we wanted to partner with a well-known charity that would give us credibility in our fundraising efforts. Partnering with a major charity also was important because we needed to piggy-back on the charity's tax-free status so donations would be tax deductible.

Getting a reputable charity to support the Ball turned out to be harder than anticipated. Charities were leery of participating in a fundraiser with a motorcycle club (even a 44%er club). They envisioned a rundown event, with unbathed people, where there likely would be violence and drugs and little money raised. They were afraid that their association with a motorcycle club might sully their own reputations.

Several charities were approached unsuccessfully, but finally Make-a-Wish Foundation agreed to participate; however, their enthusiasm for the project was tepid. We believed that advertising the Ball as benefiting Make-a-Wish would be important to our sales effort. But Make-a-Wish initially would not agree to allow us to use its name or logo.

It took some negotiation, but Make-a-Wish finally capitulated. We agreed to call the Ball the "Harley Dreams Make-a-Wish Ball." Make-a-Wish required us to enter into a Licensing Agreement that required us to do all the work and to give 100% of the net proceeds to Make-a-Wish.

We also had to provide Make-a-Wish an accounting of all revenues and expenses within 30 days after the event.

Any use of the Make-a-Wish name or logo had to be preapproved. In addition, we needed permission to solicit donations from any corporations, businesses, celebrities, sports teams or individuals that we identified as potential contributors.

Make-a-Wish was upfront in telling us that they did not plan to send any of its members to the Ball and it did not intend to provide any support to us. Clearly, Make-a-Wish did not expect much from us, but they were willing to take whatever meager funds we might raise.

The party started at Sam's Boat, where everybody gathered to participate in a police escorted ride to the Ball. This was the first Dead Man's Parade that has preceded every Ball.

The pre-party at the first Ball.

The morning after the Ball, I was in bed with the *Chic de jure* when the phone rang. The caller identified herself as Shelby Hodge. I had no clue who Shelby Hodge was.

She turned out to be the society page editor for the *Houston Chronicle*. She had attended the Ball and told me that she needed information concerning the number of guests, the amount of funds raised and similar information because she wanted to do an article on the Deacons and the Ball for the Tuesday edition of the *Chronicle*. She told me it was the best time she had had at any charity event in the last 10 years.

Of course, I had no clue about any of that data, but I dragged my lazy ass out of bed and got Shelby the information she needed.

Shelby continues to report on the Deacons Ball for *CultureMap*.

2003

The second Deacons Charity Ball was held on September 13, 2003, at Rockefeller Hall. Brian Black, Clint's brother, provided the entertainment. There were 318 guests, so attendance had gone up substantially over the first Ball. Abuso Catering once again supplied the food and booze. Our cost per person for liquor was increased substantially from the 2002 rate because we drank so much that Abuso claimed he lost money that year.

Once again, Stubb's Cycles donated a motorcycle that was raffled. This time it was a Fat Boy, and thank goodness, a Deacon did not win.

We auctioned a complete Super Bowl package that included tickets to the game, admission to all the big media events and parties and limousine service for the weekend. It went for over $10,000, but the purchaser reneged and we wound up getting nothing out of it.

The Mad Doctor was there taking pictures of all the tits and ass he could find. The photos and an article about the Ball eventually wound up in a five page spread in *Outlaw Biker* magazine. The article admitted that we were not the kind of motorcycle club normally covered by *Outlaw Biker*, but it said that the Deacons ride 5,000 miles just to get to Sturgis. A copy of the article is included in an Appendix to this book.

Best-selling author Judith McNaught was there. She arrived at the pre-party in a chauffeur driven Bentley, but she hopped on the back of a bike to ride to the Ball. She donated two unique auction items. The first was that she would write the high bidder into one of her books, using the bidder's real name and personality traits. She also agreed that if a high bidder ever wrote a book, she would present it to her publisher for possible publication.

The Ball was covered by *Outlaw Biker, Houston Chronicle, Full Throttle and Houston Hot Country Magazine*. Channel 2 News did a feature on the Ball and the Deacons of Deadwood.

We tried to attract outside corporate sponsors for the Ball. A new strip joint had opened near the Galleria, and a bunch of Deacons visited one afternoon to meet with the manager. The Club and the strip joint came to a deal: The strip joint would buy a $5,000 table at the Ball and stock it with strippers, and in return we would have at least one ride per month to the strip joint. This was a triple win. The Club would get a $5,000 sponsorship and a table full of strippers at the Ball, plus we would get to go to a strip club once a month.

While we were at our initial meeting at the strip club, Carroll Kelly's girlfriend Ann slipped off. She was spotted in a booth munching some rug. When Carroll saw what was going on, he said "Ann luuuuuuvs to eat pussy!"

The strip club wrote the Deacons a bad check for the table, so the strippers did not attend the Ball. The transaction may not have worked out, but the Deacon's entrepreneurial spirit was commendable.

We raised $59,000, $50,000 of which was donated to Make-a-Wish. Reportedly, this was the largest single donation ever made to the Houston Make-a-Wish chapter. Nonetheless, Make-a-Wish was so apathetic about our efforts that they didn't bother to send anyone to the awards ceremony to pick up the check. That attitude caused us to send our charitable donations elsewhere in future years.

The day after the Ball, we threw a post-party at which Kip Attaway played. He came in from Wyoming for the gig. Kip has recorded such love song classics as *It's Hard to Say I Love You While You're Sitting on My Face*, and *Loving You's the Dumbest Fuckin' Thing I've Ever Done*. We gave away free booze and food as a Thank You to our sponsors.

Kip has since performed for the Deacons many times, and we have taken many road trips to see him. On one of those trips to New Orleans, he was so rowdy he was kicked out of the club in which he was playing.

2004

The third Ball was held on September 11, 2004, at the Capitol Grille. Fuzzy Side Up was brought back as the entertainment. Brian Black had put on a great show the previous year, but he just didn't have the energy we needed. Stubb's Cycles donated a Heritage Softail for the raffle.

Having the Ball on September 11 caused some emotional issues. We had to have the Ball on that date because it was the only Saturday in September that we could get the venue; however, it had been only two years since the 9/11 World Trade Center bombing. We were worried that having the Ball on September 11 would be seen as a sign of disrespect.

To help mitigate that problem, we hired a violinist from the Houston Symphony Orchestra. She opened the proceedings at the Capitol Grille by playing *America the Beautiful* and *God Bless America*. This silenced 400 bikers and tears were shed.

This was the first year that we tried to use mass media to advertise the Ball. We took out ad space on the *Chris Baker Show* on Houston radio station KPRC. Lots of our friends reported having heard the radio spots, but there was little evidence that the advertising was effective in selling tickets.

The Capitol Grille did not work out quite as well as had been expected. We sold about 100 more tickets than we had planned, which was a high-class problem; however, the venue just wasn't big enough to hold all those people. Plus, the Capitol Grille stiffed us on the booze. It was supposed to be top shelf liquor, but they served second-rate stuff, which allowed the Capitol Grille to be the first venue not to lose money on booze at a Deacons event.

Before the 2003 Ball, the guests all met at Bubba's Sports Bar in preparation for the police escorted Dead Man's Parade to Rockefeller Hall. John Talbot showed up at the last minute on his Harley Ultra Classic, he was pissed off and wanted a drink.

Talbot had installed a high-end sound system on his motorcycle and planned on blasting out music all the way to the Ball. He had one of the worst looking motorcycle jackets ever made. It was black leather and had a bunch of chrome studs all over the shoulders. He had to wear the jacket because it had been a gift from his wife to be Pat. This jacket was good for Halloween parties and gay bars, but it was horrible on a motorcycle. John had thrown this jacket into the saddlebag on his bike, and one of the studs hit something that shorted out the entire sound system.

So much for Talbot's Parade concert.

Talbot's jacket remained the unanimous pick as the worst motorcycle jacket in the Club until Steve Lamb showed up with a brown jacket with some fringe and bone chevrons on the front and sleeves. This jacket also was appropriate for gay bars.

Lamb lost the title of the worst jacket when Tommy Cason showed up with a jacket and chaps with so much fringe he looked like Bigfoot. Even the gays wouldn't let Tommy around with that jacket, although it might have been suitable for a beastiality bar.

After the indifference that Make-a-Wish had shown us the previous two years, we decided to move in a different direction for our charitable contributions. Our member Randy Hale was on the board of directors of Boys and Girls Country, which took children from troubled homes and gave them a wholesome place to grow up. Some of the children had been there since before school age and stayed on through college.

The deal that we struck with Boys and Girls Country was that we would give them 75% of the net proceeds from the Ball in exchange for their helping with back office functions such as check-in and running the silent auction. The remaining 25% of the net proceeds was to go to other charities on an *ad hoc* basis. This was to be an ongoing relationship that would be renewed every year.

2004 was the first year we were able to attract corporate sponsors; however except for the donation from Cruzin' to Cure, they all came from our members or their businesses. We received the following donations:

- Cruzin' to Cure $5,000
- Porter & Hedges (my law firm) $2,500
- Sam Douglass $2,500
- SW Infinity (Fred Haas) $1,700
- Mossy Nissan (ER) $1,000

The Deacons made the following donations:

- Boys and Girls Country $50,000
- Camp for All .... $ 5,000
- Make-a-Wish .... $ 5,000
- Ronald McDonald House .... $ 4,000
- Odyssey House .... $ 1,000
- Toys for Tots .... $ 100

2005

The fourth Deacons of Deadwood Charity Ball was held on September 17, 2005, at the Decorative Center. Once again, the band was Fuzzy Side Up. There were over 400 guests. The caterer was A Fare Extraordinaire. Stubb's Cycles donated a Softail Deluxe that was raffled. Steve Lamb personally donated a Harley-Davidson for the silent auction. Also, this was the first time we sold VIP tables. Those sales have become increasingly important because they are sold at a premium price. We raised $84,500.

At the December 2004 meeting, we had determined that Boys and Girls Country would be the primary beneficiary of the Ball in 2005. That was in line with the promise we had made to Boys and Girls Country in 2004 that if they would provide certain back office services, we would donate 75% of our net proceeds of the Ball to them. Unfortunately, it did not work out that way.

The Deacons of Deadwood Motorcycle Club

The previous year, we had been introduced to Camp for All, which is a camp that allows children with debilitating maladies to experience camp life. Camp for All had become popular with the Deacons because not only was it a charity benefiting children, but it sponsored an annual charity bicycle ride in which we had begun participating as marshals. So, Camp for All was a great organization to which we could donate that also provided a fun riding opportunity.

At the March 2005 monthly meeting, after contentious debate, the Club voted to split the proceeds from the Ball between Camp for All and Boys and Girls Country. This vote was taken while I was out of town on business. When I found out about it I was furious; I had given my word to Boys and Girls Country that they would receive 75% of the proceeds.

When I called Boys and Girls Country to give them the bad news, they asked what they had done wrong. They believed that they had upheld their part of the bargain at the 2005 Ball to provide back-office services in exchange for an ongoing relationship pursuant to which they would receive 75% of the proceeds of each Ball.

I told Boys and Girls Country that they indeed had fulfilled their part of the bargain, but that the Deacons had voted to renege on its obligation. The Boys and Girls Country representative asked me why they should trust anything we told them in the future, and I told them that there was no reason they should continue to trust us.

Despite this nasty occurrence, the Ball was a success. All of the corporate donors from the 2004 Ball made similar donations in 2005. We donated $23,000 to each of Camp for All and Boys and Girls Country.

The pre-party was held at the Twelve Spot in downtown Houston. It was in one of the oldest buildings in Houston and had been the original site of the Foley's Department Store.

This was the first Ball attended by the Jersey Chicks. I had had an associate who had left my law firm to be general counsel for my biggest client. To take that job, this associate had to move to New Jersey. When he and his wife came to the 2004 Ball, they brought half a dozen women (without their husbands) from Jersey who eventually became known as the "Jersey Chicks." These Chicks started coming to all the Deacons Balls, the Rodeo and other Deacons events throughout the year.

One of the Jersey Chicks (for the sake of confidentiality, I'll call her Barbara Zychowski of 6 Deerland Trail, Monmouth Junction, New Jersey 08853; 732-522-3590) showed up in skin tight leather pants. Instead of a top, she wore no clothing at all, but had her body painted like a tuxedo. From 10 feet away it looked like a real tuxedo, but up close, you could see her nipples popping through the latex. Now that's Biker Formal!

We always get a block of rooms at a hotel near the venue for the Ball so that the Deacons and our guests do not need to drive far after having been drinking all night. In 2005, the Omni Hotel on Riverway was selected because it was close to the Decorative Center. We had experienced a good relationship with the Omni's event coordinator, but the week of the Ball, Hurricane Katrina hit New Orleans. The Omni's event coordinator was from New Orleans, and only a few days before the Ball, she quit her job to go home and help her family.

That was a problem. The Omni's management knew that a motorcycle club was coming to the hotel, but they did not know anything about the Deacons. The event coordinator had not left any information for the Omni's management to let them know that the Deacons were lovers, not fighters. As a result, the Omni's management hired lots of policeman to patrol the hotel and its grounds.

These policemen had a confrontational attitude. I had checked into the hotel earlier in the day. When I arrived at the hotel after the Ball I parked my bike near the front door. A policeman told me I could not park there, so I moved my bike.

When I was walking back into the hotel the same policeman told me that I could not park the bike in the second spot. I moved the bike again to be near a line of pickup trucks in the hotel's driveway.

The Deacons of Deadwood Motorcycle Club

The same cop told me I could not park there either and I asked why not. The policeman replied that I was parked in a fire lane. I asked about all the trucks that were parked there and the policeman responded that the trucks were going to be moved later on. I asked when that might be, considering it was already 3:00 am. I told the policeman I no intention of moving the bike again and headed into the hotel.

That's when the policeman threatened to arrest me and would not allow me to go to my room even though I already had checked in.

This cop was an asshole, but he wasn't the only asshole policeman at the Omni that night. We had rented the presidential suite for $2,500. Half a dozen policemen were posted outside the door and told us that they were just "waiting for us to fuck up" so they could arrest us all.

The next year we were again having the Ball at the Decorative Center. The Omni called me to see if we would like to come back. I told the guy that the Deacons would never come back and all of the reasons why.

A few days after the Ball, we had an embarrassing incident. One of our members named Dick Tate (no joke) had donated a mini bike painted like Peter Fonda's Captain America motorcycle from *Easy Rider* for the silent auction. He had purchased a bunch of these mini bikes and had been unable to sell them, so he donated one for sale at the Deacons auction.

Dick intended to keep an amount equal to his purchase price for the bike, so the sale of the mini-bike would be profitable only if it sold for an amount in excess of Dick's purchase price. The bike was sold at a profit, but Dick could not produce the title. We had to offer the purchaser the opportunity to take his money back.

It took a few weeks, but Ricky Cook finally got the title issue resolved and the purchaser kept the bike, but he was not appreciative of the headache he went through to get the title.

This was typical of Dick Tate. Dick had been a longtime malcontent in the Club and he later resigned in protest after the Club booted out two of his sidekicks. Good riddance!

2006

The fifth Charity Ball was held on September 23, 2006, at the Decorative Center. The band was Fuzzy Side Up. As an unexpected treat, Jeff Carlisi of the rock band 38 Special made an appearance and jammed with our band. The caterer again was A Fare Extraordinaire. Stubb's Cycles donated the motorcycle that was raffled. Once again, the Dead Man's Parade started at the Twelve Spot in downtown Houston. There were over 400 guests. Over $90,000 was raised.

One of the highlights was Barbara the Jersey Chick. She had come to the 2004 Ball dressed only in skin tight leather pants on the bottom and her top painted like a tuxedo. In 2005, she again arrived in body art. This year, instead of the upper body tuxedo, she had her tits painted like a flame job.

Before the Dead Man's Parade from the Twelve Spot to the Ball, we staged an incident with one of the motorcycle policeman who was to escort us to the Ball. He approached Barbara and told her that she was under arrest for indecent exposure. He handcuffed her and started to lead her out of the building. As soon as they got to the door, she was un-handcuffed and told to have a good time.

John Aubrey ran the silent auction and he came up with some fun innovations. He had the auction simulcast on eBay, so our guests at the Ball were bidding against the world.

Carroll Kelly was friends with University of Texas quarterback Vince Young. The Texans had won the national championship against USC in the Rose Bowl in a game that Vince, on fourth down and five, made an 8 yard game-winning touchdown run. Carroll convinced Vince to participate in our silent auction by agreeing to go to a dinner for 10 at John Aubrey's River Oaks home and Johnny Carrabba agreed to prepare the dinner himself.

The good news is that this package sold for $8,000. The bad news is that Vince stiffed us and we had to return the $8,000. Fortunately, we had held that money back from our donations to the charities we were supporting to guard against a Vince snub.

As an aside, David Kramer had bought the Vince Young/Johnny Carrabba package. Kramer was a bawdy guy who had been one of David Cook's old buds. He had been to all of Cook's Rides to Fuad's. He also had been a big Deacons supporter and had been to all of our Charity Balls. Unfortunately, between the Ball and the time we had to return the donation, Kramer died. He is missed by all of us who knew him well.

2007

The sixth Ball was held at the Decorative Center. The band was Night Beat. The caterer was A Fare Extraordinaire. Once again, Stubb's Cycles donated the motorcycle that was raffled. There were over 450 guests, which was a new record. The pre-party was at the State Grill, which is downtown in the Rice Hotel above Sambuca. When guests arrived at the Decorative Center, they were greeted by the Carlos Compean Quartet, which played Sinatra and Tony Bennett type tunes. They also played during Night Beat's breaks, which provided a nice contrast between rock and jazz standards. For the first time, we raised over $100,000 net to the charities.

The Kid and Mrs. Kid.

Justin Dossett went to the Ball dressed biker casual. He wore a silk robe with a Deacons patch on the back, and rode that way in the Dead Man's Parade to the Ball. Of course, he got drunk as shit, and Amy Aubrey and John Talbot wouldn't let him ride to the after party. Instead, he gave his bike keys to Jay McKendree, who probably was as loaded as the Kid. There is no word as to what Jay did with his own bike.

This was John Aubrey's first Ball as president. He wanted to transform the Ball from primarily a biker party to an event he thought would be attractive to a wider audience. One of his goals was to make the "River Oaks Crowd" feel comfortable coming to a biker themed party rather than a mere motorcycle club event.

John was successful in those efforts. The quality of the auction items was substantially upgraded to include things like a trip to the Masters and a trip to play golf at Oakmont Country Club. John also brought in a consignment company that specialized in providing high-end auction items for charity events. He hoped that these items would appeal to the crowd he was trying to attract.

Joe Kilchrist sold over 20 VIP tables. Joe had left the Club a year or two previously because he had moved out of town, so Joe was not a Deacon when he made this extraordinary sales effort. In appreciation, Joe was made an Honorary Deacon and was presented with a new set of colors already sewn onto a vest. It was an honor that he did not expect, and was he was very emotional when we presented his new patch to him.

2008

The seventh Deacons of Deadwood Charity Ball was held on September 27, 2008, at the Decorative Center. The band was Password. This band was led by Cecil Shaw, who wrote the 5th Dimension hit *Aquarius*. Once again, Carlos Compean's Quartet played traditional jazz during the breaks. The pre-party was at Sambuca downtown in the Rice Hotel. The caterer was A Fare Extraordinaire. Once again, Stubb's Cycles donated the motorcycle that was raffled. There were over 400 guests. We raised only $30,000, but that's because of an act of god.

The 2008 Ball was held in the aftermath of Hurricane Ike, which hit Houston less than a week before the scheduled date of the Ball. Over 100,000 homes were flooded in Galveston, and that town was declared to be uninhabitable. Electricity was out over much of Houston, and as a result, a nighttime curfew was imposed. Ricky Cook said he knew it was a real disaster because even the rich people didn't have electricity.

As the date of the Ball approached, power was slowly being restored throughout the city; however, the Decorative Center still was without power. Some members proposed postponing the Ball, but John would have none of that. John made contingency plans for supplying our own power with generators and arranged to move the Ball outdoors under tents in the Decorative Center parking lot if that became necessary.

The Thursday before the Ball, John Talbot was in his car near the Decorative Center and saw some electrical workers fixing the power lines. He asked whether power would be restored by Saturday. The electrical workers said they thought so but they couldn't be sure.

We lucked out and power was back on in time for the Ball. Unfortunately, the Decorative Center had a pungent odor caused by the power failure. In addition, there was an art exhibition that could not be taken down in time for the Ball. So John worked around the exhibit in setting up the Ball and claimed that the art made our event "edgy."

Unfortunately, we had to pay for all the generators, tents and other facilities we had rented in case the contingency plan had to be put into effect. That kind of thing is expensive and it cut into our profits; but it was the right thing to do, and we were lucky to have had somebody as organizationally proficient as John running the show.

2009

The eighth Deacons of Deadwood Charity Ball was held on September 19, 2009, at la Colombe D'or. The band was the Fab Five. They play British invasion type rock and dress the part. Orlando Sanchez arranged for the pre-party to be held at Artista

The pre-party at Artista.

in the Hobby Center in downtown Houston. That is a stylish spot and they put on a stylish party for us. For the first time, Stubb's Cycles was not the donor of the bike that was raffled. Instead, Republic Harley-Davidson made the donation. We raised over $50,000, which was donated to Camp for All.

La Colombe D'or has a Grand Ballroom with oak panels originally carved in 1715 that were installed in an estate outside of Paris in 1891. They did not charge a site fee and they gave us favorable pricing on food and alcohol. Plus, the facility had not only a Grand Ballroom, but other smaller rooms that would allow for different themes. For instance, while the main band was in the Ballroom, another room had a piano bar and still another had gambling with proceeds going to charity. This layout provided for an intimacy that had not been experienced at previous Balls.

After the Ball let out, I invited a crowd to party at my loft downtown. There was a pool on the roof of the building. One thing led to another, and everybody went to the roof to go skinny dipping.

The next afternoon, a bunch of us went back to the roof. There was a woman up there reading a book, and I was dispatched to negotiate with her. I told her we wanted to go skinny dipping in the pool and that she was welcome to join us. I also told her that if that was going to be a problem, we would hold off. She did have a problem, but we hovered around like a bunch of vultures and she finally left.

A few days later, I got a call from Holly Crawford, who was the manager of my building. Holly said she had a couple of things she needed to discuss with me. I said I had been expecting the call.

Holly said that it had been reported that I had a loud party in my apartment the previous Saturday that lasted till nearly dawn. I admitted that that was true.

Then Holly said "There's something else I need to talk to you about, but I don't know how to put it."

The Deacons of Deadwood Motorcycle Club

I said "Yeah, I did that too," and Holly asked what I had to say about it. I replied that it was the weekend of the Deacons Ball and that she should expect more skinny dipping going on the following year.

All this caused quite a stir in my building, mainly from people who wanted to be invited next time around.

2010

The ninth Deacons of Deadwood Charity Ball was held on September 11, 2010, at la Colombe D'or. This was the second time the Ball was held there, and they expanded the venue to give us access to the entire facility. The band was the Fab Five. The pre-party again was held at Artista in the Hobby Center in downtown Houston. For the second time, Republic Harley-Davidson donated the bike that was raffled. We donated $50,000 to Boys and Girls Country.

At the pre-party, I was looking for rides for about five or six of my female guests. Geoff Seaman figured what the hell, what could go wrong? He led a really tall gal and her girlfriend to the bikes. The tall chick's friend said to this female Shaquille O'Neil, "I know you haven't ridden much, but just stay over the center of the bike."

This advice was ignored. They started riding in the Dead Man's Parade, and the chick immediately began leaning left and right, and eventually swung all the way around the bike and looked at Geoff straight in his eyes. She stayed that way during the whole ride.

Ken Carr arranged for one of the most unique silent auction items we ever offered. Ken knows the producer of the Sons of Anarchy. He got the show to donate an actual Sons patch that was signed by the cast. It was sewn on a vest and framed. They also donated a show script that was signed and framed.

Steve Lamb's friend Paul Sigmond bought the vest for $8,000, making it our highest paying auction item ever. He had bought a VIP table and stocked it full of strippers. When one of them showed up at

Sam Allen

our October meeting to pick up the Son's vest, she was so hot the room almost went silent. Everyone was hiding their boners.

2011

In 2011, the Deacons held its 10th Charity Ball and we wanted to do something special. For several years, I had been pushing to increase the size of the Ball and to bring in nationally known entertainment. I attended a board meeting held at Steve' Lamb's house to discuss doing that. It was the first board meeting I had attended since leaving the board three years previously. Representatives from Camp for All were at the meeting.

I had the feeling that the fix was in to reject the proposal. Everybody seemed afraid that the financial risk necessary to increase the size and scope of the Ball was too great. I made the pitch that although all of the previous Balls had been successful, attendance and revenue had been down over the last couple of years and something was needed to jazz up the next Ball.

The Camp for All representatives agreed with me and thought the financial risk was worth taking even though a failure would affect the amount we would be able to donate. Folks promised their full support and represented that they would take a significant role in sales efforts. The board wound up approving the proposal unanimously.

The venue selected was the Verizon Center (now called The Bayou City Center), which was the premier concert hall in downtown Houston. The cost for this high profile location was nearly three times the cost of any previous venue. In fact, the Balls held at la Colombe D'or had no site fee at all. The cost of food and booze was competitive with previous venues, but the costs were increased proportionally to the number of guests we would need to attract to make the Ball profitable.

Negotiations for a nationally known band turned out to be trickier than expected. The Club budgeted $15,000 plus expenses for the band. I had been pressing for an oldies group like Eric Burdon and the Animals,

Paul Revere and the Raiders, The Turtles or The Buckingham's. Of these I favored the Animals because not only were they in the proper price range, they had over 20 chart hits, and I thought they might be a good ticket draw.

Steve was not hip on the Animals. He had listened to some recent Eric Burdon performances and thought he sucked. Plus, Steve thought that a band like the Animals would be a draw only to the geriatric set.

Steve finally settled on Foghat, which was a 1970s rock band that had a few chart hits including *Slow Ride* and *I Just Want to Make Love to You*. Steve had heard them play recently and thought they rocked out. Foghat normally would have been outside of our price range, but its lead singer, Lonesome Dave, had died and the band was trying to reestablish itself with a new lead singer that came over from 1970s rock band Humble Pie. To put an end to the controversy of which band would be hired, Steve hired Foghat and paid the band himself.

To make the Ball successful, over 500 tickets would need to be sold, with an increase price to $175, up from our traditional price of $125. Captain Kirk helped by donating $20,000 from his company, Big Dog Logistics, to be the Ball's official corporate sponsor. He set up The Big Dog Lounge at the Ball, which had special decorations and bars. He also gave away Deacons caps and other souvenirs.

Steve and his board were counting on Camp for All's help in selling those tickets. However, in July Steve got a call from Joe Kilchrist, who had been so instrumental in selling tickets for some previous Balls. His wife Eileen was on a committee called "Friends for Camp for All." She reported that no one on that committee had even heard about the Deacons Ball.

Inside the Big Dog Lounge.

Sam Allen

Steve immediately called Pat Sorrells, the head of Camp for All, and asked about this lack of support. She told Steve that Camp for All had a policy of not actively supporting sales efforts for third-party events held on their behalf, and that the Deacons should not expect significant help from Camp for All in selling tickets for the Ball.

This was a troubling piece of news. Steve's board never would have agreed to increase the size of the Ball and risk the financial outlay needed to make it a success had Camp for All not pledged its support early on. Steve was worried that without their help, the Ball might be a financial flop. Rather than panic, Steve started his own sales effort. Steve had traditionally been the most prolific Ball ticket seller, but he redoubled his efforts and sold more tickets than he had ever sold before.

By the night of the Ball, 550 tickets were sold, which was about 125 more tickets than the Deacons' previous record. Camp for All purchased only two.

Foghat came to the after party, which was held in captain Kirk's suite at the Doubletree downtown. The Captain's girlfriend got into a fight with Allen Park's girlfriend and screamed "I'll fuck you up like a nigger's checkbook!"

The Ball turned out to be the Deacons' biggest fundraising success. The net proceeds were about $125,000, which was about 100% higher than the average net proceeds from previous Balls.

Deacons at the Foghat After-Party.

We donated $84,000 to Camp for All.

2012

With one big Ball successfully completed, Steve Lamb organized an even bigger Ball for 2012. With the experience he and his board had gained in being profitable with the Foghat show, Steve felt we could upgrade the quality of the entertainment. Vince Neil, the front man for Motley Crue, agreed to play, but he backed out at the last minute. We wound up hiring Blue Oyster Cult, another 1970s rock band that had chart hits with *Don't Fear the Reaper* and *I'm Burning for You*. About 620 guests attended.

Once again, Captain Kirk and Big Dog Logistics donated $20,000 to be the official sponsor. He built a bigger and better Big Dog Lounge that was an even bigger success than in 2011.

At this Ball, Steve Skelton discovered the advantages of Biker Formal attire. He was sporting a kilt that night with a Deacons patch on his jacket. Chicks love kilts, and several of them asked Steve whether he was wearing anything under his. When he replied that he wasn't, the inquiring woman invariably gave him a grope to see (or, I guess feel) for themselves.

Wearing this kilt was a good move.

Steve had a VIP table in the front row, but as is typical at the Ball, he didn't spend much time there. Instead, he roamed the Bayou Center soliciting gropes. As the Ball was winding down, Steve happened to be at his table when a wild red head came over to check on his kilt. She more than groped. She was on her knees under the table giving Steve some mouth to dick resuscitation.

As the song says: "Every girl's crazy 'bout a sharp dressed man."

This Ball was the first time Mike Fisher worked with Workshop Houston to auction a tricked up bicycle. Workshop Houston started as a community outreach organization that taught kids how to repair bicycles. It also emphasized academic performance. It later started to teach vocational skills, including metal fabrication.

Mike got the idea for the boys at Workshop Houston to build a fancy chopper style bicycle that would be auctioned at the Ball. The kids were to pay for the materials to build the bike, but along the way, Deacons donated various parts to cut down on the kids' expenses. They created a cool bike that was finished with a paint job that was done in Fish's own paint shop. It was sold at the Ball for $10,000, and the entire proceeds went directly to Workshop Houston. The guy who purchased the bike donated it back to Workshop Houston so they could resell it or keep it for their own use.

The girls at Workshop Houston had their own project. They designed T-shirts with art work with a theme related to the Ball. Fish paid for the T-shirts and for the printing of the artwork. The T-shirts were sold to our members and the proceeds went to Workshop Houston.

Fish riding the Workshop Houston bicycle.

The Deacons raised $240,000. This was the first time the Deacons made donations of over $200,000 in a single year.

This also was the first year of Steve Lamb's plan to donate to a variety of charities rather than following our usual model, which was to give a substantial portion of our net proceeds to a single organization. Steve believed that by doing so, the Deacons would get greater name recognition in both a motorcycle world and in Houston's charitable circles. Consistent with this new policy, we made the following cash donations:

- Devereux Foundation $72,000
- Camp Quality $23,000
- Covenant House $23,000
- Workshop Houston $10,000
- Panther Creek $7,000
- Dream League $5,000
- ArtReach $2,000
- Child Advocates $1,000

Instead of making just cash donations, the Club made some community outreach type gifts. The Club donated Christmas presents to 350 families through LINC Houston. The presents were wrapped at Captain Kirk's warehouse and pre-delivered to the site. The whole Club rode their bikes to the presentation, including David Wright, who rode dressed up as Santa.

With the kids at LINC Houston.

The Club also donated 100 bicycles to children through the Kim Coleman Education Fund.

2013

Steve and his board tried to hire Night Ranger in 2013. The Club backed out of that contract when Vince Neil once again became available. Unfortunately, after Vince signed to play the 2013 Ball, he backed out because Motley Crue had been offered $2,000,000 for a one weekend gig at a casino. The big tick tock kept ticking and tocking along, and the Club did not have a band. Steve's friend Billy Gibbons from ZZ Top came to the rescue.

Billy had recently reunited with his old high school band, The Moving Sidewalks. They had played a couple of gigs together and were thinking about a national tour. Billy called Steve and asked about launching that tour at the Deacons' Ball. Billy agreed to do the gig at a cut rate price, which was in the neighborhood of $50,000.

This was a *coup* for the Deacons. It gave the Ball a national exposure that no previous Ball had experienced. Guests flew in from all over the country. Jimi Hendrix sister came as did Sharon Stone's sister. Jeff Beck and Billy Bob Thornton were supposed to come but had to cancel at the last minute.

For the third year in a row, the captain and Big Dog Logistics donated $20,000 and set up the best Big Dog Lounge of all. It had its own bar, specialty shooters and several hot motorcycles. It was a party within a party.

Once again, Mike Fisher and Workshop Houston built a bike that was auctioned. It sold for $10,000.

Over 800 guests attended the 2013 Ball and net profits exceeded $250,000.

Once again, we donated to an array of charities benefitting children in the Houston area:

- Devereux Foundation $50,000
- Camp for All.. $50,000
- Camp Quality.. $30,000
- Epilepsy Foundation.................................. $30,000
- Panther Creek... $10,000
- Workshop Houston $10,000
- Dream League $10,000
- Child Advocates... $10,000
- Gulf Coast BB&S $3,500

We also donated Christmas presents to 350 families through LINC Houston.

2014

The "Lucky 13th" annual Deacons Ball was held on September 20, 2014 at the Bayou City Event Center. It was a blow out. The bottom line: over $375,000 net to the charities. To put that in perspective, that's about 20 times the amount we raised at our first Charity Ball in 2002. Here's how we did it.

The pre-party was at Rebel's Honky Tonk. Our old friend the Mad Doctor was there talking women out of their tops for photos before the start of the Dead Mans' Parade, which had more participants than our first Ball had guests. For the Parade, the Houston Motorcycle Unit closed down Washington Street, I-10, I-45 and Highway 288 to get us the Bayou City Event Center safely.

Brett Michaels provided the entertainment, and he rocked out. He and his band donated $10,000 from the stage, and at the end of the show, they auctioned off one of the band's guitars used in the show.

We sold out the party with 1,200 guests, which is 50% greater than our previous attendance record, which was only last year. We sold 12 Platinum VIP Tables at $7,500 each, 22 Gold VIP Tables at $5,000 each, 36 Silver VIP Tables at $3,000 each and the rest were general admission tickets.

Due to the financial successes of our previous three Balls, we didn't need to have a motorcycle dealership help with the motorcycle we raffled. We simply bought a Road King and sold $100,000 of raffle tickets for it. We also bought a Street Glide Special that we raffled at the Ball for $100 per ticket. We sold all of them, giving us a total raffle profit of about $115,000.

Jamie Adams ran our auctions, and as big a pain in the ass he was all year long about it, he set a new standard of excellence. Everything sold out and we made a profit of over $175,000. Our previous record was about a third of that. Jamie came up with some unique ideas for our auctions. For the first time, we had a computerized biding system featuring a huge electronic big board showing how the bidding was going. There also were hot chicks roaming the floor soliciting bidders. There was a live auction and a special last minute auction to help a young man with debilitating disease. He was a Brett Michaels fan, and we were able to arrange for him to meet Brett and sit at one of the Platinum VIP Tables.

Mike Fisher and his crew from Workshop Houston built a Deacons bicycle for the third year in a row. This year the bike had a small motor.

Brett Michaels turned out to be a great guy. Originally, his managers would allow for a VIP Table meet and greet limited to 16 couples. Once he got there, he had pictures taken with three times that many guests. He took the time to speak to everyone he met and made our guests feel special.

Once again, Captain Kirk sponsored the Big Dog Lounge, this year co-sponsored by Turm Oil, which is in Brett Michael's home town of Butler, PA. Deacon Rodney Fields works there. The Lounge was decorated with several bikes with Deacon's paint jobs. There were strippers in cages and nude women wearing only body paint. There were special ice sculptures and an ice shot bar.

For the first time, we had professional videographers supplied by Deacon Michael Wyckoff. He and his crew interviewed Deacons and our guests before, during and after the Ball. The footage will be used to create professional quality videos and advertisements to promote the Deacons and our charitable activities.

CHAPTER 12

PATCHES

"I don't know why, but you almost have to join a club. If you don't, you'll never be accepted anywhere. If you don't wear any colors, you're sort of in between—and you're nothing."

– A retired Hells Angel

Ricky Cook and I designed the original patches. I copyrighted the patch in 2003, and Jay McKendree secured a trademark for the patch 2011. The Club has adopted a trademark policy to protect the trademark on our patch.

There now are so many patches that it has been suggested that we form a Patch Committee and give the Patch Committee members a Patch Committee Patch.

Here are the stories about all of our patches.

Dead Man's Hand

The Deacons' Dead Man's Hand patch originated from the hand Wild Bill Hickok was holding when he was shot by Jack McCall in Nuttal & Mann's Saloon (Saloon No. 10) in Deadwood, South Dakota in 1876. Everyone agrees that Wild Bill was holding black aces and black eights, but controversy exists about the fifth card. Local news accounts reported that the fifth card was either a red jack or red queen. We selected the nine of diamonds as the fifth card because that is the card that appears in the Dead Man's Hand in Saloon No. 10's logo.

The original patch had three pieces: The Dead Man's Hand with skeleton fingers on a green background like the cloth on a poker table, with top and bottom rockers with the words "Deacons" and "Deadwood." The skeleton fingers represent David Cook holding the cards to our lives from the grave. Cook's other skeleton hand is on your wallet.

The three piece patch almost immediately was abandoned because of Bandido objections. The circular Dead Man's hand patches were given out to Deacons' supporters and girlfriends. Noah "Wild Hog" Latham had one until he was patched into the Club as a full member.

MC

This is the traditional patch designating a riding group as a motorcycle club. We came across some controversy about this patch in 2014 when the Bandidos challenged why we had not joined the Confederacy of Clubs. That is an organization that the Bandidos require motorcycle clubs to join. Their purported purpose is to unify motorcycle clubs for common purposes, like lobbying for the repeal of helmet laws and other motorcycle friendly legislation. We had successfully avoided this affiliation for years by maintaining that we had nothing in common with the Bandidos. After all, we are about as far away from being outlaws as is possible.

In 2014, the Bandidos essentially told us that if we wanted to wear an "MC" patch, we had to join the CoC, and if we didn't join we would be risking bodily harm. The Bandidos told us that our alternative was to stop wearing the MC patch. Most members believed that removing the MC patch without joining the CoC would not solve the problem. So, we voted virtually unanimously to join (there was one dissenting vote from a member who was not at the meeting when the vote was taken).

The Deacons of Deadwood Motorcycle Club

Most of us now believe that joining the CoC was an important event in the evolution of the Deacons as a real motorcycle club (shades of George Bogle), and that being a CoC member will help resolve problems that might be encountered when being confronted by the Bandidos locally or by other 1%er clubs throughout the country.

44%

The 44% patch originates from two sources.

The magazine of the American Motorcycle Association once published an article stating that 99% of all bikers are solid upstanding citizens, and the remaining 1% gave bikers a bad name. The Hells Angels immediately declared itself to be part of the 1% and established their own 1%er tattoo and patch. Of course, all outlaw clubs now are 1%ers.

Many biker bars, especially out west, will not allow motorcycle club members to wear their patches. To get around this technicality, some clubs have adopted codes to help identify a person as a member or supporter of a particular MC. For instance, someone wearing a T-shirt with the number 81 can be identified as a member or supporter of the Hells Angels because H is the eighth letter of the alphabet and one is the first letter of the alphabet. So, 81=HA=Hells Angels.

The Deacons 44% patch is a combination of these two ideas. D is the fourth letter of the alphabet, so DD=44=Deacons of Deadwood, and we are only about 44% bad ass. Thus, the 44% patch.

From time to time we have considered abolishing the 44% patch because of the attention it attracts. It is the only patch about which 1%ers ever inquire. However, we consistently have determined to keep it.

Houston

This is simply a patch identifying that the Deacons of Deadwood is from Houston.

Nine of Diamonds

The Nine of Diamonds patch originates from the nine of diamonds in the Dead Man's Hand. Originally, only nine founding members were to receive this patch. However, within a few days of the founding of the Club, several other influential members joined and they also were awarded a Nine of Diamonds patch. That used to drive Elza Smith to apoplexy.

The Nine of Diamonds patch members are:

David Cook (Posthumous)	Sam Douglass
Ricky Cook	Preston Douglass
Sam Allen	Bob Mitchell
Tolly Allen	Mike Callaghan
John Aubrey	Eric Robertson
John Talbot	Ted Ricketson
Carroll Kelly	Elza Smith

No more Nine of Diamonds patches will be awarded.

Ace of Spades

The Ace of Spades patch was the first patch created after our initial patches. Seguine Al Arfsten awarded it to all the Deacons who rode their motorcycles to Sturgis in 2002, which was the year we were founded.

No more Ace of Spades patches will be awarded.

The Deacons of Deadwood Motorcycle Club

Officers and Directors

Patches are given to the Club's incumbent directors, president, vice president, treasurer, and road captain. In addition, patches are given to each past president and past director.

Long Rider

The Long Rider patch is awarded to any Deacon or guest of a Deacon that completes a ride with other Deacons of at least 1,000 miles.

Iron Butt

The Iron Butt patches are awarded to any Deacon or guest of a Deacon that completes a sanctioned Iron Butt Association ride with another Deacon and receives a patch from the Iron Butt Association confirming the completion of the ride. Iron Butt rides for which Deacons have earned patches include the *Saddle Sore 1,000* (1,000 miles in 24 hours); *Bun Burner* (1,500 miles in 36 hours); *Bun Burner Gold* (1,500 miles in 24 hours); *Coast to Coast* (from the Atlantic to the Pacific) and *Border to Border* (Mexico to Canada).

The following Deacons have completed Iron Butt rides:

Name	Iron Butt Rides
Sam Allen	Saddle Sore 1,000 Bun Burner Bun Burner Gold
John Aubrey	Saddle Sore 1,000 Bun Burner
George Bogle	Saddle Sore 1,000 Bun Burner
Mike Callaghan	Saddle Sore 1,000 Bun Burner Bun Burner Gold Border to Border Coast to Coast

Justin Dossett............................	Saddle Sore 1,000
Martin Dossett..........................	Saddle Sore 1,000
Mike Fisher	Saddle Sore 1,000 Bun Burner
Jim Row......................................	Saddle Sore 1,000
Geoff Seaman	Saddle Sore 1,000 Bun Burner
Peter Sommer	Saddle Sore 1,000 Bun Burner Bun Burner Gold 2,000 miles/48 Hrs 3,000 miles/72 Hrs Coast to Coast
John Talbot	Bun Burner
Ben Thompson..........................	Saddle Sore 1,000 Bun Burner Bun Burner Gold 2,000 miles/48 Hrs 3,000 miles/72 Hrs Coast to Coast
Johnny Williams.......................	Saddle Sore 1,000

Hard Core

This patch is awarded to Deacons who have completed a minimum of three separate Iron Butt rides, at least one of which must be a *Bun Burner Gold, Border to Border* or *Coast to Coast* ride, plus at least 25,000 additional miles of riding with the Deacons. The following Deacons have been awarded the Hard Core patch:

>Sam Allen
>Mike Callaghan
>Carroll Kelly
>Peter Sommer
>Ben Thompson

The Deacons of Deadwood Motorcycle Club

Mileage Patches

Patches are awarded to Deacons who have surpassed specified mileage goals in a year. The recipients of these patches are:

25,000	20,000
Sam Allen	Mike Fisher
Peter Sommer	Geoff Seaman
	David Reed
	David Youngblood

There also are mileage patches for 15,000, 10,000 and 5,000 miles per year, but the holders of those patches wouldn't admit to them.

Individual Ride Patches

The Club has long awarded patches to participants in our most significant rides. The Deacons' annual Patch Rides include:

Black Hills (Sturgis)	Fort Clark
Big Bend	Hot Springs
Hill Country	President's Ride

On occasion, patches have been created to commemorate particular one-time rides, such as the *Lonesome Dove* Ride. The following Deacons received the *Lonesome Dove* Ride patch:

Sam Allen

Steve Lamb	Geoff Seaman
John Lowery	Mike Fisher
Peter Sommer	LaMark Bejer
Kirk Lane	Ben Thompson

Six of Clubs

The Six of Clubs patch was awarded to all the participants in the first Fort Clark ride, which was founded by Orlando Sanchez. The following Deacons hold this patch:

Orlando Sanchez	Jay McKendree
Peter Sommer	Justin Dossett
Mike Marlowe	Ted Faleski

No more Six of Clubs patches will be awarded.

Map of the United States

The Map of the United States patch is awarded to Deacons who have ridden a motorcycle to all of the contiguous 48 United States.

The following Deacons have earned this patch:

Sam Allen
Matt Linton
Peter Sommer

The Deacons of Deadwood Motorcycle Club

Membership Stars

Deacons who have been members for 10 years are awarded a platinum star with a green Roman numeral X. Deacons who have been members for five years are awarded a gold star with a green "5":

The following Deacons have been awarded a Platinum 10-year star:

Sam Allen	Ricky Cook	Tolly Allen	John Aubrey
John Talbot	Sam Douglass	Preston Douglass	Jay McKendree
Steve Lamb	Bill Talbot	Eric Robertson	Al Arfsten
Mike Callaghan	Tommy Cason	Scott Tambourine	

The Following Deacons have been awarded a Gold Five-year star:

John Burns	Ben Thompson	Justin Dossett	Orlando Sanchez
Ken Hill	Bob Bulian	Dennis Hensley	Peter Sommer
Noah Latham	Ken Carr	Rusty Drake	Geoff Seaman
D. Youngblood	John Lowery	Aaron Seward	Selly Chinnery
Alan Parks	Andy Harris	Mike Fisher	

The 15-year stars that will be awarded beginning in 2017 have not been designed.

Flying Monkey

The Flying Monkey patch is awarded to Deacons who have had notable encounters with the Princess of Darkness. The flying monkey was selected to represent these encounters because the flying monkeys from the *Wizard of Oz* are the most frightening things most of us remember from our childhood. So too, the Princess of Darkness is the most frightening thing any of us have encountered as adults.

Here's how flying monkey patches have been earned:

Ricky Cook. Ricky has been at the center of the Princess's attention for years. She's tall, trim and attractive, and on occasion she can act in a civil way. But once she gets a few drinks in her things can get bleak pretty quickly. In the spirit of full disclosure, however, Ricky can egg her on at times.

Ricky's Flying Monkey patch is for conduct above and beyond the call of duty and relates to a continuum of events rather than any specific episode.

One time the Princess burned her condo down. Folks suggested she did it on purpose so she could move in with Ricky. Ricky let her stay with him for a while, but when she started acting up, he kicked her out of the main house and made her stay in a small apartment that had been built in his parking lot. She would have to bang on the window to get Ricky to let her back in, and Ricky wouldn't always do it.

One afternoon Ricky was having a barbecue in this parking lot. The Princess had been acting up so she was not invited. The parking lot has a fence that is nearly 10 feet tall. Somehow, the Princess scaled this fence looking like a gazelle and bopped into the barbecue. On this particular occasion she wound up acting in a pretty decent fashion, but it's a good example of how she could overcome serious obstacles when stalking Ricky.

The Club was in Bandera during the Hill Country Ride. The Princess acted up and Ricky left her at the 11th St. Bar and headed back to Kerrville, where everybody was staying. The Princess wound up having to get a ride back to Houston with Tommy "the Snake" Cason, who without question was the horniest human being in the history of the world.

In retrospect, Ricky probably should be awarded a Masochist patch for putting himself in harm's way so often over so long a period of time.

Sam Allen. Since Ricky and I are best friends, I have been present during dozens of POD episodes. However, I got my Flying Monkey from a specific event.

The Club had ridden to the Sundowner Bar after one of our regularly scheduled monthly meetings. The Princess was not with us. When it was time to head home it started to rain, so I asked Ricky if I could stay on his couch rather than have to ride downtown in the bad weather. That was fine with Ricky.

When we got to Ricky's crib, he opened the security gate so we could park our bikes inside. When Ricky got the gate open, a set of headlights went on, and a car screamed toward me. I had to dive out of the way, and the truck barely missed me, but the truck didn't miss Ricky's gate. The Princess rammed into it, causing over $1,000 of damage. The Princess then took off leaving me wet and Ricky with a broken gate.

Justin Dossett. Ricky and the Princess were at the Club's first camp out ride at Ron's Relay. Ricky asked the Kid if he would walk out to Ricky's truck with him for some reason. As they approached the truck, the POD said something to the Kid which he didn't understand, and he asked her to go back inside. The next thing he knew the POD punched him in the face. He felt violated.

John Talbot and Coy Banta. Ricky and the Princess, Coy Banta and his wife Teddi, John Talbot and I all went to the Breaux Bridge Crawfish Festival in Louisiana. On Saturday night, Talbot took the crowd to one of his favorite Lafayette nightspots. The Princess thought Ricky was paying too much attention to some of the beautiful Creole action and the POD threw a fit and started smacking Ricky around. Talbot, Coy and the rest of us were not only embarrassed, we were kicked out of the club.

19

This is the Club's most secret patch. Those who earn it are awarded the patch by those who already have it. I once refused to disclose the meaning of this patch in a court proceeding in which I was being deposed. When the deposing lawyer told me I had no choice but to answer the question, I told him I would make the disclosure as soon as I was served with a court order compelling me to answer. I was not so served so I gave no response.

Houston Livestock Show and Rodeo

This patch was awarded to Deacons and guests of Deacons who came to the Deacons suite at the Houston Livestock Show and Rodeo.

Charity Ball

This patch is given to all attendees at the Club's annual Charity Ball.

In Memoriam

Most motorcycle clubs have patches that commemorate the passing of their brothers. For the Deacons, the death of a brother is a personal thing to be shared with Club members but not with outsiders. So, rather than having a patch naming a brother who has died, we remember him with a green star with his initiation number in the center. Only Club members know the meaning.

CHAPTER 13

IN MEMORIAM

"Do not go gently into that good night.
Rage, rage against the dying of the light."

– Dylan Thomas

David Cook-001

David gave the Club our name. He used to organize trips to Sturgis each year, and he would take over the entire Bullock Hotel in Deadwood. A bunch of his crew was walking up the street in Deadwood one afternoon, and he said "There are so many of us up here that they should call us the "Deacons of Deadwood." When his son Ricky co-founded the Club a few years after David's death from pancreatic cancer, it adopted the name Deacons of Deadwood after David's remark.

There are too many stories to relate here. Many Club members believe that his ideals were the blocks upon which the Deacons of Deadwood was founded. While that is not exactly true, when given the choice of printing the truth or the legend, it's better to go with the legend.

Carroll Kelly-008

Carroll Kelly was one of the founding members of the Deacons of Deadwood. He was a prominent lawyer and businessman in Houston for decades. Carroll was born and raised in Freer, Texas. He played basketball for the University of Texas and later attended the UT Law School. He was the biggest UT sports fan on the planet, and would watch UT football at the Deacons' Charity Ball.

Carroll knew everybody, and if he met you and he didn't know you, he would get to know you immediately. He played golf regularly with Darrell Royal and Willie Nelson, among others.

He was a life-long Democrat and was strongly influenced by John F. Kennedy, who he met when he was young. He was active in local politics and knew every politician in Texas worth knowing over the course of many decades.

Carroll was one of the most opinionated members of the Deacons. He may have been right or wrong but he was never in doubt. Many viewed him as the conscience of the Club.

Carroll also was a tough SOB. When he found he was ill, a friend of his went along on a doctor's visit. The doctor told the friend in confidence that Carroll had terminal cancer and that he had just given Carroll that news. When Carroll came out of the doctor's office all he said to his friend was "Where are we playing golf today."

The day Carroll died he played golf in the morning and passed away on the way to see his grandson play little league football. He lived his life the way he wanted to live it until the minute we lost him.

Eric "ER" Robertson-008

ER was a founding member of the Deacons of Deadwood. Before joining the Deacons, he rode with a loosely knit group called the Mag 7, most of whom became Deacons.

ER was an Ohio State sports fan and a NASCAR fan. When it came to hunting, he was the Grim Reaper. He had trophies from all over the world, the most recent of which was a 9'6" Alaskan brown bear. For a little guy he shot a lot of big animals.

ER liked to drink and sometimes fight. He would say "I'm not scared." He had limited success in his fights, but he in fact was not afraid.

One time ER had a chance to go to a World Series in New York. After the game, he happened to be in the restaurant where George Steinbrenner, the owner of the Yankees, was having dinner with his family. Before he could be stopped, he was sitting next to The Boss asking a friend to take a picture of Steinbrenner and him. He told George that he had driven 24 hours straight to watch the game. Steinbrenner said "I love fans like you. Here's my card. If the Series comes back to New York, I'll fly you up to watch the game with me in the owner's box. Have your people call my people and we'll set it up."

ER replied "I don't have any people!"

ER had an engaging smile, a happy disposition, and was liked and loved by all who knew him. He loved to watch sports and drink, and it caught up to him one afternoon.

Sam Douglass-010

Sam was a founding member of the Club and was a Nine of Diamonds patch holder. He was a life-long friend of David Cook's who often had drinks on Thursday nights with David's crew at Luxury Cycles before riding to Stelter's in Downtown Houston. He also attended all of Cook's Ride to Fuad's charity events.

At the meeting at which the Deacons received their patches, Ted Ricketson's wife, the "Fly," asked where the women's patches were. I told her that the women weren't getting patches. The Fly asked me "Why not?" Sam interjected "Because we are a motorcycle club, and motorcycle clubs don't have women."

Sam Allen

Sam and his son Preston, along with ex-Deacon Fred Farner, founded the Hill Country Ride in 1997 when a group that included David Cook and future Deacons Sam Allen, Ricky Cook and Fred Haas headed to the YO Ranch Hotel in Kerrville the weekend before Memorial Day. Unlike today's Deacons, everyone trailered their bikes.

Sam continued to participate in the Hill Country Ride, as well as other rides, as long as his health permitted. During one of his last Hill Country Rides, he asked about a group of Deacons who had been causing trouble within the Club and referred to them as "The sniveling seven." It turned out that the snivelers were sitting across from Sam at the same table.

Sam went to Sturgis with David Cook's group for years and was one of the original Bullock Hotel crowd. He was in Deadwood when Cook said "There are so many of us here they should call us the Deacons of Deadwood," which was the origin of our name. In most years, Sam, Preston, Fred and other guests would stop at Sam's place in Aspen for some Colorado riding before getting to Sturgis.

Sam was one of the Club's early corporate sponsors. He and Preston would buy a VIP table at each of our Charity Balls even when they couldn't attend.

Sam won the motorcycle we raffled at our first Charity Ball. Since Sam and Preston had just bought Corpus Christi Harley-Davidson and our guests consisted almost entirely of people who knew David Cook, there was worry within the Club that folks might have though the raffle was rigged. Of course it wasn't, but after that we adopted a policy prohibiting a Deacon from wining the raffle.

There are many stories about Sam that could be related here. But Sam had a rule that "What happens with Sam, stays with Sam." He never spoke out of school, so there will be no speaking out of school here. But there is no need to do that. All of us who knew Sam have our own fond remembrances.

In 2011, Sam became the only Deacon to be honorably retired from the Club. We held a retirement ceremony at Capone's Restaurant. There was virtually 100% attendance. Preston came in from Corpus Christi and other friends of Sam's came in from other parts of the country. We presented Sam a sterling silver tray from Tiffany's engraved with Sam's name and initiation number, along with the Deacon's patch.

We lost Sam on Thanksgiving Day 2014. He was a much respected Deacon who had a greater influence on the formation and development of the Club than he likely would have acknowledged himself. Plus, he was just a hell of a good guy.

Sam Allen

Sam Douglass

1932 - 2014 | Obituary
SAM PRESTON DOUGLASS
1932-2014

Sam Preston Douglass was born in Houston, Texas on the eve of All Saints Day in 1932. He died with his beloved Paula by his side, on Thanksgiving Day, at the age of 82.

Sam graduated from San Jacinto High School in 1950. Attending the University of Houston, he earned a Bachelor of Business Administration degree, with majors in Management and Finance. He was President of the graduating class of 1954 and of the Cavaliers, which later became Sigma Nu fraternity. Sam was also a Cougar cheerleader in 1952, 1953 and 1954. Graduating as a distinguished Military Graduate, Sam received a regular Army Commission, where he served as a Captain in the Quartermaster Corps.

After attending Baylor College of Law for one year, Sam moved to Austin, where he earned a Doctor of Jurisprudence degree from the University of Texas Law School. He was a member of the Moot Court Team and a member of Phi Alpha Delta Legal Fraternity.

Sam was a natural born leader. He worked during the summers as a counselor at Ozark Boys Camp and Brown and Root. His business career began as Vice President, Director and General Counsel for Marine Exploration and American Sulphur companies. Sam was a Vice President, Director and General Counsel for the River Oaks Bank & Trust Company. He later became a partner in the Yarborough, Brigman, Talley and Lucas law firm.

The Deacons of Deadwood Motorcycle Club

Sam left the practice of law to become Co-Founder of Service Corporation International, NYSE: SCI, where he served as President and Chairman of the Executive Committee. Later, he Co-Founded the Wedge Group of Companies. During his tenure at Wedge, he participated in the acquisition or formation of P&S Rice Mills, Rice Sales and Services Inc; Schoelman Lines of Texas, Inc., Locassine Rice Dryer, Inc. Kaplan Rice Mill, Inc., International Grain Management Corp., Market Produce, Inc., Saudi International Rice Company, Ltd., and American Foods. As Chairman and Co-Founder of Energy Services International, Sam was President of P.A. Incorporated, Petroleum Services International, Inc. and Zaploc, Inc.

Sam founded the Equus Group of Funds in 1978, where he served as Chairman of the Board of Directors and CEO until his retirement. He occupied the same office in the Wortham Tower as his respected mentor, Gus Wortham, Founder and Chairman of the American General Insurance Company, to whom he always referred as, "'Mr. Gus'". His most cherished and meaningful negotiation was with Mr. Gus, for the acquisition of some chairs from Suite 8-F, of the Lamar Hotel. It was a well- remembered and fond farewell.

Active in the Houston community, Sam served for many years on the boards of the University of Houston School of Law, The C.T. Bauer College of Business and The Jesse H. Jones Graduate School of Business at Rice University. The Sam P. Douglass Courtyard was dedicated upon the completion of Herring Hall on the Rice campus. Later, the Sam P. Douglass Library was installed in the University of Houston Alumni Center. Sam was blessed to have received many awards during his lifetime but was most proud to be the recipient of the Distinguished Alumni award from the University of Houston College of Business and the 1989 Distinguished Alumnus Award from the University of Houston Alumni Organization.

Sam was a member of River Oaks Country Club, where he particularly enjoyed his time in later years with CO in the men's locker room. He was also a member of the Coronado Club and the Argyle Club in San Antonio.

Sam was a Co-founder and Director of Chub Cay Associates, serving as its President. He loved the Bahamas and shared many years of fun adventure with his family and friends on the private island of Chub Cay. A one in the world, Flo's Conch bar was an out island ""destination"" favorite at high tide and the boat ride itself, was worth the trip. Sam loved summers in Aspen, especially Harley rides in the mountains with Preston and friends. Breakfast at the ""country club"" was a frequent stop and cigars on the Roaring Fork, with a good book, was his ideal respite.

A man of diverse interests, Sam was a voracious reader and took great delight in the exclusive Bookclub of Two, in which he shared books with Bennie. Sam rode cutting horses and was especially fond of ""Chi Willy"". He had a deep respect for the land, instilled by God and nurtured by his adored Grandfather and namesake, Sam Preston, of Midland, Texas. Sam enjoyed the years he spent as a Santa Gertrudis, Brangus and Exotic game breeder at his Kirschburg and Whiskey Canyon Ranches. His soul will always fondly hover in South Texas, Africa and the English Countryside, where the art of the shoot is perfected. A great shot, he treasured the many hunts with dearest friends and leaves a field legacy of good form and sportsmanship.

The Deacons of Deadwood Motorcycle Club

Sam was a founder of the Cowboy Artists of America Museum in Kerrville, Texas and was a member and former Director of the Tejas Vaqueros for 41 years. Membership in this fine organization was shared with his son, Preston. Their adventures on horseback were of great importance to him and he looked forward to the week in the canyon with his close vaqueros each year.

Sam was honored to be elected a delegate from St. Martins to the Diocesan Council of the Episcopal Church. He loved smoking cigars during reflections with the Bishop and many priests on sunny days in God's gardens. At the time of death, Sam was an active member of Christ Episcopal Church of Aspen and St. John the Divine Episcopal Church in Houston. Sam felt the collective Love of the Body of Christ through all of his health challenges and was most grateful for this most precious gift from God.

All who knew Sam will remember his warm smile and zeal for all of life. He was strong but gentle, delighting in teaching and helping others and loved deeply, including special friends Emma Cate, Bella Francis, Bruno and Beau Jaune.

He is preceded in death by his parents, Tommie Preston Douglass and Louie Earle Douglass; and Emma Chase.

He is survived by Paula, his wife of 36 years, with whom he had a life long partnership and love affair. He is also survived by his mother-in-law and friend, Bonnie Callahan Terry, ""Zette"" of Houston; Brother-in-law Ira James Terry, Jr. and wife Susan of Pittsburg, Pa; daughter, Brooke Douglass Graubart and husband Marc, of Houston; son Sam Preston Douglass, Jr. and wife Kate, of Portland, Texas; grandchildren, Treva Grace Graubart of Houston; Emily

Sam Allen

Douglass Murdock and husband Bailey, of Charlottesville, Va., Sarah Park Douglass of Oxford, Miss; Sam Preston Douglass, III of Ft. Worth, Texas; Cody Sachse, Bryanna Sachse and Will Sachse of Portland, Tx; nephews Christian Griffin Pendley and wife Marci, of Houston; Ira James Terry, III and wife, Erin, of Wake Forest, NC and Jonathan Terry of Atlanta, Ga; Sam took great delight in his Great nephew, Preston Pendley of Houston, Texas and his Great niece, Lauren Terry, of Wake Forest, NC and good friends and cousins, Preston Bridgewater, of Houston, Texas and Gary Babb of Huntsville, Alabama. Sam will always have a special place in his heart for Carmen and the Villacorte family, including Lala and faithful companion, Alberto Aburto. He is grateful for the loyal devotion of Dawn Clark and his trusted friend and ally, Molly Alonso. One of the best, last gifts Sam received were bedside visits from twins, Owen and Carlyle and his beloved, brilliant physician, Dr. James L. Pool, M. D.

Pallbearers will be Robert L. Waltrip, James H. Greer, R. W. Wortham, III, Allen Lawrence Berry, Charles R. Ofner, Dan Moody, III, Ira James Terry, III and William Bailey Murdock. Honorary Pallbearers will be The Honorable James A. Baker, III, Jerry E. Finger, Robert A. Day, The Honorable George Argyros, John P. Wade, Frank D. Adams, J. Thomas Bagby, John H. Duncan and the Membership of Tejas Vaqueros.

Friends are invited to a visitation fiesta with the family from 4 o'clock in the afternoon until 7 o'clock in the evening on Tuesday, the second of December, 2014, at the Douglass family residence. A service of holy burial will be conducted at 1 o'clock in the afternoon on Wednesday, the third of December, 2014, in the Sanctuary of St. John the Divine

Episcopal Church, 2450 River Oaks Boulevard in Houston, Texas. The Rev. Dr. Clay A. Lein, Rector, The Rev. Dr. Douglas W. Richnow, Sr. Associate Rector and The Rev. Bruce McNab, officiating. A private Interment will follow the celebration of the Rite of Burial.

In lieu of flowers, memorials can be made to The Kelly Day Endowment at the Baker Institute for Public Policy; C.T. Bauer College of Business; The Jesse H. Jones Graduate School of Business at Rice University, Agape Development in Houston, Texas or the charity of one's choice.

Almighty Father, we thank You for providing warriors, doctors and nurses who have cared for us, prayed with us, come to the Lord's Table with us, shared their lives with us, comforted us. Especially hold safe the one who sees us all, as ""her family"". Protect, guide and strengthen them, day in and day out, as they continue to care for Your weak, wounded and sick. ""Come unto to me all ye that labor and are heavy laden, and I will give you rest."" Matthew 11:28

- See more at: http://www.legacy.com/obituaries/houston-chronicle/obituary.aspx?n=sam-preston-douglass&pid=173327155&fhid=6290#sthash.ufiFIOn5.dpuf

Duke Nunn-019

Duke joined the Deacons during its first year. He was a roofer by trade.

Duke used to like to go to Big John's Icehouse on Sunday mornings and work the New York Times crossword puzzle. If you peeked over his shoulder you could see that at least half the words he had filled in were wrong.

Duke was proud to be a Deacon. He didn't have much money, but he paid his dues on time every month. He was a good example to some real dead beats the Club had in those days.

Duke was drinking one Sunday morning and had a high speed wreck on his bike. He sustained a severe head injury and needed help from others for the rest of his life. He would show up at Club functions now and then or we might run into him on occasion, and he always mustered a smile for his brothers. It's an indictment of the Club that we did not keep up with him better than we did.

Tommy "The Snake" Cason-021

Tommy joined the Deacons during its first year, and other than our founding members, he was the fourth longest serving member when he died.

Tommy spent most of his life in Pasadena, Texas. When he was very young, he would make money shining shoes, and later mowing lawns. He graduated from Pasadena High School when he was only 16 years old, and he immediately entered into a four year masonry apprenticeship. By the time he was 21, he had his own masonry contracting company, which he operated for the rest of his life.

Tommy loved the ladies and the ladies loved him. He sure wasn't shy. Even his past girlfriends and ex-wives remained his friends.

Tommy had been sick for quite some time before he went to a doctor. His throat was so constricted that he could barely swallow. When he found he had throat cancer, he was scared, but faced it with a determination to beat it.

Predictions of Tommy's demise were often and always premature. It seemed like he had three months to live every three months for his last three years. He was like the guy in the old joke "My doctor gave me three months to live. I told the doctor I didn't have the money to pay him, so the doctor gave me three more months."

Tommy faced death with the same quiet dignity that defined his life. That is the mark of his character. He was one of the most loved members of our Club.

Sam Allen

Eulogy for Tommy Cason

June 8, 1951-May 28, 2013

Welcome.

We are here to celebrate the life of our friend Tommy Cason. My name is Sam Allen, and I'm one of the founders of the Deacons of Deadwood Motorcycle Club and a long-time friend of Tommy's. Many months ago, Tommy and his family asked that I speak at his funeral, and I'm honored to have been asked to do so.

Thomas Michael Cason was born on June 8, 1951 in Galena Park, Texas. He was the son of Pete Cason and Patsy Hill. Tommy spent most of his life in Pasadena, Texas. When he was very young, he would make money shining shoes, and later mowing lawns. He graduated from Pasadena High School when he was only 16 years old, and he immediately entered into a four year masonry apprenticeship. By the time he was 21, he had his own masonry contracting company, which he operated for the rest of his life.

Tommy was married twice, and from one of those marriages came his daughter Breeze. Breeze and his grandson Ethan, who lit up his life, as did Tommy's sister Sissy. Tommy and Sissy were devoted to each other and Sissy's care for Tommy during his illness added years to his life. They were lucky to have each other.

Tommy was a gentle man, but there was nothing soft about him. He worked hard his whole life in a tough business. Through a combination of hard work, personal integrity, and quiet dignity, he was a force in both his personal and professional life without ever having to act forcefully.

The Deacons of Deadwood Motorcycle Club

Tommy was an avid National Rifle Association member and once was a licensed gun dealer. He owned his own gun shop and would travel to gun shows. He was an expert marksman and won shooting contests when he was as young as 11 years old.

Tommy liked to read about Texas history, and became quite a Texas historian. He particularly liked histories about the early days of Texas and biographies about Sam Houston and the other Texas founders.

During this Service, two songs that Tommy loved are being played. There were other choices, like "Girls Girls Girls," or maybe "To All the Girls I've Loved Before." Or since Tommy liked country music, there could have been the John Anderson tune "Swingin'."

Yes, Tommy loved the ladies and the ladies loved him. It may because he was such a gentleman, or maybe it was because he was so persistent. He sure wasn't shy. But even ex-wives and his past girlfriends remained good friends. It never seems to work out that way for me. One of my ex-wives tried to run me down in her truck and the other tried to stab me with a butcher knife!

The stories about Tommy and his various exploits are abundant, and no remembrance of Tommy's life would be complete without those stories. Unfortunately, I can't think of any I can tell at this venue. I can't tell you about Tommy's adventures with the House Mouse or at the Miller House. I can't tell you about the anatomy lesson Tommy gave Steve Lamb during one of our Club's charity rides. I'm sure plenty of stories will come out at the Reception following these Services, so I hope all of the curious among you will attend.

Tommy had been sick for quite some time before being diagnosed with throat cancer. His throat was so constricted that he could barely swallow. When he found his inability to swallow was due to throat cancer, he was scared, but faced it with a determination to beat it. His battle with cancer went on for several years, and during that time he faced other severe health problems, like the heart attack Ken told you about. No one thought he would survive. I visited him in the hospital during his recovery from that heart attack. He was hooked up to all kinds of artificial breathing and other equipment that was keeping him alive. When I left his hospital room that day, I believed that it was the last time I would see him alive. When the doctors unhooked everything, he just kept on breathing.

That was a couple of years ago.

Predictions of Tommy's demise were often and always premature. It seemed like he had three months to live every three months for the last three years. He was like the guy in the old joke "My doctor gave me three months to live. I told the doctor I didn't have the money to pay him, so the doctor gave me three more months."

Dylan Thomas wrote a poem about facing death. He said: "Do not go gentle into that goodnight. Rage, rage against the dying of the light."

Tommy didn't have much rage in him, but he certainly had no intention of going gentle into that good night. Tommy was not looking toward some better place in the hereafter; he wanted to live as many days as he could right here. The last time I saw Tommy, he told me he went to sleep every night wondering if he would wake up in the morning. But he didn't act like each day might be his last; he acted like each day was like the day before.

Tommy always was a sharp dresser, and the last time I saw him, he was being fed intravenously because he no longer could eat solid food, but he was wearing a button down shirt and starched jeans.

He ran his business literally until the last few days of his life. And I mean he really ran it. He had his relatives drive him around to pick up materials; he visited his job sites; and he got payrolls out. He just kept on living his life as best he could until his body could no longer support his spirit.

A man's character is defined not so much by achievement and how he acts during good times, but by his conduct in facing adversity. Of course, no one can know what Tommy thought privately, and he was a particularly private man. However, to those around him, Tommy never complained about the pain he was suffering. He never lamented about his misfortune in getting cancer at such a young age. He always seemed more concerned about his family and friends than about himself.

Tommy faced death with the same quiet dignity that defined his life. That is the mark of his character. I am sure that if asked, Tommy would have insisted that nobody inconvenience themselves to come here today. I also know that he would have been warmed and pleased that his family and friends gathered here today to remember him.

Tommy Cason died on May 28, 2013. He was at home and surrounded by his family. He is survived by his sister Sissy, his daughter Michelle Breeze and his grandson Ethan Smith. He also is survived by his 70 Deacons of Deadwood Brothers who loved him.

Good bye, dear friend.

Sam Allen

"Seguin Al" Arfsten-025

The Mad Doctor introduced "Seguin Al" Arfsten (aka "Rodeo Al"; aka "Al the Pimp") to us during our first year.

Al got the nickname "Seguin Al" during the Club's annual ride to Big Bend. A large group departed on a Thursday night during good weather intending to make it to San Antonio. Another group was to leave Friday morning, but the weather forecast was for rain. Al sent out an e-mail offering to lead members who were not used to riding in the rain to San Antonio, where they would meet up with the Thursday group and head on to Big Bend.

Al's group made it as far as Seguin, Texas, which is about 60 miles outside of San Antonio. The rain was so bad, he had the whole group turn around and head back to Houston. The problem was that the weather system was going west to east, and by the time he turned around, the weather was clear in San Antonio. So, rather than riding another 30 miles west into clear weather, his group followed the rain 150 miles all the way back to Houston.

So, Al became Seguin Al. The Club even had a proclamation made up and signed by the mayor of Seguin giving him that name, and it stuck.

Years later, Al recruited a few gorgeous under age college girls into the Deacon's suite at the Houston Rodeo. They got loaded and one was taken out on a stretcher with alcohol poisoning. The members decided that Al had redeemed himself sufficiently to shed the Seguin Al nickname, and he was offered either "Rodeo Al" or "Al the Pimp." He decided to stick with Seguin Al.

Although it was fun to poke some fun at Al now and then, he always was a good member. He rarely missed a meeting and he went on all the long rides. In fact, he was the first Deacon to get to the Sturgis Rally wearing a Deacons patch. He also recruited good prospects for the Club and was ready to help any member who needed assistance.

Al was proud to have been a Marine and a Vietnam veteran.

Al had a congenital problem with blood clots, and would get hundreds of tiny clots in his brain at one time. This syndrome apparently killed Al's father, and we lost Al to the same thing. There was no public funeral, but his friends put on a memorial service that drew folks from many of the motorcycle clubs around Houston.

Tom Murphy-083

Tom Murphy was new to the Houston area in 2009. He moved here from the Midwest where he had worked in the car business holding many senior level positions, including General Manager, Sales Manager, Finance Manager and Parts Manager for new car dealerships. His last position was Finance Manager at the local Volvo dealership. He moved here with his wife, Becky, and shortly afterwards joined the Club. They both rode motorcycles and participated in all our rides to Galveston, Kemah, the Hill Country, and wherever the Deacons wanted to go to get in 150 - 250 miles in one day. He loved to ride and tell stories, and was happy to raise a beer to celebrate your health and good fortune.

Tom had not been a member long before he contracted throat cancer. As his health diminished his participation in the Club dropped off. He was a private guy and did not want to burden us with his problems, even though we encouraged him to remain as active as he could. We only had Tom for a while, but he was a Deacon and is missed by those of us who knew him.

LaMark Bejer-097

LaMark came to the Deacons in an unlikely way.

He liked to hang out at the Alabama Icehouse. One night, half a dozen bikers who go there showed up at one of our monthly meetings, and that meeting happened to be the night at which LaMark's Club sponsor was going to introduce LaMark to us. These guys just were not what our Club was looking for, and they all were politely discouraged from trying to join. LaMark was bundled with those guys, and we all thought that would be the last we would see of him.

Turned out we were wrong. His sponsor told the Club that LaMark was not part of the grimy crew that had showed up uninvited, and that LaMark was a great guy who would be an asset to the Deacons. We rounded him up and he became our 97th member.

LaMark was all at once outgoing but reserved; happy but not boisterous. He was one of those guys who always was around without calling attention to himself. LaMark logged thousands of miles on his bike with our Club. He was with us in Sturgis, the *Lonesome Dove* Ride, Big Bend, the Hill Country, the Ozarks and all the other long rides we take. He did not have an extended family, and in many ways, the Deacons became his family.

LaMark's business was called LaMark of Excellence, which was the most respected fine art display company in Houston. He hung artwork in many of Houston's museums, and he was the turn to guy for folks like Bob McNair, owner of the Houston Texans, and oil man J.P. Bryan, who owns the Gage Hotel in Marathon, Texas. The Gage is the finest hotel in west Texas, and is a long time Deacons' destination. LaMark hung all the artwork at the Gage, including the striking white buffalo in the bar.

LaMark is the only Deacon to be killed on his bike. He came up fast on an accident that was being worked by an EMS Unit. He hit his brakes to avoid the accident and went down. A car following too close ran him over and he was dead at the scene. The news of LaMark's passing was sudden and filled the Club with both shock and grief. The love for LaMark shown by our members was a testament to the man he was.

When he passed, his family asked that in lieu of flowers, donations be made to the Deacons' Charity because they knew that's what LaMark would have wanted.

The Deacons of Deadwood Motorcycle Club

Eulogy Delivered by John Lowery

LaMark Bejer

    LaMark of Excellence — that was what he called his company. LaMark hung works of art for many people. But he himself was a work of art, if not a piece of work. He was both a diamond in the rough and a perfectly crafted machine. LaMark's life was marked with interesting contrasts.
    I first met LaMark about nine years ago at the Alabama Ice House. He was obviously a nice person. Everybody knew that. At first he was quiet. But he always smiled. But like a diamond in the rough you had to rub a bit to see the shine from within. Once you got to know him he never stopped talking.
    Before we were both Deacons, LaMark and I did a bunch of riding together. Right off the bat I loved his riding style. He kept up in traffic, but on the open roads he liked to drift back a bit. Sometimes so far back that I could barely make out his headlight. I called him the Distant Star. He and I both were interested in the Deacons. Al Arfsten was a regular here. He was my sponsor and I joined the Deacons first. Not long after, I got LaMark to come to a meeting. I was his sponsor. He wanted to belong to something. He was hooked. I am so proud of all my brothers that welcomed him into the Club. Like me, it did not take you guys long to get close to him. He loved you all.
    Wanting to belong was somewhat of a theme with LaMark. He did not have the best of a family life growing up. But he always thought of himself as a lucky guy. He did not have, as he would put it, a rich person's education. But he was a diamond in the rough. He persisted. Through the pressure

and hard work he built a shining business. His clients are a Who's Who of the rich and famous. But he never felt he belonged with them. I am not sure he ever knew how much he actually meant to them. The next time you are at the Gage Hotel in Marathon look around —everything hanging on a wall is there, perfectly placed, because of LaMark.

He was a hard worker and a perfectionist. LaMark owned a fleet of trucks. I once asked to borrow one of his vehicles to buy some televisions for my new house. Not only did he loan me the truck, he came along. He also helped me bring new furniture over and insisted on helping me get the pieces into my new house. I was amazed at how strong he was, lifting things I could not lift and telling me to "take it easy" and "that I belonged in an office." He would not let me pay him. All he wanted was a home-cooked meal. He loved my wife's cooking and also loved her and my daughter. That first night he was over he left telling me I was a lucky man to have such a great family. As he left he saw the artwork I had hung myself and said he would be back to straighten up my sloppy work. He was blunt but always followed a sharp comment with that coyote laugh. His laugh was more like a Schmedley giggle. When he came back not only did he help me hang the new stuff, he wanted to rehang all of my art. I had to be his helper. The only person worse at math than me was LaMark. He would measure a length, ask me half the value and when I did not answer fast enough he would bend his tape measure in half and mutter the number. I would think he must be off by a mile. But he would be spot-on correct. Like his math, he invented hanging methods that should be patented. In fact, I can never move now that he is gone, because I will never be able to get the art off my wall! But before anything was hung permanently, he always wanted to check with the boss, as he called my wife, to make sure she was happy. I think he knew he would get another home cooked meal. Which, of course he got. On the way out from every meal he would say, "John, you are a lucky man to have Laurie. You have a great family."

LaMark was fascinated by science and technology. The things that most of us never noticed were on his mind. Did you hear about the cooling suit idea? I did. All of the time. He loved to talk about his ideas. He was one of the first people to get the super bright LED lights for his headlight. One day at my house he noticed some art I did when I worked for NASA as an artist. He loved space and art, and in that order. He wanted to know more about what I did. He also wondered why I did not still paint. It always bugged him. He thought of me as an artist and I thought of how he hung art as artistry. Just a month ago I finished a painting and hung it myself. I chuckled to myself that the next time he was over he would want to rehang it. Now when I come home and see it hanging crooked, I am sure it is LaMark toying with me.

I went on many trips with LaMark. Everywhere we went, he and I always shared a room. What an easy roommate. He and I also, no matter the weather, would find a swimming hole at our stops. He knew how to chill. He took the time to gaze at the stars.

LaMark rarely asked for help. LaMark and I were at a stop light in Santa Fe, New Mexico, on the Lonesome Dove ride. We got separated from the main group. So when the light turned green I took off like a banshee catching the group just ahead. Once we all stopped, I was asked where LaMark was and I said, "you know, he is the Distant Star, he will be along." But no LaMark. So Fish went back to find him. Darn LaMark's luck. His drive belt snapped at the light. He would not of asked for our help and would assume we would ride without him. But Fish stayed in town for an extra day and took the scenic route to Amarillo the next day. With LaMark's luck, he missed out on the treacherous sand trip that snagged Geoff Seaman, now known as Sandman, and he and Fish had a much more enjoyable trip. That is an example of how LaMark's luck put him in a better place. The next day LaMark and I found the swimming pool in Fort Worth at the hotel and shared stories about how lucky he was to have a mechanical failure and avoided the sand pit.

On that same ride Lambo had the idea to play Credit Card Roulette with every dinner and bar tab. All of us lost at least three times. Except for Lambo and, of course, Mr. Lucky himself – LaMark.

I thank LaMark for so many great times together. I thank LaMark for making much of the art in my home hang straight. I thank LaMark for pointing out how lucky I am to have my wife and my daughter. His words will continue to ring in my head and to not take them for granted. He left his LaMark of Excellence on me.

So now, I raise a Bud Light, LaMark's premium beer of choice. The next time you gaze at the stars, one of LaMark's favorite past times, imagine that one of those lights is LaMark on his Road King. His super bright LED headlight is not far behind. It is LaMark, the Distant Star. Make a wish upon that star. It is our brother not far behind. He has your back. I love all my brothers. I love you, LaMark — you will be missed!

CHAPTER 14

WHERE NO MAN HAS GONE BEFORE

"Let the word go forth, from this time and place, to friend and foe alike, that the torch has been passed to a new generation of Americans – born in this century, tempered by war, disciplined by a hard and bitter peace, proud of our ancient heritage – and unwilling to witness or permit the slow undoing of those human rights to which this Nation has always been committed, and to which we are committed today at home and around the world.
– John F. Kennedy, *Inaugural Address*

"Hey, Mr. space man, won't you please take me along for a ride"
– The Byrds

Steve Lamb is the last of the Deacons admitted in the first year of the Club to serve as president. The Club now has been handed off to a newer generation of members. Kirk Lane, the Deacons' current president has been in the Club for fewer than five years. About 60% of our members have known only Steve Lamb or Kirk Lane as president. Fewer than 20% of our members were around during the difficult years when we had to expel two members and another group left to form their own club. Even fewer were around when we had trouble getting any major charitable organization to be willing to take our money for fear of being associated with a motorcycle gang.

For years, our presidents would nearly beg our members. "If everyone sells four Ball tickets and two books of raffle tickets, our whole Ball will be sold out." That sounds so easy, but most of our early members would not bother to even try to meet that goal. In some years, between Steve Lamb and I, we would sell two thirds of all Ball tickets sold.

Today, we not only put on the premier motorcycle-based charitable function in Houston, but we now are one of Houston's most significant charitable organizations. Between 2011 and 2014 we raised more money than in the previous nine years combined. That's a long way from our first Charity Ball, at which 218 guests attended and $22,500 was raised. We now raise over four times that much on our motorcycle raffle alone.

As for riding, several inquiries each day are sent over our e-mail system from members looking to ride with other members, and there always are plenty of respondents ready to go. We have more long rides than ever before, and at any given time, we might have four or five groups riding at different destinations around the country. That was the goal of our founders, but it took close to 10 years to be realized.

None of these successes arose out of some serendipitous coincidence. We enjoy the strong Club we have today due to the hard work and persistence of our earlier membership. These members held our Club together when the acrimony was so severe that coming to meetings was more of a burden than fun. They stuck to it when we could not muster a single person to show up for Club rides. They took the risk of doubling down on our charitable efforts by hiring nationally known bands and presenting them in premier venues when success would require sales efforts that we had never come close to achieving. Mostly, we had a succession of presidents who worked their asses off and wouldn't consider the possibility of failure.

Now it's the next generation's turn.

The Deacons of Deadwood Motorcycle Club

From time to time younger members ask me, with a combination of wonder and apprehension, about what might happen when the longer standing members are no longer in the Club. I think they look at the achievements we have made in the last few years and wonder how they would be able to duplicate them if the older members were to disappear. The answer is easy. They either will have to do the work themselves or they will have to scale back. I suspect they will do just fine.

These days, many of our sales are generated by our newer members. Every week, I see e-mails congratulating newer members for selling VIP tables or big bunches of raffle tickets. There seems to be an atmosphere of pride among them that we older guys never generated, at least not in terms of sales. Even our silent auction is being run by a relatively new member who is almost giddy with enthusiasm for the job.

Our future success will depend on the quality of our leadership and its vision for our Club. My dear old dad once told me to always set my goals high, because I would be surprised at how easy it would be to achieve them. Kirk Lane seems to have that philosophy.

We met the Captain through Steve Lamb, who had invited him to our early Charity Balls. His girlfriend Kim also was instrumental in introducing the Captain to the Club. The Captain met Kim at Sam's Boat. The Captain was there with a stripper he had flown in from Los Angeles. Kirk's friend Todd was at the Boat and he called up Kim to stop by. The Mad Doctor was there taking pictures of the stripper's tits when Kim arrived. The Captain and Kim hit it off and Captain wound up giving the stripper to Todd. As it turned out, Kim knew David

Captain Kirk is leading us to where no MC has gone before.

Cook, Sam Douglass and a bunch of other long-time Deacons, and the Captain wound up bringing her to the Ball that year.

The Captain was apprehensive about becoming president because he was afraid his duties for the Club would interfere with running his company, Big Dog Logistics. Kirk and Big Dog Logistics had been our corporate sponsor for our Charity Balls in 2011, 2012 and 2013. In each of those years, the Captain donated $20,000 to set up the Big Dog Lounge at the Ball, and he did it again in 2014 along with a co-sponsor. The most important of these donations was in the first year, when the Club brought in Foghat at an expensive venue under circumstances where we were unsure whether we would generate enough funds to pay our expenses. Having Kirk's $20,000 in the bank must have been a comfort to Steve Lamb that first year.

Kirk's first year as president started on a rocky note. He had been in office less than a month when he was summoned to a meeting with the Bandidos, who essentially told the Captain that the Deacons were going to have to join the Confederacy of Clubs or face potential physical harm. He was told that some of our members were not showing due respect to the Bandidos and some other Houston area MCs, and if he did not rein in our members, the Bandidos would take retribution against him and the other Deacons' officers personally.

That scared the shit out of the Captain, which is not surprising. Some of the members of his board advised him to commit the Club to joining the CoC without telling our membership as a whole that he was taking unilateral action.

Of course, that was bad advice because it was a controversial issue over which many older members had strong opinions. Word of joining the CoC without a Club debate leaked out, and there was a negative reaction by some members, most notably me. The Captain finally decided to put joining the CoC to a Club wide vote. That was the right thing to do. He lobbied our membership in favor of joining by explaining the benefits we would receive while acknowledging the downside. The Club wound up approving joining the CoC by a nearly unanimous vote.

That experience seemed to put the Captain's presidency on an even keel. He learned that being up front with his brothers on controversial matters was the only way to garner the respect and loyalty of our membership. He has continued to lead us with that "everything out in the open" philosophy, and that attitude has served him well.

Kirk now has nearly completed his first term as president, and he put on our most successful Charity Ball ever. Entertainment was provided by Brett Michaels and he rocked out. We had 50% more guests than in 2013. We raised nearly $400,000 net to the charities we are supporting.

The Captain's vision for the future is clear: he wants to expand our membership and fundraising activities. In the last three years we had our Charity Ball at the Bayou Center in downtown Houston, which could accommodate about 800 guests. We already have outgrown our 2014 venue, which can accommodate 1,200 guests. The Captain has his sights on the Toyota Center or Minute Maid Park.

Captain Kirk will need a lot of help to achieve his goals. I spoke with the Captain about the younger guys that will be providing that help. Here are a few of them.

Mike Fisher

I was unsure whether to put Mike in this part of the book or in the Epilogue where I discuss hard-working members who don't get the recognition they deserve. I'm putting Mike here because although he has contributed much to the Club already, he

The Fish at the 2013 Ball.

is now flowering and his future contributions to the Club are likely to surpass his past performance.

Mike was the chairman of the charity committee when it was expanded and charged with vetting an array of potential charities to which we would donate. Although we always had a charity committee, it did not have as significant a set of responsibilities as had Mike's committee. He and his committee did yeoman service in identifying quality charities and expanding our exposure in Houston's fundraising circles.

In our Charity Balls in 2012, 2013 and 2014, he teamed with the boys at Workshop Houston to build hot bicycles that were auctioned for $10,000 the first two years. The 2014 bike had a motor and sold for nearly $4,000. He also teamed with the girls at Workshop Houston to make T-shirts commemorating our Charity Balls. While Mike spends a substantial amount of his time in these projects, he also finances them so 100% of the proceeds go to Workshop Houston.

Mike was elected as a director in 2013. In his first year as a director he has become the Club secretary and is reconstructing our books and records. Hopefully, some of the information I gathered in writing this book will help him in that project.

I suspect we will see Mike in our senior management for a long time.

Jamie Adams

Jamie was in charge of the silent auction for the 2014 Charity Ball. We have never raised more than $60,000 in our silent auction. Jamie's goal was $150,000 and we topped $175,000.

Running the silent auction traditionally has been viewed as a thankless job, but

Jamie Adams revolutionized our silent auction.

Jamie tackled it with enthusiasm. For the first time we had a computerized auction system that featured a big board showing the highest bids on the most significant items. We had hot chicks patrolling the Ball with iPads to keep track of the bidding and to send messages to bidders to let them know how they were faring. He also had our first live auction.

Mark Graber

Mark has taken over the charity committee. Given the amount of money we now raise, this committee has become of increasing importance. In 2014, Mark and his committee screened about 20 charities that applied for donations from the Deacons. They conducted a complete vetting of every applicant and narrowed the recipients down to about 10. Mark is doing an outstanding job in chairing this committee and he seems to be destined to higher office in the Club.

Mark Graber soberly chairing our charity committee.

The only real concern about Mark's chairmanship is that apparently they do not drink during the meetings. I guess Mike Callahan will never serve on that committee.

John Asta

John Asta also serves on the charity committee. John is responsible for our association with the Dream League, which is a division

The Assman at the Ball.

of the First Colony Little League program. Its roster consists of approximately 60 physically or mentally handicapped players.

Matt Hillman

Matt ("Money") Hillman used to make a living playing high-stakes pool. He has played for over $10,000 per game. He now works at Morgan Stanley, where gambling in the financial markets is more risky.

Matt has become Ricky Cook's assistant in the treasurer's office. I'm sure he will find working with Ricky to be infuriating; oops, I mean interesting. In any event, being the treasurer is one of the toughest jobs in our Club, and Matt is embracing his new duties with vigor.

Matt "Money" Hillman sans pool cue.

Fred Tyler

FredEx is not serving on our board or any committee; however, he's a guy with great enthusiasm for the Club. He was involved in the Workshop Houston project and came up with the idea of putting a motor in the 2014 bicycle. He also is looking into getting a famous custom bike maker to build us a Deacons bike to auction at our Ball.

FredEx at a Deacons meeting.

He has written some hilarious articles about our Club and our members that he has mocked up to look like they came from the Houston Chronicle. He has expressed an interest in becoming the Club Historian.

James LaFountain

This is another new member who has a lot of enthusiasm. He told Captain Kirk he wants to run for president someday. He sold a bunch of Ball tickets and was a big help at the Ball generally. He is considered one of the leaders of the younger set and is under consideration for 2014 Deacon Rookie of The Year.

Nick Nesterenko

Nick is another member who is up for 2014 Deacon Rookie of the Year. Not only did he excel in his sales efforts for the 2014 Ball, he took charge of our social media program and through his efforts our public exposure has been much expanded.

James "Chopper" LaFountain

Nick practices mixed martial arts fighting, and in 2014 he sponsored a night of fights, all of the proceeds of which went to the Deacons' charity account.

Nick's job has taken him overseas, but he has remained as active as possible during his absence.

Steve "Chinchilla" Mink

Steve is the third potential 2014 Deacon Rookie of the Year. He has come to the Club with great enthusiasm and is a leader among the new members. He bought a Platinum VIP Table to the 2014 ball and sold another one. The Club is expecting great things from Steve.

EPILOGUE

I wrote the Forward to this book on January 19, 2014. In that Forward, I said that I was about to dig into the Deacons' books and records to start writing this history, and I had no idea what I was going to find. It is now November 30, 2014, and the book is done.

I made a diligent effort to get things right. I did not rely solely on my own recollections. Each of the past presidents reviewed the chapters concerning their tenure in office and gave me additions and corrections to the original text. Their input was especially helpful in connection with recounting the events surrounding the expulsion of David Lee and Bruce McDonald and with the departure of the Sovereign Souls. We also had pretty good written records of those events. They happened just like they are described in this book. Ricky Cook, John Aubrey, John Talbot and my brother Tolly, all who were founding members of the Club, read the early chapters to be sure the history of those years was accurate. The descriptions of our most notable rides are based on interviews with those who participated in the rides.

We had a record of our founding and our organizational meeting in April 2002, then no records until June 2003. Between June 2003 and the beginning of 2010, we had pretty good minutes of our member and board meetings. After that, our records again are sparse. Since our records are incomplete, I had to piece together our history from personal experience and by interviewing our members.

Carroll Kelly was our secretary for most of the middle years, and although he kept minutes of meetings, they often were lacking detail.

He did, however, keep many of the e-mails and other documents surrounding the expulsion of David Lee and Bruce McDonald. Those records confirmed just what assholes they were.

Our records with respect to our Charity Balls are thin. Surprisingly, the records of the 2011-2013 Balls, when we had Foghat, Blue Oyster Cult and Billy Gibbons, are less complete than our records about the early Balls. Almost all of the information about these Balls comes from interviews with our members.

Records concerning rides are almost non-existent. All of that information comes from the recollections of our members.

I saw no records from the Deaconess Chapter. All of the information about them came from my personal recollections and from interviews with Sally Gracia (now Leidel), Lisa Talbot and Angie McKendree.

When I started editing the book, it became evident that there are several of our members who have been more influential and have contributed more to our Club than may be apparent from my narrative. They deserve some additional attention, and here it is.

Ricky Cook

Ricky was our second president, and hopefully the narrative about him in this book makes clear he was a good one. However, there are two areas in which Ricky doesn't get the recognition he deserves.

The first has to do with the founding of the Club. I generally have been credited with being the founder. That's because I was the first president, I was the face of the Club in the early years and I did much of the heavy lifting in getting us going. But Ricky deserves recognition as co-founder. He and I collectively came up with the idea of forming the Deacons. We both participated in designing the patches and forming our culture. Ricky knew many of our founding members before I knew them. It is unlikely that the Deacons would have been formed without Ricky.

Ricky also deserves recognition for his long service as our treasurer. That is the second most thankless job we have (the worst being running the silent auction), and Ricky has performed in a superlative fashion for years. He may be cantankerous about collecting money from those who owe it, and he may drive our presidents crazy by being out of touch from time to time, but our financial books and records have been perfect during his tenure.

John Aubrey

John Aubrey now spends a good bit of his time in Wyoming, so we don't see him as often as we would like. Still, he attends enough meetings every year to remain a voting member. He also continues to support our Club in many quiet but important ways, including making himself available to give advice to our Club's management and supporting many of our activities financially.

At the 2013 Ball, Steve Lamb and John auctioned a trip through Wyoming and Montana, and they paid for everything, including airfare, motorcycle rental, hotel rooms, food and booze. Neither Steve nor John is likely to tell anyone how much they spent, but we received over $15,000 in auction proceeds that went directly to our bottom line. John recently has expressed interest in helping the Club solicit donations from major corporations.

Discussion of John's participation in our Club would not be complete without mentioning his wife Amy. She has been indispensable in helping with our silent auction and decorations committees. She has been a quiet but influential member of the Deaconess Chapter who has donated both her time and her home to advance their activities. Most of all she is John's companion and best friend.

John Talbot

Talbot is one of our founding members and has served our board of directors several times. He also served as vice president. He often has been a voice of reason when such a voice was needed. He could have been elected president had he chosen to run. For years he was in charge of getting the bands for our Charity Ball. He always found good entertainment at a great price. He still helps in quiet ways, such as serving on our current charity committee.

Similarly to the other John, no discussion of Talbot's contribution to the Deacons would be complete without mentioning his wife Pat. She has been a quiet helper and supporter of ours since the beginning.

Preston Douglass

Preston has been in the Club from the beginning. Even though he always has lived out of town, he has supported us both in spirit and financially. For years, he bought a VIP table to our Ball even though he could not attend himself. He has organized the Hill Country ride for 17 straight years. He has put together other unique rides, like the rides he organized with NASCAR driver Terry Labonte. He gives our members great deals on motorcycles. He never asks anything in return. He's just a great guy and it's too bad we don't get to see him more often.

John Talbot in search of wildlife to run down.

Preston Douglass during his annual Hill Country Ride.

The Deacons of Deadwood Motorcycle Club

Jay McKendree

Although I have been appointed Club historian, Jay has been our *de facto* historian for years through the photographic record he has developed.

David Youngblood

Blood is our most old school member and currently serves on our board and as vice president. He has been an un-appointed ambassador for our Club throughout the motorcycle world by attending every rally and going to every biker bar everywhere. He was one of the biggest proponents of our joining the Confederacy of Clubs.

Blood on a ride to who knows where.

Peter Sommer

The Commodore was elected as a director the first year he was eligible to hold that position. He has served as road captain several times and was instrumental in developing the ride program we enjoy today. Peter helped take on the task of running our silent auction and decorating our Ball venue a couple of times. Those are the thankless kinds of tasks that no one enjoys doing but need the guiding hand of someone responsible to get them done correctly, and Peter fit the bill. He has been on every major ride we have and he has organized a bunch of great rides himself. He is one of those kinds of guys who can be relied upon in a pinch, and the Club has relied on Peter for more things than most members know.

Geoff Seaman

Geoff is a lot like Peter. He has great organizational skills and was elected as a director at his first opportunity. He also has run our silent auction and has taken on many other burdensome tasks, including being in charge of the decorations committee for the 2014 Ball. He goes on all the big rides and organizes rides himself. After his three-year stint as a director expired, he probably could have been elected president, but he decided to take a year off, and Steve Lamb wound up serving a third term. Geoff ran for president the next year and was defeated by a narrow margin. Geoff currently does not hold an office within the Club, but he remains highly respected for his views on important club matters, such as our joining the Confederacy of Clubs. Geoff also is in charge of running a Deacon's on-line store.

I suspect we'll see Geoff in our management again.

David Reed

David has been a hard working behind the scenes member since he joined the Club. He has taken on burdensome jobs like decorating our Charity Ball venues and being in charge of setup and breakdown. He also has been in charge of our patch and t shirt sales for the last several tears.

The Agent riding like a pro.

David is an insurance agent, and lots of our members have started buying their motorcycle insurance from him. To help with rates and promote safety, David has arranged for the Club to have several private Ride Like a Pro classes so we can all hone our riding skills.

David contemplated running for president and later ran for director. He has served as road captain for several years. Also, he has worked hard on our silent auction and has donated some interesting things, such as a Sugar Land Skeeters jersey signed by Roger Clemens.

ACKNOWLEDGMENTS

The Club's records are incomplete. I could not have written this book without tapping into the recollections of our members. I'd like to thank everybody who took the time to help me.

First of all there is Jay. He provided all the photos and helped in the layout before it was sent to Book Nook, which turned the manuscript into a professional looking book. He also helped with proofreading and is responsible for the removal of the excessive number of commas that were in the original text.

Ricky Cook, John Aubrey, Jay McKendree and Steve Lamb all let me interview them about the Deacons' early years and reviewed and commented on those portions of the book, as well as the portions of the book about their presidencies. Captain Kirk met with me to talk about his early participation in the Club, his presidency and his vision for our future.

John Talbot also sat down with me to reminisce about our founding and about many of the rides we took together both before and after we were founded. In addition, he reviewed and commented on the chapters on the founding of the Club and its early years.

Sally Gracia, Lisa Talbot and Angie McKendree were of indispensable assistance on the material about the Deaconess Chapter. They reminded me of much I had forgotten and added things about which I never knew.

Sam Allen

Mike Fisher gave the book a thorough proofreading and identified lots of typos and several factual errors. He improved the book.

My brother Tolly proofread the book, but he lost it and never sent me his edits. Therefore, every typo, every phrase using poor grammar, every misquote, every mistake in fact and every other error in this book is his felt.

Thanks to all!

APPENDIX A

MEMBERSHIP

The Club's membership records are incomplete and confusing. Early on, there was no set application process. Members were admitted informally at the monthly Club meetings. There are no minutes of these meetings between the Organizational Meeting in April 2002 through the June 2004 meeting. So, membership data for the first 14 months are based on the recollections of the early members.

The members generally are listed in the order they were admitted; however, the membership rolls are confusing because of our initiation number system. This system was not implemented until nearly a year after the Club was founded. There are some early members who never were assigned an initiation number. As members resigned, some remaining members were assigned the lower initiation numbers of the resigning members. Some members have more than one initiation number. This has occurred when someone left the Club and then came back, or where we have a record of both an initial number and a lower number assigned from a departing member. We once attempted to reconstruct the records to determine the original initiation numbers for each member, but our records were not sufficient to complete that project accurately. But we are pretty close.

I originally was going to include a record of when members left the Club, but those records are so incomplete I decided to omit that information.

We have had six honorary members:

- Casey Campbell was the long-time manager of Saloon No. 10 in Deadwood. He was made an honorary member in 2003 when we thought it would be good for our Club to have a presence in Deadwood. At one time, we were a member of the Deadwood Chamber of Commerce, and Casey was our representative to the Chamber.
- Kip Attaway is a musician and comedian who originally was from Mt. Pleasant, Texas, but now claims Jackson Hole, Wyoming as his home. Kip has played for us many times. He was made an honorary member and he used his patch to make a Deacons of Deadwood guitar that he uses in his performances.
- Richard Van Aukin was made an honorary member after his wife Lovinia was killed on a Deacons ride to Boys and Girls Country to present a $50,000 donation. He later converted to a regular membership and eventually became a voting member. His interest in the Club waned after a few years and he resigned his membership.
- Joe Kilchrist was a regular member who resigned when he moved out of town. He later moved back to Houston and was so productive in his Ball ticket sales that we made him a lifetime honorary member.
- Noah Latham was my former girlfriend Melanie's son. When Melanie was killed in a gun related accident, the Deacons made him an honorary Deacon. He was nine years old. He now is 15, and worked for Deacon Ben Thompson for the summer of 2014.
- Dave Andrews, a.k.a. Outlaw Dave, was made an honorary member during Steve Lamb's presidency. Dave has a local biker-related radio show and has used that show to great effect in supporting the Deacons. Dave's membership no doubt will be converted to a regular membership.

Although the honorary members technically are members for life, they are included in the tables below only in the year they were made honorary members and in years in which they actively participated in Club activities.

The Deacons of Deadwood Motorcycle Club

The initiation numbers appearing below are the current initiation numbers for each existing and former member. The initiation numbers appear only the first time a member appears.

2002
Start of Year

David Cook (1)	Sam Allen (3)	John Talbot (6)	Carroll Kelly (8)
Ricky Cook (2)	John Aubrey (5)	Elza Smith (7)	Tolly Allen (12)
Ted Ricketson			
Total: 9			

New Members

Bob Mitchell (4)	Monte Jones (14)	Duke Nunn (19)	Scott Tamborine (24)
Eric Robertson (9)	Steve Lamb (15)	Rusty Drake (20)	Al Arfsten (25)
Sam Douglass (10)	George Bogle (16)	Tommy Cason (21)	Fred Hass (26)
Preston Douglass (11)	Randy Hale (17)	Chris Blackledge (22)	Harding, Aubrey
Mike Callaghan (13)	Ted Faleski (18)	Ken Carr (23)	Fred Farner
Total: 20			

2003
Start of Year

Allen, Sam	Carr, Ken	Faleski, Ted	Mitchell, Bob
Allen, Tolly	Cason, Tommy	Hale, Randy	Nunn, Duke
Arfsten, Al	Cook, David	Harding, Aubrey	Robertson, Eric
Aubrey, John	Cook, Ricky	Hass, Fred	Smith, Elza
Blackledge, Chris	Douglass, Sam	Jones, Monte	Talbot, John
Bogle, George	Douglas, Preston	Kelly, Carroll	Tamborine, Scott
Callaghan, Mike	Drake, Rusty	Lamb, Steve	
Total: 27			

Sam Allen

New Members

Dan Bezborn (27)	Scott Lutwak (32)	Joe Kilchrist (37)	Dick Tate (42)
Coy Banta (28)	David Lee (33)	Don Stavinoah (38)	Jim Christensen (43)
Matt Linton (29)	Jeff Roberts (34)	Larry Bolander (39)	David Moss (44)
Bill Talbot (30)	Brent Henry (35)	David Henry (40)	Casey Campbell
Johnny Bish (31)	Robert Garcia (36)	Jay McKendree (41)	
Total: 19			

2004
Start of Year

Allen, Sam	Carr, Ken	Hass, Fred	McKendree, Jay
Allen, Tolly	Cason, Tommy	Henry, Brent	Moss, David
Arfsten, Al	Christensen, Jim	Henry, David	Nunn, Duke
Aubrey, John	Cook, David	Jones, Monte	Roberts, Jeff
Banta, Coy	Cook, Ricky	Kelly, Carroll	Robertson, Eric
Bezborne, Dan	Douglass, Sam	Kilchrist, Joe	Smith, Elza
Bish, Johnny	Douglas, Preston	Lamb, Steve	Stavinoah, Don
Blackledge, Chris	Drake, Rusty	Lee, David	Talbot, Bill
Bogle, George	Faleski, Ted	Linton, Matt	Talbot, John
Bolander, Larry	Garcia, Robert	Lutwak, Scott	Tamborine, Scott
Callaghan, Mike	Hale, Randy	Mitchell, Bob	Tate, Dick
Total: 44			

New Members

Randy Hicks (45)	Patrick Browning (48)	Bruce McDonald (51)	Mike Morris
Lance Bradley (46)	Chris Pendley (49)	Arvel Martin (52)	Joe Allen
Jim Langsdale (47)	Adan Ortiz (50)	Al Rubio (53)	Robert Odom
Don Clements (55)	Kip Attaway		
Total: 14			

The Deacons of Deadwood Motorcycle Club

2005
Start of Year

Allen, Joe	Callaghan, Mike	Henry, Brent	McKendree, Jay
Allen, Sam	Carr, Ken	Henry, David	Moss, David
Allen, Tolly	Cason, Tommy	Jones, Monte	Nunn, Duke
Arfsten, Al	Christensen, Jim	Kelly, Carroll	Odom, Robert
Aubrey, John	Cook, David	Kilchrist, Joe	Ortiz, Adan
Banta, Coy	Cook, Ricky	Lamb, Steve	Pendley, Chris
Bezborne, Dan	Douglass, Sam	Langsdale, Jim	Roberts, Jeff
Bish, Johnny	Douglas, Preston	Lee, David	Robertson, Eric
Blackledge, Chris	Drake, Rusty	Linton, Matt	Rubio, Al
Bogle, George	Faleski, Ted	Lutwak, Scott	Smith, Elza
Bolander, Larry	Garcia, Robert	Martin, Arvel	Stavinoah, Don
Bradley, Lance	Hale, Randy	McDonald, Bruce	Talbot, Bill
Browning, Partick	Hicks, Randy	Morris, Mike	Talbot, John
Clements, Don	Hass, Fred	Mitchell, Bob	Tamborine, Scott
			Tate, Dick
Total: 57			

New Members

Jim McConnell (54)	John Burns (55)	Don Lightfoot (57)	Tom Hanbury (58)
Doug Growden			
Total: 5			

Sam Allen

2006
Start of Year

Allen, Joe	Cason, Tommy	Henry, David	Moss, David
Allen, Sam	Christensen, Jim	Jones, Monte	Nunn, Duke
Allen, Tolly	Cook, David	Kelly, Carroll	Odom, Robert
Arfsten, Al	Cook, Ricky	Kilchrist, Joe	Ortiz, Adan
Aubrey, John	Douglass, Sam	Lamb, Steve	Pendley, Chris
Banta, Coy	Douglas, Preston	Langsdale, Jim	Robertson, Eric
Bish, Johnny	Drake, Rusty	Lee, David	Rubio, Al
Blackledge, Chris	Faleski, Ted	Lightfoot, Don	Smith, Elza
Bogle, George	Garcia, Robert	Linton, Matt	Stavinoah, Don
Bolander, Larry	Growden, Doug	Martin, Arvel	Talbot, Bill
Bradley, Lance	Hale, Randy	McConnell, Jim	Talbot, John
Browning, Partick	Hicks, Randy	McDonald, Bruce	Tamborine, Scott
Burns, John	Hass, Fred	Morris, Mike	Tate, Dick
Callaghan, Mike	Hanbury, Tom	Mitchell, Bob	
Carr, Ken	Henry, Brent	McKendree, Jay	
Total: 58			

2007
Start of Year

Allen, Joe	Cason, Tommy	Henry, David	Moss, David
Allen, Sam	Christensen, Jim	Jones, Monte	Nunn, Duke
Allen, Tolly	Cook, David	Kelly, Carroll	Odom, Robert
Arfsten, Al	Cook, Ricky	Kilchrist, Joe	Ortiz, Adan
Aubrey, John	Douglass, Sam	Lamb, Steve	Pendley, Chris
Banta, Coy	Douglas, Preston	Langsdale, Jim	Robertson, Eric
Bish, Johnny	Drake, Rusty	Lee, David	Rubio, Al
Blackledge, Chris	Faleski, Ted	Lightfoot, Don	Smith, Elza
Bogle, George	Garcia, Robert	Linton, Matt	Stavinoah, Don

The Deacons of Deadwood Motorcycle Club

Bolander, Larry	Growden, Doug	Martin, Arvel	Talbot, Bill
Bradley, Lance	Hale, Randy	McConnell, Jim	Talbot, John
Browning, Partick	Hicks, Randy	McDonald, Bruce	Tamborine, Scott
Burns, John	Hass, Fred	Morris, Mike	Tate, Dick
Callaghan, Mike	Hanbury, Tom	Mitchell, Bob	
Carr, Ken	Henry, Brent	McKendree, Jay	
Total: 58			

New Members

Joe Blount (59)	Bob Cavnar (61)	Fred Farner (63)	Kevin Phelps (65)
Ben Thompson (60)	Justin Dossett (62)	Chris Mabry (64)	Rich Van Aukin (70)
Total: 7			

2008
Start of Year

Allen, Joe	Cason, Tommy	Hanbury, Tom	Morris, Mike
Allen, Sam	Cavnar, Bob	Henry, Brent	Moss, David
Allen, Tolly	Cook, David	Henry, David	Nunn, Duke
Arfsten, Al	Cook, Ricky	Jones, Monte	Odom, Robert
Aubrey, John	Dossett, Justin	Kelly, Carroll	Ortiz, Adan
Banta, Coy	Douglass, Sam	Kilchrist, Joe	Pendley, Chris
Bish, Johnny	Douglas, Preston	Lamb, Steve	Phelps, Kevin
Blackledge, Chris	Drake, Rusty	Langsdale, Jim	Robertson, Eric
Blount, Joe	Faleski, Ted	Lightfoot, Don	Rubio, Al
Bogle, George	Farner, Fred	Linton, Matt	Smith, Elza
Bolander, Larry	Garcia, Robert	Mabry, Chris	Stavinoah, Don
Bradley, Lance	Growden, Doug	Martin, Arvel	Talbot, Bill
Browning, Patrick	Hale, Randy	McConnell, Jim	Talbot, John
Burns, John	Hicks, Randy	McKendree, Jay	Tamborine, Scott
Callaghan, Mike	Hass, Fred	Mitchell, Bob	Thompson, Ben
			Van Aukin, Richard
Total: 61			

Sam Allen

New Members

Orlando Sanchez (66)	Ken Hill (69)	Jim Row (73)	Peter Sommer (76)
Nowrey Smith (67)	Martin Dossett (71)	Alan Davidson (74)	Randy Felicia (77)
Bryan Krause (68)	Bob Bulian (72)	Dennis Hensley (75)	
Total: 11			

2009
Start of Year

Allen, Joe	Cook, David	Hill, Ken	Row, Jim
Allen, Sam	Cook, Ricky	Jones, Monte	Rubio, Al
Allen, Tolly	Davidson, Alan	Kilchrist, Joe	Sanchez, Orlando
Arfsten, Al	Dossett, Justin	Krause, Bryan	Smith, Elza
Aubrey, John	Dossett, Martin	Lamb, Steve	Smith, Nowrey
Banta, Coy	Douglass, Sam	Langsdale, Jim	Sommer, Peter
Bish, Johnny	Douglas, Preston	Linton, Matt	Talbot, Bill
Blount, Joe	Drake, Rusty	Mabry, Chris	Talbot, John
Bogle, George	Faleski, Ted	McConnell, Jim	Tamborine, Scott
Bulian, Bob	Falicia, Randy	McKendree, Jay	Thompson, Ben
Burns, John	Farner, Fred	Mitchell, Bob	Van Aukin, Richard
Callaghan, Mike	Garcia, Robert	Nunn, Duke	
Cason, Tommy	Hanbury, Tom	Phelps, Kevin	
Cavnar, Bob	Hensley, Dennis	Robertson, Eric	
Total: 53			

The Deacons of Deadwood Motorcycle Club

New Members

Noah Latham (78)	D. Youngblood (82)	John Manlove (86)	Selly Chinnery (90)
Ken Carr (79)	Tom Murphy (83)	Frog Castellano (87)	Ken Carr (91)
Geoff Seaman (80)	John Lowery (84)	Tuffy Hogue (88)	Allen Parks (92)
Mike Marlowe (81)	Bob Loiseau (85)	Aaron Seward (89)	Mike Perperski (93)
Total:16			

2010
Start of Year

Allen, Joe	Cook, Ricky	Lamb, Steve	Robertson, Eric
Allen, Sam	Davidson, Alan	Langsdale, Jim	Row, Jim
Allen, Tolly	Dossett, Justin	Latham, Noah	Rubio, Al
Arfsten, Al	Dossett, Martin	Linton, Matt	Sanchez, Orlando
Aubrey, John	Douglass, Sam	Loiseau, Bob	Seward, Aaron
Carr, Ken	Douglas, Preston	Lowery, John	Seaman, Geoff
Froggy Castellano	Drake, Rusty	Mabry, Chris	Smith, Elza
Banta, Coy	Faleski, Ted	Manlove, John	Smith, Nowrey
Bogle, George	Falicia, Randy	Marlowe, Mike	Sommer, Peter
Bulian, Bob	Farner, Fred	McKendree, Jay	Talbot, Bill
Burns, John	Hensley, Dennis	Mitchell, Bob	Talbot, John
Callaghan, Mike	Hogue, Tuffy	Murphy, Tom	Tamborine, Scott
Cason, Tommy	Hill, Ken	Nunn, Duke	Thompson, Ben
Cavnar, Bob	Jones, Monte	Parks, Allen	Youngblood, David
Chinnery, Selly	Kilchrist, Joe	Perperski, Mike	
Cook, David	Krause, Bryan	Phelps, Kevin	
Total: 62			

Sam Allen

New Members

Andy Harris (94)	LaMark Bejer (97)	Kirk Lane (100)	David Stoerner (103)
Mike Turner (95)	Russell Morgan (98)	David Wright (101)	Homer Adams (104
Lou Cinquemano (96)	John Asta (99)	Johnny Williams(102)	Steve Skelton (105)
Total: 12			

2011
Start of Year

Adams, Homer	Cook, Ricky	Latham, Noah	Skelton, Steve
Allen, Sam	Dossett, Justin	Lowery, John	Smith, Nowrey
Allen, Tolly	Dossett, Martin	Manlove, John	Sommer, Peter
Arfsten, Al	Douglass, Sam	McKendree, Jay	Stoerner, David
Asta, John	Douglas, Preston	Morgan, Russell	Talbot, Bill
Aubrey, John	Harris, Andy	Murphy, Tom	Talbot, John
Banta, Coy	Hensley, Dennis	Nunn, Duke	Tamborine, Scott
Bejer, LaMark	Hogue, Tuffy	Parks, Allen	Thompson, Ben
Bulian, Bob	Hill, Ken	Robertson, Eric	Turner, Mike
Burns, John	Jones, Monte	Row, Jim	Williams, Johnny
Callaghan, Mike	Kilchrist, Joe	Sanchez, Orlando	Wright, David
Cason, Tommy	Lamb, Steve	Seward, Aaron	Youngblood, David
Chinnery, Selly	Lane, Kirk	Seaman, Geoff	
Total: 51			

The Deacons of Deadwood Motorcycle Club

New Members

Mike Fisher (106)	David Reed (108)	Mike Arabucki (110)	John Bevcar (112)
Mike Candalaria (107)	Johnny Prejean (109)	Tom Davidson (111)	Dwayne Tuttle (113)
			H. Fishman (114)
Total: 9			

2012
Start of Year

Adams, Homer	Chinnery, Selly	Lamb, Steve	Seaman, Geoff
Allen, Sam	Cook, Ricky	Lane, Kirk	Skelton, Steve
Allen, Tolly	Davidson Tom	Latham, Noah	Smith, Nowrey
Arabucki, Mike	Dossett, Justin	Lowery, John	Sommer, Peter
Arfsten, Al	Dossett, Martin	Manlove, John	Stoerner, David
Asta, John	Douglass, Sam	McKendree, Jay	Talbot, Bill
Aubrey, John	Douglas, Preston	Morgan, Russell	Talbot, John
Banta, Coy	Fisher, Mike	Murphy, Tom	Tamborine, Scott
Becvar, John	Fishman, Howard	Nunn, Duke	Thompson, Ben
Bejer, LaMark	Harris, Andy	Parks, Allen	Turner, Mike
Bulian, Bob	Hensley, Dennis	Prejean, Johnny	Tuttle, Duane
Burns, John	Hogue, Tuffy	Robertson, Eric	Williams, Johnny
Callaghan, Mike	Hill, Ken	Row, Jim	Wright, David
Candalaria, Mike	Jones, Monte	Sanchez, Orlando	Youngblood, David
Cason, Tommy	Kilchrist, Joe	Seward, Aaron	
Total: 59			

Sam Allen

New Members

Mark Graber (115)	Brian Bennett (118)	S. LaBauve (121)	Jason Johnson (124)
Cliff Love (116)	Mark Carreon (119)	Gary Mann (122)	
Jamie Adams (117)	Chris Block (120)	R. Northcutt (123)	
Total: 10			

2013
Start of Year

Adams, Homer	Prejean, Johnny	Johnson, Jason	Row, Jim
Adams, Jamie	Candalaria, Mike	Kilchrist, Joe	Sanchez, Orlando
Allen, Sam	Carreon, Mark	LaBauve, Shannon	Seward, Aaron
Allen, Sam	Cason, Tommy	Lamb, Steve	Seaman, Geoff
Allen, Tolly	Chinnery, Selly	Lane, Kirk	Skelton, Steve
Arabucki, Mike	Cook, Ricky	Latham, Noah	Smith, Nowrey
Arfsten, Al	Davidson Tom	Love, Chris	Sommer, Peter
Asta, John	Dossett, Justin	Lowery, John	Stoerner, David
Aubrey, John	Douglass, Sam	Manlove, John	Talbot, Bill
Banta, Coy	Douglas, Preston	Mann, Gary	Talbot, John
Becvar, John	Fisher, Mike	McKendree, Jay	Tamborine, Scott
Bejer, LaMark	Fishman, Howard	Morgan, Russell	Thompson, Ben
Bennett, Brian	Graber, Mark	Murphy, Tom	Turner, Mike
Block, Chris	Harris, Andy	Northcutt, Ronnie	Tuttle, Duane
Bulian, Bob	Hensley, Dennis	Nunn, Duke	Williams, Johnny
Burns, John	Hogue, Tuffy	Parks, Allen	Wright, David
Callaghan, Mike	Hill, Ken	Robertson, Eric	Youngblood, David
Total: 68			

The Deacons of Deadwood Motorcycle Club

New Members

Rodney Fields (125)	Rusty Drake (132)	Jimmy Alaniz (139)	Bob Rota (146)
Nowrey Smith (126)	Fred Tyler (133)	Jeremy Dill (140)	Dean Mlazgar (147)
David Stevens (127)	W. Schroeder (134)	Jeff Justice (141)	John Sallaz (148)
Matt Peterson (128)	Steve Weems (135)	Ken McCorkle (142)	Outlaw Dave (149)
Matt Hillman (129)	Dorsey Parker (136)	David Mills (143)	Bill Parker (150)
P. Detweiler (130)	Mike Tessari (137)	N. Nesterenko (144)	
Brian Baumer (131)	Ron White (138)	Al Nava (145)	
Total: 26			

2014
Start of Year

Adams, Homer	Cook, Ricky	Love, Chris	Sanchez, Orlando
Adams, Jamie	Davidson Tom	Lowery, John	Schroeder, Warren
Alaniz, Jimmy	Detweiler, Parker	Mann, Gary	Seward, Aaron
Allen, Sam	Dill, Jeremy	Mills, David	Seaman, Geoff
Allen, Sam	Dossett, Justin	McCorkle, Ken	Skelton, Steve
Allen, Tolly	Douglass, Sam	McKendree, Jay	Smith, Nowrey
Arabucki, Mike	Douglas, Preston	Mlazgar, Dean	Sommer, Peter
Asta, John	Drake, Rusty	Morgan, Russell	Stevens, David
Aubrey, John	Fields, Rodney	Murphy, Tom	Stoerner, David
Banta, Coy	Fisher, Mike	Nava, Al	Talbot, Bill
Baumer, Brian	Fishman, Howard	Nesterenko, Nick	Talbot, John

Sam Allen

Becvar, John	Graber, Mark	Northcutt, Ronnie	Tamborine, Scott
Bennett, Brian	Harris, Andy	Outlaw Dave	Tessari, Mike
Block, Chris	Hensley, Dennis	Parker, Bill	Thompson, Ben
Bulian, Bob	Hill, Ken	Peterson, Matt	Turner, Mike
Burns, John	Hillman, Matt	Parks, Allen	Tuttle, Duane
Callaghan, Mike	Johnson, Jason	Prejean, Johnny	Tyler, Fred
Callaghan, Mike	Justice, Jeff	Robertson, Eric	Williams, Johnny
Candalaria, Mike	Kilchrist, Joe	Parker, Dorsey	Wright, David
Carreon, Mark	LaBauve, Shannon	Prejean, Johnny	Youngblood, David
Cason, Tommy	Kilchrist, Joe	Reed, David	Weems, Steve
Candalaria, Mike	LaBauve, Shannon	Rota, Bob	White, Ron
Carreon, Mark	Lamb, Steve	Row, Jim	Williams, Johnny
Cason, Tommy	Lane, Kirk	Row, Jim	Wright, David
Chinnery, Selly	Latham, Noah	Sallaz, John	Youngblood, David
Total: 100			

New Members (through October 15, 2014)

S. Cimerhanzel (151)	Bill Bridges (155)	Micahl Wycoff (159)	D. Funkhauser (163)
Mike Kennedy (152)	Kavin Hanz (156)	Stan Davis (160)	Steve Abney (164)
A. Bertagnoli (153)	J. LaFountain (157)	Steve Mink (161)	L. Burnside (165)
Tony Masraf (154)	Gaylon Slagell (158)	Hugo Luna (162)	J. Yarborough (166)
Total: 16			

APPENDIX B

DIRECTORS AND OFFICERS

2002	2003
Directors Sam Allen John Aubrey Elza Smith **Officers** Sam Allen.......................... President Elza Smith .... Vice President, Road Captain and Sergeant at Arms John Aubrey .... Vice President; Keeper of the Exchequer and Secretary Ricky Cook........................ Vice President John Talbot .... Vice President Tolly Allen .... Vice President Ted Ricketson .... Vice President	**Directors** Sam Allen John Aubrey Mike Callaghan Ricky Cook Carroll Kelly Steve Lamb Bob Mitchell John Talbot **Management Committee** Sam Allen John Aubrey Ricky Cook Carroll Kelly **Officers** Sam Allen............................President John Talbot ....Vice President, Road Captain and Sergeant at Arms John Aubrey ....Keeper of the Exchequer Carroll Kelly ....Secretary John Talbot ....Road Captain (June – September) Ricky Cook..........................Road Captain (October – December)

Sam Allen

2004	2005
Directors Sam Allen John Aubrey Monte Jones Carroll Kelly Steve Lamb John Talbot **Officers** Sam Allen .... President Carroll Kelly .... Vice President; Secretary John Aubrey .... Keeper of the Exchequer Matt Linton .... Ride Captain (January – March) Dan Bezborn .... Ride Captain (April – December)	**Directors** Sam Allen John Talbot Carroll Kelly Steve Lamb Bob Mitchell Joe Kilchrist (resigned in March) John Aubrey (filled vacancy created by Kilchrist resignation) **Officers** Ricky Cook......................... President John Talbot .... Vice President Carroll Kelly .... Secretary John Aubrey .... Keeper of the Exchequer Dan Bezborn .... Ride Captain (January – February) Dick Tate .... Ride Captain (March – May) Rusty Drake....................... Ride Captain (June – September) Tommy Cason .... Ride Captain (October – December)
2006	**2007**
Directors George Bogle Tommy Cason Sam Allen John Talbot Carroll Kelly Steve Lamb **Officers** Ricky Cook.........................President John Talbot ....Vice President Sam Allen...........................Keeper of the Exchequer Mike Callaghan..................Road Captain (term uncertain) David Lee...........................Road Captain Doug Growden...................Road Captain	**Directors** Mike Callaghan Adan Ortiz George Bogle Tommy Cason Sam Allen John Talbot **Officers** John Aubrey .... President John Talbot .... Vice President Sam Allen........................... Keeper of the Exchequer David Lee........................... Road Captain Ken Carr............................ Road Captain

The Deacons of Deadwood Motorcycle Club

2008	2009
Directors Steve Lamb Bob Cavnar Mike Callaghan Adan Ortiz George Bogle Tommy Cason **Officers** John Aubrey .... President John Talbot .... Vice President Sam Allen .... Treasurer David Lee .... John Talbot Ken Carr .... Road Captain	**Directors** Justin Dossett Orlando Sanchez Steve Lamb Bob Cavnar Mike Callaghan Bill Talbot **Officers** Jay McKendree .... President John Talbot .... Vice President Ricky Cook......................... Treasurer Sam Allen........................... Secretary Peter Sommer .... Road Captain
2010	**2011**
Directors Peter Sommer Bob Bulian Justin Dossett Orlando Sanchez Steve Lamb Bob Cavnar Mike Callaghan Bill Talbot **Officers** Jay McKendree .... President John Talbot .... Vice President Ricky Cook......................... Treasurer Sam Allen........................... Secretary Peter Sommer .... Road Captain	**Directors** Peter Sommer Bob Bulian Justin Dossett Orlando Sanchez Geoff Seaman Kirk Lane **Officers** Steve Lamb .... President Geoff Seaman .... Vice President Ricky Cook......................... Treasurer Peter Sommer .... Road Captain

Sam Allen

2012

Directors
Steve Skelton
Aaron Seward
Peter Sommer
Bob Bulian
Geoff Seaman
Kirk Lane

Officers
Steve Lamb .... President
Geoff Seaman .... Vice President
Ricky Cook .... Treasurer
Aaron Seward .... Secretary
Peter Sommer .... Road Captain
David Reed .... Road Captain

2013

Directors
David Youngblood
David Wright
Steve Skelton
Aaron Seward
Geoff Seaman
Kirk Lane

Officers
Steve Lamb .... President
Geoff Seaman .... Vice President
Ricky Cook .... Treasurer
Aaron Seward .... Secretary
Peter Sommer .... Road Captain
David Reed .... Road Captain

2014

Directors
Mike Fisher
Ken Carr
David Youngblood
David Wright
Steve Skelton
Aaron Seward

Officers
Kirk Lane .... President
David Youngblood .... Vice President
Ricky Cook .... Treasurer
Mike Fisher .... Secretary
David Reed .... Road Captain
David Stevens .... Sergeant at Arms

APPENDIX C

DEACONESS CHAPTER MEMBERS, DIRECTORS AND OFFICERS

Members

2004

Aubrey, Amy	Chester, Carmen	Gracia, Sally	McKendree, Angie
Banta, Tedi	Chester, Sylvia	Jackson, Tracy	The Raisin
Bogle, Julie	Cox, K.C.	Jones, Brandy	Point, Melanie
Brister, Pat (Talbot)	Gibbons, Sherry	Mattison, Lynnie	Talbot, Lisa

2005

Aubrey, Amy	Chester, Sylvia	Hartley, Marilyn	Elaine, the "Raisin"
Banta, Tedi	Cox, K.C.	Jackson, Tracy	Point, Melanie
Bogle, Julie	Gibbons, Sherry	Jones, Brandy	Talbot, Lisa
Brister, Pat (Talbot)	Gracia, Sally	Linton, Dayna	
Chester, Carmen	Faleski, Nancy	McKendree, Angie	

2006

Aubrey, Amy	Cox, K.C.	Jones, Brandy	Talbot, Lisa
Banta, Tedi	Gibbons, Sherry	Linton, Dayna	
Bogle, Julie	Gracia, Sally	McKendree, Angie	
Brister, Pat (Talbot)	Faleski, Nancy	Elaine, the "Raisin"	
Chester, Sylvia	Jackson, Tracy	Point, Melanie	

Sam Allen

2007

Aubrey, Amy	Cox, K.C.	Jones, Brandy	Point, Melanie
Banta, Tedi	Gibbons, Sherry	Linton, Dayna	Talbot, Lisa
Bogle, Julie	Gracia, Sally	Little, Debbie	
Brister, Pat (Talbot)	Faleski, Nancy	McKendree, Angie	
Chester, Sylvia	Jackson, Tracy	Elaine , the "Raisin"	

2008

Aubrey, Amy	Chester, Sylvia	Gracia, Sally	McKendree, Angie
Banta, Tedi	Cox, K.C.	Faleski, Nancy	Point, Melanie
Bogle, Julie	Croix, Vanessa	Linton, Dayna	Talbot, Lisa
Brister, Pat (Talbot)	Emery, Ann	Little, Debbie	
Bulian, Sharon	Gibbons, Sherry		

2009

Aubrey, Amy	Carr, Tanya	Gibbons, Sherry	McKendree, Angie
Banta, Tedi	Chester, Sylvia	Gracia, Sally	Row, Maggie
Bogle, Julie	Cox, K.C.	Faleski, Nancy	Seward, Alicia
Brister, Pat (Talbot)	Croix, Vanessa	Linton, Dayna	Sommer, Ellen
Bulian, Sharon	Emery, Ann	Little, Debbie	Somyak, Linda
			Talbot, Lisa

2010

Asta, Julie	Carr, Tanya	Gracia, Sally	Row, Maggie
Aubrey, Amy	Chester, Sylvia	Faleski, Nancy	Seward, Alicia
Banta, Tedi	Cox, K.C.	Linton, Dayna	Sommer, Ellen
Bogle, Julie	Croix, Vanessa	Little, Debbie	Stoerner, Lori
Brister, Pat (Talbot)	Gibbons, Sherry	McKendree, Angie	Talbot, Lisa
Bulian, Sharon			

The Deacons of Deadwood Motorcycle Club

2011

Asta, Julie	Carr, Tanya	Gibbons, Sherry	Seward, Alicia
Aubrey, Amy	Carver, Becky	Gracia, Sally	Sommer, Ellen
Banta, Tedi	Chester, Sylvia	Little, Debbie	Stoerner, Lori
Brister, Pat (Talbot)	Cox, K.C.	McKendree, Angie	Talbot, Lisa
Bulian, Sharon	Croix, Vanessa	Row, Maggie	

2012

Asta, Julie	Carr, Tanya	Davidson, Diane	Row, Maggie
Aubrey, Amy	Carver, Becky	Gibbons, Sherry	Seward, Alicia
Banta, Tedi	Chester, Sylvia	Gracia, Sally	Sommer, Ellen
Brister, Pat (Talbot)	Cox, K.C.	Little, Debbie	Stoerner, Lori
Bulian, Sharon	Croix, Vanessa	McKendree, Angie	Talbot, Lisa

2013

Asta, Julie	Carr, Tanya	Davidson, Diane	Row, Maggie
Aubrey, Amy	Carver, Becky	Gibbons, Sherry	Seward, Alicia
Banta, Tedi	Chester, Sylvia	Gracia, Sally	Sommer, Ellen
Brister, Pat (Talbot)	Cox, K.C.	Little, Debbie	Stoerner, Lori
Bulian, Sharon	Croix, Vanessa	McKendree, Angie	Talbot, Lisa

2014

Aubrey, Amy	Cimmerhanzel, Lisa	Martinez, Maria	Seward, Alicia
Baldwin, Kim	Cox, K.C.	McKendree, Angie	Sommer, Ellen
Banta, Tedi	Croix, Vanessa	McMillin, Kim	Stoerner, Lori
Brister, Pat (Talbot)	Davidson, Diane	Mlazgar, Tammy	Talbot, Lisa
Buckley, Mary	Drury, Leslie	O'Hara, Maureen	Weems, Collat

Sam Allen

Bulian, Sharon	Gibbons, Sherry	Peterson, Tiffany	Wyckoff, Courtney
Carr, Tanya	Gracia, Sally	Prejean, Karen	Youngblood, Stacey
Carreon, Cynthia	Justice, Allison	Reed, Susan	
Carver, Becky	Leverett, Heather	Row, Maggie	
Chester, Sylvia	Little, Debbie	Seaman, Eija	

Officers

2004	2005
Sally Gracia.............................President Lisa Talbot...............................Vice Pres.	Sally Gracia.............................President Lisa Talbot...............................Vice Pres. Angie McKendree..................Secretary Angie McKendree..................Treasurer
2006	**2008**
Sally Gracia.............................President Julie Bogle ....President Lisa Talbot...............................Vice Pres. Tedi Banta ....Vice Pres. Angie McKendre....................Secretary Sally Gracia.............................Secretary Angie McKendree..................Treasurer	Angie McKendree..................President Tedi Banta ....Vice Pres. Sherry Gibbons ....Secretary Julie Bogle ....Treasurer
2009	**2010**
Angie McKendree..................President Tedi Banta ....Vice Pres. Sherry Gibbons ....Secretary Julie Bogle ....Treasurer	Sharon Bulian ....President Vanessa Crio...........................Vice Pres. Alicia Seward.........................Secretary Ellen Sommer.........................Treasurer

The Deacons of Deadwood Motorcycle Club

2011	2012
Sharon Bulian .... President	Ellen Sommer .... President
Vanessa Criox .... Vice Pres.	Sylvia Chester .... Vice Pres.
Alicia Seward .... Secretary	Maggie Row .... Secretary
Ellen Sommer .... Treasurer	Julie Asta .... Treasurer

2013	2014
Ellen Somme .... President	Becky Carver .... President
Sylvia Chester .... Vice Pres.	Angie McKendree .... President
Maggie Row .... Secretary	Eija Seaman .... Vice Pres.
Julie Asta .... Treasurer	Diane Davidson .... Secretary
	Angie McKendree .... Treasurer
	Tedi Banta .... Treasurer

APPENDIX D

WEBSITE ARTICLES BY MEMBERS

When George Bogle was head of the Club's technology committee, he instituted a program under which members would be selected to author articles that would be posted on our website. Each member's name would be put into a hat and one name would be drawn to determine the member who would write the article for the next month. The member who was selected could write on any topic he chose.

When Matt Linton and George left the Deacons to form the Sovereign Souls Motorcycle Club, our website left with George because he had been hosting it through his own Internet company. Jay McKendree had to build an entirely new website and find a new host. A good bit of content was lost, but fortunately, Jay was able to save the articles that appear in this Appendix.

These articles were fun for all of us to read at the time they were written, and they are of even greater interest today because they reflect the attitudes of the members and the issues that we faced in our early years. The articles that Matt, George and Ted Faleski wrote are particularly interesting because they give an indication of their views about the Deacons before they decided to leave.

The dates that these articles were written and the order in which they appeared on our website have been lost, so they appear in no particular order. In addition, I have not edited them, so they appear with all the typos and grammatical errors that were included in the original postings.

Sam Allen

Carroll Kelly

"AN UNFORGETTABLE CHARACTER"
By Carroll Kelly – AKA "Speedy"

I know most of you are aware that the Readers Digest has, for many years, featured an article in its monthly publication entitled "The Most Unforgettable Character I Ever Met." I was never given the opportunity to write an essay in Readers Digest, but obviously, I have been given the privilege and task of writing an article for our Club's website, and I am titling my essay - - - "An Unforgettable Character."

This story begins in 1995 when I approached a strapping young man at Ninfa's Restaurant on Navigation. I asked this fellow if the motorcycle outside was his. He reluctantly admitted to the ownership of the bike. I related to him that I also owned a motorcycle and further, inquired as to whether or not he might be going to Sturgis, South Dakota in August. He responded by a statement along the lines of "yes, but what's it to you?" Notwithstanding his unfriendliness, I forged ahead. He then related to me that he and a "large group" of people would be going to Sturgis. I asked him if I might include myself in that "large group" of people. He said, "Well I guess you can if you insist."

At any rate, I got this fellow's name and phone number and early the next week I called him to attempt to move forward with this trip that would include several bikes and multiple riders. The fellow finally seemed reconciled to the fact that I was going to make this trip to Sturgis with him and his group of friends.

The Deacons of Deadwood Motorcycle Club

As things progressed it became apparent that the only people that were going on this trip in this context were this fellow that I met at Ninfa's and me. The "large group" obviously dissipated to he and I. As the trip grew closer to its beginning, we were making plans to have our bikes shipped, fly to Rapid City, South Dakota, pick up our bikes, and begin the odyssey in and around Rapid City, Sturgis, Deadwood, etc. I soon learned that the "large group" of people that this fellow was talking about were people who, likewise, hauled their motorcycles to the Sturgis area, stayed in Deadwood, and casually rode around the area sightseeing, viewing ladies in scantily clad outfits, and hanging around the bars in the area acting like Macho Bikers.

My new friend and I met David Cook, the GURU of Deadwood at that time, and his entourage of bikers at the Bullock Hotel in Deadwood, South Dakota. Needless to say, David Cook did not have rooms for my new friend and me. So, we stayed at a third-rate motel on the outskirts of Deadwood, but were accepted into the David Cook group at the Bullock Hotel for refreshments, food, general BS, etc. Those activities went on for several days and at the conclusion of the time in Deadwood, David Cook and his entourage loaded their classic motorcycles into their trailers and headed back to Houston. My new friend and I, however, undertook to return to Houston by taking a rather circuitous route through the Little Big Horn Battlefield; Billings, Montana; Bear Tooth Mountain; the Range Rider Hotel at the entrance to Yellowstone National Park; Yellowstone National Park; Jackson Hole, Wyoming; Cheyenne, Wyoming; Denver, Colorado; and points south.

By this time my friend and I were on rather friendly terms and both of us seemed to be enjoying the trip, the sights, the food, and the camaraderie. My friend did, and has developed, a habit of somewhat narcissistically taking times on many of the mornings of the trip to work on various projects from his hotel room with his office in Houston. During those times, I would twiddle my thumbs in my room and wait for my friend to finish his work so that we could continue our trip. About 8 days into the trip, and on a Sunday evening, we located a lively biker bar in Pueblo, Colorado. After food and drinks, we returned to our respective rooms and I was told by my friend that we would not be able to leave the next day until sometime in the afternoon since he planned to work from his room in Pueblo with his office in Houston. We went to bed. During the night I decided that the camaraderie, fellowship, and adventure of the trip to-date had been enough for me. I decided to tell my friend the next morning that I was going to mount my 1980 Shovelhead Harley (which, by the way, used about as much oil as it did gasoline on the trip) and take out on my own for Houston. This is what I did and my friend continued his trip through Albuquerque and Santa Fe, New Mexico; Tombstone, Arizona; and points south and west.

This trip was my first motorcycle trip, and I also learned it was my friend's first motorcycle trip of any significance. We would travel as much as 300 miles a day and would be totally exhausted from the day's activities. As many of you know, my friend and I have now ridden together over 40,000 miles, and on many days we have covered 700 to a 1,000 miles a day. So, we have learned to be better bikers with much more stamina and know-how concerning the handling and manipulation of an 800 lb. motorcycle. All of the trips we have taken together have been wonderful, but this first trip was obviously a learning experience for both my friend and me.

The Deacons of Deadwood Motorcycle Club

At any rate, I made it home safely in about a day and a half from Pueblo, Colorado; and my friend made it home safely to Houston in about four more days of sightseeing and riding. As we all know, in the world of Harley Davidson Motorcycles, it is "not the destination but the journey that counts." This trip was, of course, a wonderful experience for me. I met many interesting and friendly people and because of my friend's generosity, I was included in this, my first trip to Sturgis. I know today that this trip with my new friend was one of the reasons for his idea, along with Ricky and David Cook, to form a motorcycle club in Houston that would be named the Deacons of Deadwood. Through my friend's hard work, this Club was formed. I am honored to be one of the founders of the Club. If you have not guessed by now – my new friend was and is "SAM ALLEN."

As I have stated previously, Sam and I have, with others, traveled across this Country and Canada on our motorcycles together. Those trips have also been unforgettable, but I know without Sam's leadership and tenacity, that many of the trips would not have taken place and that in all probability, the Deacons of Deadwood Motorcycle Club would never have been founded. It now has a membership of well over 50 members, has generated several hundred thousand dollars for charity, and has given me the opportunity to meet and become friends with other "unforgettable characters."

"Thanks Sam"
September 19, 2008

Sam Allen

JayMckendree

A Deacons Fairy Tale

(In order to get the effect, read like you were reading to a small child

Once upon a time there was a band of merry men that religiously road their steel horses across the countryside in search of the next great watering hole with fair maidens. These great men were known as the Deacons.

The children of the countryside loved the Deacons because the Deacons worked very hard to put on a royal banquet attended by the wealthy city folk who brought their bags of gold for the children in order to attend the best banquet in the land.

Some of the Deacons did not want to work so hard. The Sounds of Silence as they came to be known, continued to ride their steel horses in the southern knolls. They continued to eat, drink, and be merry, but without any responsibility they were able to frolic free and travel with men who were less merry and appeared to be more scary.

When the SS left the Deacons, a cloud of "woe is me" was lifted. The Deacons were a better group and more merry men wanted to join.

But, the SS want to remain friends with the Deacons, but mostly under their own terms. The SS, flying the flag of their land, wanted to come to the Deacons monthly vigil to the center of town where many Deacons gathered to slap each others back and regale in Deacon business.

Many of the SS also wanted to come to the royal banquet waving their flag to the crowd: "look at me – look at me; we are the same as the Deacons."

The Deacons of Deadwood Motorcycle Club

Some of the Deacons were perplexed because they thought the royal banquet was a special night where the Deacon armor always shined the brightest. They were concerned the rust of the SS armor and maybe that of their friends would cast a spell over the city folk causing them to take their bags of gold back to their castle never to be seen again.

Other Deacons were concerned that the many challises of spirits, testosterone, and resentment would lead to a melee and bring the sheriffs of Nottingham. Also, seeing the melee, the city folk may never return to the banquet with their bags of gold.

After all, the royal banquet was not the average steel horse ride or even a roasted hog festival. It was a gala ball without comparison. It was music, food, drink, and more importantly, a purpose. It was attended by the wealthy city folk so they could give away their bags of gold while letting go of some of their inhabitations with the best merry men in the land.

The SS were sad when they thought they could not fly their flag at the royal banquet. Many prayed to the Lord of Friendship: "Dear Lord, woe is me. If I cannot fly my flag at the royal banquet, how else can I show my support of the Deacons and the children they help without giving away any bags of gold and doing any work? Yes I know Lord of Friendship, that is why I left the Deacons, but I deserve to fly my flag wherever I ride my steel horse without question because I am the most hardy of merry men in the land."

And, the Lord of Friendship said to the Deacons, this is your decision. Not that of any king, knights of the roundtable, or just the wise elders. You must make the decision. Is this your royal banquet to shine or is it just another steel horse event?

Jay

Sam Allen

Seriously, the Deacons of Deadwood are a unique group in the community, including the motorcycle community. We have a special event not attempted by any other club. We have a charity ball with a motorcycle theme because that's who we are. It is not a motorcycle ride or a $5 barbeque plate benefit. We ride hard all over the country because we want to and we raise serious money for great children with additional hard work.

The SS want to continue as a *de facto* subchapter by continuing what they did before – not doing the heavy lifting, but getting some credit for showing up. They want special concessions by asking for a free table just for buying several ball tickets and kissing of their ring for donating auction items.

I've wasted entirely too many brain cells and too much time on the SS and their demands. They are gone. Our Club is better than it has ever been before with quality people wanting to join. Importantly, we remained friends with the SS. But, they are not Deacons. Riding together and going to informal parties and get togethers is one thing. But, the choice is yours about whether they attend our meetings in their colors and show up at the Ball - in their colors - on a night that is ours.

The Ball is seven weeks away. This is the time where we do the most work, but also the time where we celebrate being Deacon. Let's concentrate on our business and less on what others demand from the best damn motorcycle club anywhere.

As my friend and mentor Forrest Gump says, that's all I have to say about that. See you at the August meeting.

DFFD

The Deacons of Deadwood Motorcycle Club

Justin Dossett

After months of planning and numerous phone calls to various hotels in Colorado, South Dakota, Kansas and Nebraska, my dad and I had finally set our sights on our first trip to Sturgis, South Dakota for the biggest motorcycle rally in the world. With the time upon us, we head out on our first journey together. We are both beaming with excitement ready to tackle the open road and all that could possible come out of it.

We pull out of the driveway and start to get settled in. When we get to the end of the street, we test out our new Harley Davidson CB walkie-talkies for the first time. We notice that mine is working and he can hear me but I cannot hear him. We drive to the nearest Harley shop and ask for a quick fix, but they say they can't help in a quick amount of time. We decide to head north to the Woodlands Harley shop, thinking they may be able to fix it more quickly. They inform us that they think they have it fixed or at least diagnosed, but the part needed is going to take 3 days to get in the shop. We decide to drive on without the walkie-talkies being fixed and expect a quite ride.

After hearing the not so good news, dad and I shrug off the bad news and continue our journey thinking our worries are behind us or so we thought. In all honesty, the best feeling I get on these long runs, is when you get to the outskirts of town around beltway 8 and look in the side mirrors and know that it is just me and this bike and my most minimal luggage that I could cram in the saddlebags for the next 10 days. Very liberating I think... So back to the story at hand, we head north of the Woodlands Harley destined for Dallas a little bummed about the communications debacle, but still excited.

Blazing north on interstate 45 I noticed in my side mirrors that my dads headlamps were not turned on and in my 9 years of riding knowledge with Harleys, your headlights are to be turned on as soon as you turn on the key. I signal to my dad to pull up next to me that his lights are not on. Now it is starting to get dark and luckily we are just coming into beautiful Buffalo, TX. After figuring out the that his high beams and that none of his lights on his bike are working, I begin to start pulling his bike apart to see where the problem may be. After tearing down his bike in a Texas Burgers parking lot I noticed his light fuse is blown as well as my dads anger/frustration fuse. I attempt to replace with spares, but still get same result. Now it is coming upon 9:00 PM and dad's blood pressure cannot take anymore and we both decide to get a 12 pack of beer and call it a night. Admitting defeat, we piece his new Street Glide back together and begin to look for a hotel and beer. Finding shelter was first on the list after doing so we set our sights on beer. After a nice little walk to the store we notice there are no beer signs like you normally see in a convenient store, so we ask the clerk where they hide the beer? To add salt, vinegar, acid and anything else that could possibly burn to our wounds the very nice clerk informs us that we are in a dry county and that the closest place is about 30 minutes down the road and that the place just closed 30 minutes ago.

Now we have truly hit a new low and we are still only on our first 4 hours of our 10-day trip. Now what? We finally get some shut-eye and found out that the North Texas Harley shop opens at 8:00 AM. If we leave Buffalo at 5:30 am we should be there right as the garage doors open. As expected, my father has always been a 5:00 AM early riser and I have always been an 8:00 AM early riser, he muscles me out of bed and onto the bikes. We pull up to the North Texas Harley shop right as they are opening; luckily I had bought my first Harley from there and had had a tech that I preferred that remembered me. We explain the Lemony Snickets series of unfortunate events and he laughs and tells us that he will take a look at it. Within 30 minutes, dad's street glide is back in business with ALL problems fixed and a very rare event, no charge from the service shop. We tip the tech very generously and have all new winds in our sails and head north to Sturgis, South Dakota.

So after the worst first day out of our ten-day trip, the next 9 days were as perfect as it could be. By far one the best Deacons and father/son trips ever.

Justin "The Kidd" Dossett

Sam Allen

Dennis Hensley
THE REASON WE ARE DOING THIS
By Dennis Hensley

Sometimes when we perform our "mission" of helping the kids, the concept can be somewhat abstract. Each of us probably knows a handicapped kid somewhere. Maybe a cousin or distant relative and, although it is heartbreaking to see a kid in pain or one that doesn't fit in because of some physical challenge or condition, it can be really hard to relate. This is the story of Nick, my son, who benefited to no end from his experiences.

It started with a headache and fever. I was in Midland on business when four year old Nick's Mom called and said he had a slight fever. Rule of thumb from our family doctor was to bring him in if the fever lasted more than 24 hours so that is what we decided to do. Next morning the fever was gone. Cool. I got home the next afternoon and Nick seemed OK but said his head hurt. Fever was back and it went downhill from there. Soon he was crying uncontrollably and we were on our way to the emergency room. I am not sure whether they we not busy or if they were concerned, but we got right in and, having been called, our family doctor was there. He had his first seizure while being examined and within minutes was on his way to the children's pediatric unit at Herman hospital where they cut a hole in his head the size of a quarter for a biopsy.

The prognosis was not good. We were faced with a 1/3 chance of survival and if he did survive, the likelihood that Nick would have require constant care and not have much quality in his life and would be profoundly retarded. Chances were better if they administered an "experimental" drug at the time (acyclovir - 1984). That and the constant attention of the medical staff saved his life, but not without after effects. Against predictions, Nick was left with a seizure disorder and slight retardation.

As Nick was growing up, many were willing to help, but the organization that stood out, offering the most support for Nick was The Epilepsy Foundation of Texas. In addition to the many things they offer, there was a summer camp for kids, Camp Spike and Wave, that gave Nick a chance to function in surroundings where he was not "different" and no-one cared if he had a seizure in the middle of some activity. It was just Nick in surroundings where he was not different and could develop the confidence to function in the real world.

Sounds a lot like "Camp for All". Nick is all grown up now, proudly holding down a job sacking groceries at H.E.B. and the seizures, which still happen occasionally, are for the most part under control. He even has the confidence, to practice Tai Kwan Do, where he holds a Brown Belt.

I am not sure whether it is our primary mission to ride motorcycles and secondary to provide help to organizations that help kids like Nick, or the other way around. I Guess it doesn't make much difference. The point is, Nick's Mom and I could not give him everything by ourselves and thanks to organizations like The Epilepsy Foundation of Texas, Camp for All, Boys and Girls Country and many others, the quality of life of "God's Special Kids" can be exponentially improved. Thanks to them and thanks to the organizations, such as the Deacons, that supports them.

Sam Allen

Kevin Phelps

Kevin Phelps

As a novice rider just a few short years ago, I set out on a typical Sunday ride with one of my best friends. He had been riding just a short time longer than I, yet we both had similar riding styles which are ride fast, pass anyone you can, take drinking breaks, and ride faster. This Sunday started like virtually every one before and since. We would wake up at the crack of 1pm after a hard night of over indulgence and call one another to set up a time, usually within the hour, to meet at Sam's Boat in Sugar Land . Lunch and several beers later and we were off.

One of our favorite routes is 359 North out of Sugar Land to 529 West to Bellville, then catching 159 West to Fayetteville and back home again. It's not a long ride, but always eventful, has great scenery, and the ability to ride fast and frequently pass slower traffic.

On this cool March day we blasted out of Sam's parking lot to start our weekly adventure. When riding with someone your comfortable with, you don't have to worry about what they're going to do, which way they're going to turn in the event of an obstacle, or waiting for them to keep up because it becomes almost instinctual. We had established this type of riding pattern.

So we were flying through the countryside, executing precision passes, and frequently sprinting to 100+mph and back just because we could on the open road. As we traveled down a tree lined portion of 529, I had an encounter with an unidentified object. It was one of those moments where things seem to happen in slow motion. Out of the right corner of my eye, the black object came out of the trees. I gripped the bars tightly, closed my eyes, and prepared for the impact as I knew I had no time to turn. I then felt an intense pain in my right knee as my foot was pulled from the floorboard. My friend, who was behind me, instantly sprinted up next to me as I was looking down at my outstretched leg to see if there was any damage. Not seeing any, I gave him the ok and we continued riding. We stopped at our usual gas and beer store to refuel on both. He came up and asked if I knew what happened. I stated the obvious, something hit me, and he proceeded to enlighten me as to the culprit. It used to be, and he emphasized used to be, a bird. Laughing hysterically, he described the event as if a giant clump of freshly cut grass had exploded on my knee, disintegrating into a mass of feathers. Particularly astonishing, in light of the carnage he described, was the fact that there was not even a mark of blood on my jeans. We pondered the obvious luck of the placement of the hit over a couple of beers as we sat on the gas station's curb.

It was then decided that we change course and head North on 159 eventually ending up on 105 East heading to our final stop at Papa's on the Lake . Neither of us had ridden this newly picked route, but he had a general idea how to get there so we went for it. This leg of the trip proved almost as fun as the first. The entire ride was only marred at the end by a couple of near accidents while pulling into Papa's.

We waited behind a pickup in the left turn lane. I saw that we didn't have a green arrow but instead just the standard green light. My friend apparently was not able to see past the pickup as he was in the left side of our lane. Well, the pickup had a gap and pulled across several lanes into Papa's, with one lone motorcyclist following. I sat in horror as the oncoming traffic finally came into view of my friend as the pickup cleared the turn in front of him. With a judicious application of throttle that sent his back tire slightly sideways, he narrowly avoided a head-on collision with what I can only assume were a few terrified motorists. Now, sitting there alone and admittedly nervous from what I just witnessed, I too had to navigate the decreasing radius turn. Keeping my focus, in retrospect for way too long, on the approaching cars as I made the turn, it became apparent that I had overshot my intended destination. Potentially riding through the grass didn't really bother me. It was the foot deep trough next to the pavement, forged by so many vehicles that had done what I was now about to do, that was the problem. I could either turn too hard and go down, or jump off the road and take my chances in the trough. So the trough it was. I easily made it over the edge of the pavement with the tires, but the left side of the bike wasn't so lucky. The scraping and abrupt end to my downward motion into the hole was quite startling. I continued my forward progress despite the noise and ended up safely in a space at the front door. The underside of my chromed primary was surprisingly free from drastic damage, albeit the two inch long and eighth inch deep area missing the aforementioned chrome. It was time for another beer and for me to tell him how close he came to death, and how my lack of focus on the road ahead could have caused my own demise. In the end, it was a great day of riding and one of my most memorable.

    It's interesting how these feats of survival are always met with laughter and the hope that we won't be that stupid the next time. Yet, the thought of switching from beer to water never really entered our minds.

The Deacons of Deadwood Motorcycle Club

Richard Van Aukin

The Road Ahead

At 58 I find myself thinking more and more about retirement and "The Road Ahead".

Born and raised in upstate New York I bought my first motorcycle in 1971, a 550 Honda. In 1976 I traded her in for a 750 and rode that bike all over the eastern states to Midwest, covering ground from Virginia to Ohio end even up into Canada. I hit lots of rough weather, including snow and slept on a few rest stop picnic tables.

In 1978 I moved to Florida and the following year ended up in Houston bringing that old bike with me. With gas hitting $1 per gallon I rode that bike back and forth to work every day, putting over 80,000 miles on her.

My first Harley was a 1994 Heritage Classic Softail. I loved that bike but felt like a weekend warrior as I spent what seemed like more time cleaning her than riding her. Lovenia and I were out for a ride one day when we met Tommy Cason while he was peddling tickets for the Biker Ball in "05". We went with the anticipation of meeting everyone at the 12 Spot and participating in the bike parade. Unfortunately as we were mounting up for that parade we noticed the rear tire was flat. Tommy like a superhero took off in his white long tailed tux and returned with a can of fix a flat...we missed the parade but had a great time anyway with the rest of the ball. Our first real meeting of the Deacons.

Lovenia loved motorcycles and looked forward to riding with the Deacons. We were married in Las Vegas, made the Lone Star Ralley in "06"...that was a great weekend. I'm hoping to make Daytona and Sturgis but for a few more

Sam Allen

years work will be in the way of long extended rides. If I stay healthy I am looking forward to retirement and getting out on "The Road Ahead".

By Richard Van Aukin

The Deacons of Deadwood Motorcycle Club

Matt Linton

The Deacons: a club, a brotherhood, an organization.

April 26th saw the Fifth Anniversary of the Deacons of Deadwood M/C. In 2002, a group of friends who had been riding to Sturgis together for years decided to formalize their group in honor of brother, friend, and father, David Cook, who fell to his battle with cancer. Five years have passed and for the anniversary party, the club returned to Blanco's in Houston, the bar where the club was first formalized. It reminded all the members of the club's roots and humble beginnings. It has been historically said in jest that the Deacons were a drinking club with a motorcycle problem and you can bet that this sentiment was fully exploited at the party.

Truth be told, the Deacons are a motorcycle club, first and foremost. Like all major clubs across the US and world, they are a close-knit group of motorcycle enthusiasts. They happen to run the gamut from those that live and breath the lifestyle 24/7, enthusiasts who ride every weekend and sunny day they can, as well as the sport touring lovers who regularly travel the country on two wheels collecting every honor and award the Iron Butt Association has to give out. These members come from all walks of life, white collar and blue collar. The group destroys financial boundaries making everyone equal. This is a big part of the Brotherhood of the Club.

Brotherhood is not something that is taken lightly by the members. Each individual goes through a regular "hang around" or "prospect" phase that allows members to get to know him, and for he to get to know the club. This is particularly important as it takes 100% vote of members to get into the group. This process may seem harsh or overly cut and dry to some, but it is necessary for the strength of the group as a whole. This does not mean every member is the best of friends, but it does mean that every member will be there if any other member needs him. Unlike larger clubs, the Deacons do not have formal chapters. In the natural order of proximity, those that frequent the same haunts tend to hang with one another most often. However, all members meet at the clubhouse once a month to take care of club business. And business is a big part of the Deacons.

Perhaps it was David Cook's battle with cancer and the trauma it caused friends and family, but the group rallied around the idea of charity work, specifically for children. Now many clubs make an effort to reach out to the community at large with fundraisers, toy runs, and charity drives; but the Deacons of Deadwood (as they were now known) decided to go above and beyond by not only participating in other groups efforts, but to put on the biggest and best party/fundraiser the biker world had ever experienced. With the exception of a few major fundraisers held by events such as Sturgis and Daytona, the Deacons have succeeded in meeting their goals. In fact, this small group of Brothers and Sisters has raised over a quarter million dollar in just five short years... that is two hundred fifty grand actually getting placed into the hands of the charities.

The Deacons will continue to grow their party and fundraising, grow their membership, and foster their Brotherhood. Like every club and organization; growth is important, diversity is important, and the true friendships are important. If you truly love motorcycles, truly want to devote time, money, and attention to a club, and feel that you are looking for a group of Brothers to support and to support you, then we would like to encourage you to take a closer look at the Deacons. There are a good handful of powerful, patch holding clubs in our area, but we are a bit different. Find out for yourself and consider if this lifestyle is for you. If so, drop by the clubhouse and introduce yourself, we would love to have more of us at the next anniversary party.

Article submitted by Comrade

Sam Allen

George Bogle

Deacon´s Most Commented Patch

Of all the patches on my vest, the one that I am asked about most often is the Deacon 44% patch. Four years ago, about the first time I donned my vest, I was standing in the original Stubbs by the parts counter when one of the guys behind the counter asked, "what does the 44% stand for"?

Since then, I´ve been asked in 1% biker bars north of Dallas; been asked by police officers while sitting on the veranda drinking a beer at our favorite stop in Keystone, SD; and a litany of other places over the years. Thankfully when I first joined, I received a pretty good explanation from Sam Allen of the original thinking behind how the Deacon´s were formed.

My answer to the question is fairly standard and I usually succeed in having some fun for myself when I answer it. I begin by telling the inquisitive questioner that the 44% patch has several meanings.

Number one, you know what a 1%er is? The typically response is "yes" with my reply being "we´re 44% of that". The bigger they are, the harder they chuckle. Second, you´ve heard of the 81 patch for the Hells Angles, 8 being "H" and 1 being "A"? The 4, 4 stands for "DD", Deacons of Deadwood. I finish by telling them there are other private meanings among the members of the club.

The answer seems to appeal to everyone, they usually give me a nod of the head or a salute of tapping beer bottles. If you´re wondering what the other meanings are, obviously I can´t say here in this newsletter or they wouldn´t be private any more. Actually, there are several meaning, with

The Deacons of Deadwood Motorcycle Club

some being better than others. If you´re a new Deacon and haven´t heard em all, just belly up to the bar and listen; you´ll eventually learn a few reasons of why it´s special to be a Deacon.

Deacons forever, forever Deacons.

Written by Ambassador

Sam Allen

Ted Faleski

FIRST HARLEY TRIP

By Ted Faleski

Both children are done with their BS degrees and working. Life is good! I suggest we get a Harley and Nancy (Red Dog) says yes. (I later find out she is not serious just humoring me – what's new) Under a cloak of secrecy my son researches and finds exactly what Harley we want. We visit David Cook (World's best sales man) act fast and buy the 96 HLSTC. When I bring the scooter home Nancy is beyond angry – this is a whole story in itself. We visit David and he gently tells Nancy that if she isn't on the back of this beautiful scooter someone else will! Red Dog acquiesces and David helps us plan our Sturgis trip (Our first long distance scooter trip) and suggests upgrades to the scooter (Now known as FURYII) FURY II is now faster, more reliable and better outfitted for a long distance ride. We are excited and ready to launch!

We load FURY II and leave at 3 AM to beat the heat. We get on 45N go a few miles and something feels loose. I stop to tighten up the pack and almost drop the bike. Great start for an adventure! We get to Waco and figure we would watch the Cowboys training camp. We have a few drinks and go the training camp. As we are watching there is Jerry Jones screaming and cursing at players like a wild man. I yell "Hey Jones you got a big stupid mouth"! We really didn't care about watching the training camp (Since I'm a Buffalo fan) as we were escorted out of the camp by security guards. Must be Jerry doesn't appreciate criticism!

The Deacons of Deadwood Motorcycle Club

We make our way to Raton, New Mexico and thru the Raton pass. What spectacular beauty. Makes us wonder why we haven't been doing this before now! We stop for gas and a hard tail chopper pulls in to fill up. The bikers look very tough and very mean. Driving a hard tail chopper all day will make anyone mean! As he starts to fill up I yell at him to stop! He continues and I grab his arm. Before he has a chance to tear me up I tell him "You're putting in diesel!" We both start laughing and he thanks me, buys us a beer and he gives us some tips on the trip and Sturgis.

Next stop Denver. We stop in Pueblo Colorado to visit the Harley shop, lunch and drinks. What a perfect day! We leave Pueblo without a care in the world! We get about 60 miles and FURY2 starts to sputter, OH NO I forgot to gas up! We are screwed. I go a mile or so and there it is a place called the Long Branch. Help Marshal Dillon! As we approach all I see a contingent of Hells Angels. We stop (With our shiny new over loaded wanna be biker look) and I ask if they know if there is gas ahead. They said they would fill us up (They had a big chase vehicle with gas and I didn't want to know what else) and cover FURYII since it was going to rain. Of course I happily said "Great", but in my mind I had a vision of rape, sodomy, murder and parts of FURYII all over the western US. I noticed the back door and told Red Dog that if anything started I would start shooting and she should run out the door and hide in the woods. Well quite the contrary happened. The Angles bought us drinks and lunch and told war stories. I told them my Mom used to ride Hogs in 1934. They thought that was very cool. We had a great time and got some travel tips.

After the rain stopped we said good bye and continued our trip to Denver, Leads and then Sturgis. We had it set up to meet a friend at the Broken Spoke. I couldn't find a parking spot so Red Dog hopped off to look for our friend while I parked. As I walked to the Broken Spoke my very excited friend says "The Hells Angels have Red Dog!" Sure enough it was the group from the Long Branch and a few more. I bought drinks for all and toasted the Angles thanking them again for helping a fellow biker.

We rode to Mt Rushmore, Badlands, Needle Highway, Devils Tower, Crazy Horse Monument, Beartooth pass, Cody and Yellowstone. What a beautiful country we live in! We met interesting people who were all more than happy to help us anyway they could. What an absolutely fantastic adventure! We also learned any biker in need is befriended by another biker. We are all from varied walks of life, but under the biker bond we are all brothers! We discovered a new life – biker life on the road – our greatest enjoyment!

Red Dog and I could not have made this first trip without the help and encouragement from our friend David Cook who we think of often. We have logged over 30,000 miles on FURYII and have never broken down one time thanks to David.

The Deacons of Deadwood Motorcycle Club

Bob Cavnar
Riding, Therapy or Both

It had been a long day; I was weary with talking on the phone and dealing with reality. Besides, I had an Ultra sitting at the house (my first Screaming Eagle) that I could hear calling me. I checked the calendar on my laptop, saw it was clear for the rest of the afternoon, grabbed my briefcase and headed for the door. When I got home, I changed into jeans, shrugged on my colors, went down to the garage, pulled off the cover and fired 'er up. That first throaty rumble is always the best, especially when you've had enough of that afore mentioned reality thing.

It was a beautiful late spring day, perfect weather where a vest and long sleeve shirt is enough to stay comfortable behind that big batwing fairing. I started up the tunes, and selected the "On the Road" playlist, one that I had assembled for a prior long road trip. Out the Westpark Tollway to Fulshear, then north. I decided just to go, with no particular destination. I rode up 359 to Highway 90, crossed and kept north. Somewhere between that crossing and Monaville, I hit the groove that all bikers live for – that oneness with the bike, a comfortable confidence, yet clear awareness of all around you, aided by the rumble of the pipes, the wind rushing by your ears, the great music from the front and rear speakers.

From there, I don't remember my specific route. I turned northwest, west, then south, not paying the slightest bit of attention to where I was. Being a weekday afternoon, the roads were void of traffic but for the occasional farm truck. It's these times you notice everything and nothing...the texture of the pavement, the vibration of the 110 below, the feel of the seat, yet no discomfort. I can ride forever. Tapping my toe on the footboard to the beat of the music, I reach a stretch of long empty road, roll on the throttle, kick it up to 6th. 6th is a sweet gear – when you toe it in, the revs drop off just right so the pipes build that big sound. When you roll on more throttle, the rumble gets deeper. You watch the revs, ignore the speedo. Go like that 'til the next sharp turn, back it down to 5th, ease to cruising speed. Back in the zone.

I rode like that for a while, rocking to the tunes and enjoying just being there. Just outside of Burton, I finally wake up and realize the sun's getting low and it's time to head for the house. DAMN IT. Just like that, the road buzz was gone, but the warm feeling remained. I run over to 290, head east and merge into the reverse commuter traffic back into the beehive. Houston.

To me, the meditative quality of long riding is golden, and not always attainable. Alone or riding with the Brothers, that unity between body, bike, road, and air is what it's all about. When you get it, you use, and savor, every minute to keep it. That is the ultimate goal, at least for me when I'm on the road.

Enough of this keyboard tapping...I'm going riding. Later.

Bob "Jefe" Cavnar

APPENDIX E

OUTLAW BIKER ARTICLE

The Mad Doctor came to the pre-party for our second Charity Ball to do an article about the Deacons for *Outlaw Biker* magazine. Doc is the national head photographer for that publication and has been a member of the 1%er club the Invaders for 50 years. The article is set forth below.

Doc couldn't resist some artistic license. There are plenty of photos of tits and ass, but about half of the chicks were not at the party. No matter. You can't have too much tits and ass in an *Outlaw Biker* article, or for that matter, in an article about the Deacons.

This article was done over a decade ago, so it's fun to see how our old timers looked in the early years.

On the far left, a trim Sambo; Carroll Kelly on the front bike; Matt the "Comrade" Linton and his then wife Dayna;

Lower left: Lynnie Mattison and me accepting the Cruzin' to Cure Helmet on behalf of the Deacons for having the greatest attendance of any MC at their poker run.

Lower middle: Mike Callaghan, Al Arfsten and some chick.

Lower right: Al Arfsten and Steve Lamb.

Some businessmen bikers called the Deacons of Deadwood, organized this event. Now these guys wear "44%'ers" on their colors, I think it means that they're not even half bad. Most of 'em are lawyers and the like, who get together to ride to Sturgis every year (and bunk in Deadwood, hence the name). It's a different take on the biker lifestyle but don't think they can't ride; some turn their annual cruise to Sturgis into a 5,000 mile trip—just gettin' there. Real iron butt rides. They do that because there are so many roads and so little time.

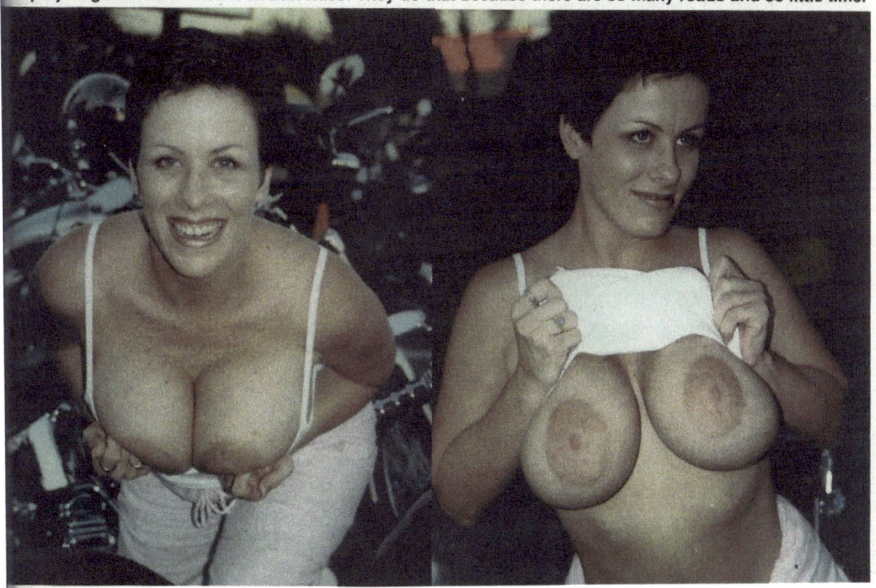

Arriving at Rockefeller Hall, we parked where we could and then watched the hot babes hop out of fancy cars and limos in front. Tickets for this party went for $150 each. Stubb's Cycles donated a 2004 Harley-Davidson Fat Boy for the raffle and Tours of Enchantment donated a complete Super Bowl package that was auctioned off. The whiskey flowed from the open bar, there was a never-ending supply of food served by waiters, and music was supplied by Brian Black and his Orchestra.

2ND ANNUAL HARLEY DREAMS MAKE-A-WISH BALL

In the top photo going from left to right: An unidentified chick; Mike Callaghan; Ted Faleski; Seguine Al Arfsten; four folks I don't know.

In the bottom photo to the right are Erick "ER" Robertson and his girlfriend (later wife) Gay Lynne and ER's other girlfriend Harley.

Left: One of Giggilo Gene's hotties.

This Biker Ball managed to raise $65,000 for the Make A Wish Foundation. God bless all these little children with life threatening illnesses and thanks to folks like the DDs for helping make a few of their wishes come true. The 2004 Charity Ball will be held at Rockefeller Hall in Houston on September 11, 2004.

Far right: A sexy looking Lynnie Mattison.

www.ingramcontent.com/pod-product-compliance
Lightning Source LLC
Chambersburg PA
CBHW042054290426
44111CB00001B/4